P9-CJW-832

Al Gore:
A User's Manual

◆

ALEXANDER COCKBURN
AND
JEFFREY ST. CLAIR

VERSO
London • New York

First published by Verso 2000
©Alexander Cockburn and Jeffrey St. Clair 2000
All rights reserved

VERSO
UK: 6 Meard Street, London WIV 3HR
USA: 180 Varick Street, 10th Floor, New York, NY 10014-4606

Verso is the imprint of New Left Books

ISBN 1 85984 803 6

British Library Cataloguing in Publication Data
A catalogue record for this book is available from the British Library

Library of Congress Cataloging-in-Publication Data
A catalog record for this book is available from the Library of Congress

Typeset in Century Schoolbook by Total Graphics, Skokie, IL
Printed in the United States of America
August 2000

Contents

1	Executive Overview	1
2	Gilded Youth	8
3	Only Five Years A Private Man	31
4	Snaildarter Soup	52
5	Shabbes Goy	67
6	Midgetman	76
7	The Sound of Dirty Music	95
8	Aiming High, Aiming Low	119
9	Whitehouse Doppelganger	144
10	Trade Wars	160
11	REGO	172
12	War on the Poor	188
13	"The Price Is Worth It"	210
14	Temple of Doom	233
15	The Green Game	245
16	The Prozac Lady	268
	Acknowledgements	274
	Index	276

1 EXECUTIVE OVERVIEW

Gore and the decay of liberalism; his life-long propensity for a double standard; absence of noble moments; troubling eagerness to please a marked feature of the young Gore; his brittle make-up; exploitation of sister and son; Humphrey evoked.

Al Gore distills in his single person the disrepair of liberalism in America today, and almost every unalluring feature of the Democratic Party. He did not attain this distinction by accident but by sedulous study from the cradle forward. A lad, and then a man who has never spent a minute of his life in ignorance or uncertainty as to where the next meal was coming from, or how the next mortgage payment might be met, Gore was nurtured to power by parents certain of his destiny. At his father's knee he learned the liberal idiom of the New Deal, and he has spent his adult life using the rhetoric to destroy the substance. At Harvard he became a disciple of Martin Peretz, the man who would later guide the liberal *New Republic* into neoconservative support for the Reagan doctrine.

Like a street mountebank fluttering a handkerchief to distract attention from his sleights of hand, Gore has always used his proficiency with the language of liberalism to mask an agenda utterly in concert with the desires of the Money Power. Nowhere is this truer than in his supposed environmentalism, which nicely symbolizes the chasm that has always separated Gore's professions from his performance. He denounces the rape of nature, yet has connived at the strip-mining of

1

Appalachia and, indeed, of terrain abutting one of Tennessee's most popular state parks. In other arenas, he denounces vouchers, yet sends his children to the private schools of the elite. He put himself forth as a proponent of ending the nuclear arms race, yet served as midwife for the MX missile. He offers himself as a civil libertarian, yet has been an accomplice in drives for censorship and savage assaults on the Bill of Rights. He parades himself as an advocate of campaign finance reform, then withdraws to the White House to pocket for the Democratic National Committee $450,000 handed to him by a gardener acting as carrier pigeon for the Riady family of Indonesia. He and wife Tipper were ardent smokers of marijuana, yet he now pushes for harsh sanctions against marijuana users.

It's hard to find noble moments in Gore's political career. Such was not the case with his father. Albert Sr. stood against the war in Vietnam, was a prime architect of the ABM Treaty (which his son is trying to undo) and a proponent of the Comprehensive Test Ban Treaty. Although Albert Sr. reproached himself in later life for having lacked courage on the civil rights issue, he did tell Strom Thurmond to shove it when the latter approached him on the floor of the Senate with his Southern Manifesto, calling on the states to resist court-ordered demands for desegregation.

There are Oedipal cross-currents in Gore's make-up. Of the obvious signs of healthful filial rebellion there have been no traces in the man. But indirectly the spoor is there. Push Gore into any corner and he'll do the wrong thing, which he'll then dignify as the consequence of an intense moral crisis. Gore is brittle, often the mark of the overly well-behaved, perfect child. When things start to go wrong, he unravels fast. Who can forget the panicked performance when his image of moral rectitude shattered at the impact of the fundraising scandals associated with the Buddhist temple in Los Angeles? Then, faced with evidence of illegal fundraising calls made from his White House office and surrounded by an unwontedly hostile press, all Gore could do was bleat out the foolish phrase that "no controlling authority" had prevented him from doing so. When Dan Quayle and later Bill Bradley taxed him with the antiabortion stance he held for most of his Congressional career, earning him an 84 percent Right To Life rating, Gore opted for rigid denial, claiming preposterously that he'd always been pro choice.

"He was an easy child, he always wanted to please us", his mother, Pauline, once said of him. This desire to please, to get the attention of often-absent parents, has been an incentive to exaggerate accomplishments. He claimed that his investigative reports at *The Tennessean* had "got a bunch of people indicted and sent to jail". Not true. He claimed that he and Tipper were the models for the couple in Eric Segal's book *Love Story*, a claim Segal was forced to deny, saying he was puzzled by Gore's assertions.

He is a stretcher in every sense of the word, either with full-blown fibs or the expansion of some modest achievement into impossible vainglory. He claimed to have created the Internet, a ludicrous pretension, although he would have been safe and truthful in describing his early support for federal funding for the Internet. He claimed to have been the author of the earned income tax credit, which had been enacted two years before Gore entered Congress.

When Gore takes an action it's as if the body politic is part of his family. The action is portrayed as having at its root some personal epiphany or trauma. He advertises crisis, depicts an interlude of anguish and claims to have achieved a higher level of moral awareness. There are the family romances with the truth. In interviews, in his book *Earth in the Balance* and, famously, in his acceptance speech at the 1992 Democratic convention, Gore shamelessly milked the accident in which his 6-year-old son was badly hurt from being struck by a car. Gore described how, amid his anguish beside the boy's hospital bed, he peered into his own soul and reproached himself for being an absentee dad. He narrated his entry into family therapy. But Tipper and the children didn't see more of him as a consequence of all that. Despite that dark night of the soul beside Al III's bed, he plunged even deeper into Senate business and spent whatever hours of leisure were available holed up away from the family, writing *Earth in the Balance* in his parents' old penthouse in the Fairfax Hotel. Soon after, he accepted Clinton's invitation to run for vice president in '92.

The epiphanies end when the family drama goes sour. When Albert III was busted for pot at St. Albans, the Gores successfully lobbied the Washington press not to run with the story. When St. Albans publicly disciplined little Albert, the Gores yanked him out of the school and enrolled him in Sidwell Friends, the elite Quaker-run prep school attended by Chelsea Clinton. When Karenna was at Cathedral, she was, by her admission, pretty wild. Sarah, the third daughter, was busted for under-age drinking at a Washington party. But Al Gore learned nothing from these experiences as a father, and preaches self-righteously about the need for the "personal responsibility" of errant children, signing on to vicious laws that hit minority teenagers hardest.

To a Democratic convention in Chicago in 1996, Gore described in vivid emotional detail the death of his sister, Nancy, from cancer. Many thought his description a wholly inappropriate and exploitative way of advocating a policy—-in this case, reduction in smoking.

That remembered psychodrama was also bogus. "She couldn't speak", Gore proclaimed to the crowd in Chicago. "But I felt clearly I knew she was forming a question, 'Do you bring me hope?' All of us had tried to find whatever new treatment, new approach might help, but all I could do was to say back to her with all the gentleness in my heart, 'I love you.' And then I knelt by her bed and held her hand and in a very short time, her breathing became labored and then she breathed her last breath. And that is why until I draw my last breath, I will pour my heart and soul into the cause of protecting our children from the dangers of smoking." *CounterPunch*, the newsletter edited by the authors of this book, was one of the first to point out, a week later, that Nancy's death from cigarette smoking scarcely had as brisk an effect on her brother as he claimed. After she breathed her last, Al Gore went on accepting tobacco company money, and went on accepting government subsidies for his own tobacco allotments in Tennessee. He stayed addicted to his tobacco allotments and tobacco industry cash for seven long years after she died before finally claiming that he'd tested clean.

Confronted with this protracted time lag between resolve and the consummation of that resolve, Gore said it had been "a process of growth". "I felt the numbness", he said, "that prevented me from integrating into all aspects of my life the implications of what that tragedy really meant."

As for the Gores' favored drug of the early 1970s, in 1999 about 700,000 people were arrested for marijuana offenses, about 87 percent for possession. That is more than double the number in the early 1990s. Of the federal prison population of 150,000, about 60 percent are in for drug law violations, the largest proportion for marijuana. Drug offenders comprise about a quarter of the 1.2 million in state prisons and about the same fraction of the 500,000 in local jails. Maybe Gore should feel a special kinship for these inmates; instead he cries for punishment.

Al Gore knows all about addiction. His sister was unable to kick the cigarette habit even as she was breathing with one cancerous lung. He knows about congenital dispositions. His wife, Tipper, is a depressive. He knows about therapy too, having communed with shrinks when he was having the midlife sag that partly prompted *Earth in the Balance*.

Suppose that some day tobacco becomes a criminalized drug. Booze too. Suppose Sister Nancy were still around and got put in prison for manslaughter while driving under the influence of alcohol (an option under current law). How would Brother Al feel if she were given more jail time, because she couldn't quit smoking? How would he feel if she were out on parole, then locked back up because nicotine or alcohol showed up in her blood in a routine test when she applied for a job? How would he like it if someone told Tipper that she should just "snap out" of her depression?

Gore is both credulous and cynical at the same time. A child sick with whooping cough conjures up for him global epidemics. A hot summer in Indiana prompts him to cry that the earth is on fire. His son's injured body in a hospital bed is projected as a metaphor for the ailments of mankind. His wife's depression is magnified into a national campaign to persuade Americans they are all depressed. Al Gore never projects optimism. The Malthusian doomsayers he studied at Vanderbilt remain his models. His favorite mode, adopted in *Earth in the Balance*, is as the herald of catastrophe.

In 1968, Robert Sherill and Harry Ernst published a short book, *The Drugstore Liberal*, on the Democratic candidate for the presidency that year, Hubert Humphrey. It was a hilarious demolition of bankrupt liberalism couching itself in all the tumid homilies of a man who genuinely did believe that the world could be improved by good intentions. As *Al Gore: A User's Manual* shows, the Democratic Party has moved onward and downward since then, and this is not surprising since the center of gravity of the entire system has moved to the right. Studying the economic record of the Clinton administration the economist Robert Pollin has rightly pointed out that "a Republican incumbent of one period can easily be less reactionary than a Democrat in the next, as we have repeatedly seen from the data – Nixon presiding over higher wages and less poverty than Clinton." The Democratic Party platform for 2000, drafted by Gore's people, would have been unimaginable to Humphrey or Nixon.

Presidents are captives of history and national circumstance. Yet they can make their mark, for better or for worse. What does Al Gore have in him to accomplish? What sort of accomplishments would they be? To many, his record is blurry. Yet the evidence is there for us to form a judgement.

2 GILDED YOUTH

A child eager to please demanding parents.
Unfavorable assessment of our hero by schoolmates.
Life below stairs with Donna; Tipper and "animal
magnetism"; school and indifferent grades; Harvard
and Martin Peretz. Gore prays for Hubert Humphrey
and marches off to war. Back home, Al and Tipper
most definitely inhale.

Gore's grandparents on his father's side were tobacco and hog farmers in Possum Hollow in middle Tennessee.

From the rigors of farm life Gore's father, hereinafter identified as Albert Sr., extricated himself via a teaching job and then a law degree from the Nashville YMCA, though he was never a practicing lawyer, unlike his wife, Pauline LaFon, who hailed from the town of Jackson, in northwest Tennessee.

Beyond acknowledgement that she played a major role in planning the political careers of her husband and son, the standard Gore literature scants the career and personality of this formidable woman, born a Huguenot, whose father was a shopkeeper who had gone bankrupt not long before she met Albert. The two major biographies of Al Jr. don't even record the name of her first husband, whom she married in her teens, seemingly as the only available path out of poverty. This tactical alliance collapsed after less than a year, but it was enough to set Pauline on a course that eventually led her to Vanderbilt law school, where she became that institution's second female graduate, and to Albert Sr., whom she met in the coffee shop of the Andy Jackson Hotel while working her way through school as a waitress.

Pauline wasn't the last person to note a certain stodginess to the Gore men, saying of Albert Sr., "I couldn't tempt him to leave any serious work, no matter how fancy a party we were invited to. That's what bothered me the most at that age." In 1936 Albert Sr. and Pauline took the bar exam and then parted, she going off to work at a tiny firm in Texarkana.

In 1937 Albert Sr. got a big break, appointed by Governor Gordon Browning as the state's first labor commissioner. Having quit her job (later she would say she was being sexually harassed by her law partner), Pauline returned from Texarkana to discover that he had attained this promising altitude, suppressed what qualms she might have had about his austere view of the lighter things in life and married him. "I was not only ambitious for him but for myself too." They effected this union in a civil ceremony in Kentucky, taking pains that the marriage license would escape scrutiny back home. Pauline was already carrying Nancy, Al Jr.'s elder sister.

Political opportunity soon knocked, in the form of a vacant House seat in their Tennessee district, and they threw themselves into Albert Sr.'s first race. Pauline's natural political skills certainly helped. So too did Albert Sr.'s cousin Grady Gore, a real estate tycoon based in Washington DC. Although vigorously conservative himself, Grady seems to have calculated that it would do no harm to have a New Deal liberal in his debt. As detailed by Gore Vidal, Grady Gore was something of a king-maker, one of a fistful of Tennessee millionaires to have survived and indeed prospered during the Depression. He had been a loyal financial backer of Senator Kenneth "Old Formidable" McKellar back in the time when senators had nicknames like battleships and there were no limits on how much cash you could stuff in the pockets of politicians. In the 1930s Grady asked McKellar for a small favor: hire his cousin Al for a junior staff position, a job that Grady was happy to underwrite. But McKellar refused. Why, Grady enquired. "Don't like him," McKellar snarled. Grady called Albert Sr. to break the news. "I was to give that old bastard $40,000 for his re-election, but not now. I'm going to give it to you." So he staked Albert Sr. with the $40,000, a hefty sum in middle Tennessee in the late 1930s.

Albert Sr. had other useful connections. Among his father's youthful companions, rafting down the Cumberland River and enjoying other boyhood adventures, had been Cordell Hull, later to become FDR's Secretary of State. Hull took a keen interest in Albert Sr.'s political career. With such patrons at his elbow Albert Sr. sailed into the House, ensconcing himself and his family on the top floor—two bedrooms, lino on the floor—of the Fairfax Hotel, owned by Grady Gore. There they lived rent-free for the rest of Albert Sr.'s political career in Washington.

By the time Al Jr. was born, on March 31, 1948, his father had enjoyed a gratifying ascent in the House, marked as one of FDR's hand-picked defenders of the New Deal. Albert Sr. was gaining seniority on the powerful Banking and Commerce Committee. Even more pertinent to the fortunes of the Gore family and those of Tennessee, he was chairman of the subcommittee that oversaw the Atomic Energy Commission.

This was the era in which the political geography of Tennessee was changed forever by two immense federal programs. The first was the network of dams and power plants that formed the infrastructure of the Tennessee Valley Authority, created by Congress in 1933 to supply cheap power to the rural South. The second was the Oak Ridge atomic laboratory, part of the Manhattan Project. For any Tennessee politician, TVA and Oak Ridge are as potent symbols of the fructifying powers of the federal dollar as the Hoover dam and Los Alamos labs are for Westerners. Albert Sr. and Pauline never lost their profound respect for vast pork barrel projects. Although he was later to gain fame as an opponent of the Vietnam war Albert Sr. also sat on the Senate Armed Services Committee, and tended to the needs of defense contractors from caterers to ship-builders, uniform manufacturers to arms makers.

No sooner had he been inaugurated as US Senator from Tennessee in 1953 than Albert Sr. was elevated by the Democratic Bourbons to head the Roads Subcommittee of the Senate's Public Works Committee, a post more accurately described as Assistant Minder of the Pork Barrel. At that time there was civil war, bloody and terrible, among the primers of the pork barrel. On one side was the potent lobby for country roads; on the other the men of vision, gazing across the American landscape and seeing the trillions of yards of concrete and the billions in bribes for easements, for rights of way, for strategically placed off-ramps, for all the endless corrupt arrangements required to build an interstate highway system, now the concern of the Eisenhower Administration.

There is in the genes of the Gore family a propensity to boast excessively. Long before young Al even imagined the Internet, Albert Sr. was claiming he was father, or at least midwife, to the National Highway Defense Act, the $50 billion program to build 40,000 miles of interstate highway, at that time the largest public works program in the history of the world. In truth, Albert Sr. was a lowly facilitator in establishing the fortunes of thousands upon thousands of building contractors and heavy equipment operators. The real

11

hero on the Hill was Representative Hale Boggs. It took a Louisiana good old boy rather than the Solon of Tennessee to reconcile the Guelphs and Ghibellines of the warring lobbies to work harmoniously for the greater enrichment of all. Evidently Boggs held Albert Sr. in low esteem as a consequence of their work on the highway bill, making a spirited though failed bid in the late 1960s to get Albert Sr. investigated by the SEC for stock fraud.

Young Al grew up a public child of public parents, mostly left on his own at the Fairfax Hotel, though always available as a display item to his parents' political associates and the press. Every student of Al Jr. encounters the "woodenness" factor. It's not so mysterious. Al Gore has been watching his act almost as long as he's been alive. Youthful rebellion was never a part of his psychic c.v. Even his mother described him as "fairly much a conformist". She also said, "Al was an easy child, very sensitive to our feelings. He wanted to do what we wanted him to do... Al never wanted to be the person to make an unhappy noise." To the sermons and injunctions of his father, worthy of Polonius in their earnest protraction, Al Jr. invariably lent a dutiful ear. His sister, Nancy, had spark, but was a decade older. By the time Al was in his early teens she was long since out of the home, making her career in the Peace Corps.

For his education the Gores dispatched Al Jr. to St. Albans, stentorian in its professions of high moral tone, labile in its recognition of the realities of its role as forcing ground for the political ruling elites of the morrow. His classmates at St. Albans remembered Al Jr. to reporters and biographers as "a stuffed shirt, even as a kid", "too well behaved", "too grown up", "excessively competitive", with "no sense of play", living "in a world of his own", "not a risk taker". Pitiless as schoolboys often are, they put under Gore's entries in the yearbook "a wooden Apollo", "Ozymandias" and the yearbook editors affixed beneath his photo a quote from Anatole France, "People without weaknesses are terrible".

Barbara Howar, a friend of Al Jr.'s more rebellious sister, described him as "an egregious little tattletale". She was on the mark. As center on St. Albans' woefully unsuccessful football team, Gore played the sneak, visiting the coach privately one Saturday morning to confide virtuously that he was concerned that his teammates were violating rules by staying out late, smoking cigarettes and drinking beer.

Gore's teachers remember him as a plodding and passive student who seemed energized only by art. "He forced himself to be good at sports and win school elections", one of his teachers recalled in 1998, "but he wasn't a natural at anything except painting, where he was really first rate. Miniatures. They were exquisite."

Gore's biographers invariably turn with relief from this arid teenage life in Washington to Al Jr.'s summers in Tennessee on the Gore family farm on the Caney Fork River outside Carthage. As always, his parents supervised their son's life script diligently. His father said in 1992 that he had carefully blended the two worlds of DC and Carthage, inculcating in Al "the rural influences and political society". Chores around the farm? It was not enough to paint a picket fence. Albert Sr. devised purgatorial tests for his son, planting tobacco, slopping hogs and forcing the prentice Cincinnatus to plow a hillside with a horse team. When even Pauline questioned the exhausting regime, Albert Sr. loftily replied, "I think a boy, to achieve anything he wants to achieve, which would include being president of the United States, ought to be able to run a hillside plough."

Al Jr. did find a warmth lacking in Washington, but his later recollections of associations with tenant farmers and farmers' daughters have a certain predictability to them, like the below-stairs adventures of Prince Hal, or the frontier escapades of Teddy Roosevelt in the Dakotas. He spent much time with the Thompson family, tenant farmers who worked the Gore plantation. The Thompsons lived in a small cabin without indoor plumbing or electricity, in pastoral contradiction to the marble mansion of Albert and Pauline.

Al Jr. fell in love with a local girl, Donna Armistead, two years his senior. They enjoyed a bucolic romance of drive-ins, soda shops and lovers' lanes. Al also became close to Donna's working-class family. "What he didn't get from his family, he picked up from our own", Donna Armistead said years later. "I guess he got a nurturing he was lacking." Gore wrote to her once a day.

But parental vigilance was unremitting. On Donna's account, Pauline interrupted a necking session in the basement of the Gore manse with the words, "Hey, you kids, let's not get into trouble here. You could work out in the gym for an hour. And there's always cold showers." Al never did invite Donna to Washington; maybe Pauline, reviewing her own history, feared that the young woman might have seen her son as a passport out of middle Tennessee. Albert Sr. and Pauline tried to engineer a strategic alliance for their son with the daughter of the exuberant senior Senator from Tennessee, Estes Kefauver. Diane Kefauver would have none of it, later declaring that Al Jr. "had an ego as big as a house".

Al Jr. had barely left St. Albans when, in the spring of 1965, he met Mary Elizabeth Aitcheson at his graduation party. Tipper, as she was known from childhood, lived with her mother across the Potomac in Arlington. Her father, Jack, had flown the nest when she was 14 months old. Margaret Aitcheson complained in the divorce papers that her husband had beat her. "By the time we were married a month, he went out, stayed out all night and came home with a broken nose. He was drinking. When he couldn't find words to express his displeasure, he would hit me." For his part, Jack Aitcheson, who owned a plumbing company, riposted that Margaret "lacked the normal maternal instincts". He charged that she slept late, dallied in bed and neglected to feed or clothe their daughter properly.

In fact Margaret suffered from chronic depression, a malady that surfaced in Tipper some years later. These days Tipper and Al still own the house in the Aurora Hills neighborhood of Arlington, where Tipper was raised, mostly by her grandmother and grandfather, a DC-area banker.

Tipper was a lot more fun than Al. She'd dated her way through some of the football team at St. Albans, supposedly played drums in a garage rock band called the Wildcats (a feat vigorously disputed by some musicians who tangled with her during the porn rock battles of the mid-80s) and drove a blue '64 Mustang. "Pure animal magnetism" was the way she excitedly described her first encounter with Gore. "We put on a record and danced and danced. It was just like everyone else melted away. And that was it. We've been together ever since."

More or less. Actually, Al returned to Tennessee that summer, and Donna Armistead says they broke up only in his first year at Harvard. By the fall of 1966 Tipper was heading for Boston to be near Al, and Donna was on her honeymoon with her new husband in a cabin on the Cumberland River near Carthage. There, so Donna rather cattily disclosed some years later, she espied her former boyfriend in a neighboring cabin two nights running with another Carthage woman. Donna wasn't the only one to be less than thrilled by Al's new girlfriend. Diane Kefauver edgily recalled that "I was always struck by how protective she was of him. She always seemed to be keeping him away from other people, jealously guarding him."

As for Gore's parents, the good-time girl from a broken home in Arlington was not what they'd hoped for. Albert Sr. eyed the Mustang with disapproval, while Pauline fumed at Tipper's pedigree in commerce. To his credit Al took parental fire without flinching and beckoned Tipper to Boston. Soon enough she had enlisted in Garland Junior College in 1966, before ultimately attending Boston University, where she majored in psychology.

There's a familiar refrain in the biographies and profiles of Al Gore, to the effect that vivacious intelligence and uproarious wit flower in Gore's private moments but become shrouded when he moves beyond his intimates. It's hard to find much material evidence for intellectual prowess in Gore's student years. Granted, grades and SAT scores are a racket, and certainly no reliable guide to intelligence and mental verve. Winston Churchill famously liked to suggest that at Harrow he'd been a poor student, which shows just how smart Churchill was, since in fact he was a rather good student but knew that a legend of youthful failure would increase his popular appeal. But Gore's blatantly lousy academic record is pertinent, if only to show just how inert he was. No sign of extracurricular energy balances the dimness of his scholastic activities. Derided by Gore and many others as a blockhead, George W. Bush had a better academic record as a history major at Yale.

At St. Albans Gore's record was mediocre. Only in art

class did he display enthusiasm and a measure of originality. That was the one course (he took it every year) in which he consistently got As. He got Bs and Cs in English; Bs and Cs in history; Cs in math and French; and a lonely A in sacred studies. He ended up ranking 25th in his class of 51. (At Hot Springs High School, Bill Clinton ran fifth out of a class of 200.)

On the other hand Gore did display a mature understanding of the manner in which elites are formed and sustained in the United States, since he displayed no qualms about the effect those poor grades might have on his higher education. The Senator's son put down Harvard as his only choice and was not disappointed. As John Davis, assistant headmaster at St. Albans, put it baldly thirty-five years later, "In Al's case, he was what Harvard most wanted at that time. What they wanted was competent academic performance, plus future potential. Plus they were very impressed by the fact that he was a political son. Colleges like Harvard, Princeton and Yale are just as excited to get important sons as top academic scholars. They want our boys as much as our boys want them."

At Harvard, Gore's grades were mostly Cs, with not a single A to lighten the darkness in his first two years. The best he could manage in a course called Man's Place in Nature was a D. Defeated by Chaucer, he abandoned English as a major for political science and the flattering attentions of Martin Peretz and Richard Neustadt.

When he got to Harvard in 1965, student activism was already surging. As the son of a Senator from Tennessee young Gore was certainly sensitive to the great issues. A stock anecdote from the Gore thesaurus has young Al calling his father in 1964 to upbraid him for voting against the Civil Rights Act. Such indignation was not apparent in the Harvard freshman in the fraught year of 1965. No sooner had he arrived than Gore threw himself into a race for class president. He won, but after a year of reviewing cafeteria menus and attending to similarly weighty matters, he retired to the basement of Dunster House and abandoned all forms of politics in favor of mopery. Many who visited Dunster House at that time remember Al as a youth who would arise from marijuana-induced reveries on the couch to ask them if they cared to "shoot a little pool".

He did see Tipper. *The Washington Post* pundit Roger Rosenblat, at that time a tutor at Dunster House, returned late one night well after curfew to see Al hustling Miss Aitcheson out of the dorm. "There was but one path connecting us and no escape for the future vice president. I saw the terror in his Boy Scout eyes, which might have read 'There goes the presidency.' We passed each other quickly on the path. I greeted Al and Tipper, 'Good evening, boys.'"

Al and Tipper found each other, and so did Al and Marty Peretz. Peretz was engineering for himself a certain acclaim with his leftish seminars on the state of modern civilization, leading carefully selected students helter-skelter through a tour of the big thinkers such as Marx and Freud. Out of a hundred or so students, all carefully scrutinized by the young professor, Gore was one of the chosen twelve, showing that, though lacking in theoretical substance, Peretz was capable of applying political science at the tactical level. (Also in the final cut was Don Gilligan, son of a Democratic Congressman from Ohio.)

In 1967 Peretz's intellectual divagations acquired the substantial ballast of one of America's major fortunes, or that portion of same supervised by the trustees of Anne Labouisse Farnsworth, heiress to the Singer sewing machine empire. Freighted with the responsibilities of this new union in the fall of that same year Peretz drew a line in the sand on the precise nature of his radicalism.

In Chicago hundreds of young leftists gathered for a National Conference on the New Politics. As the great radical journalist Andrew Kopkind described it in an essay at the time, this was the moment when "the liberal-left coalition finally and permanently split on the basic principle of support for the black liberation movement. Until that time the coalition had been led by those in the process of becoming radical—the civil rights workers, the SDS anti-war demonstrators, the community organizers. But a new set of social and political conditions was turning young people's heads around, and the papered-over splits began to widen."

Peretz had bankrolled the convention. Kopkind describes the convulsive climax: "The blacks and the white left refused to realign the coalition with liberal leadership. Martin Peretz stalked out of their Palmer House ballroom and announced to the TV cameras, 'The movement is dead.' And so it was, on its old terms. But implicit in the political system was the need for a 'liberal' front to mediate divisive political conflict; thus, it was not long before Peretz, Allard Lowenstein and several other drop-outs from the old movement began putting together a New Politics coalition focussed on capturing the reformist wing of the Democratic Party. The forum for their efforts became the McCarthy campaign."

In this striking paragraph, Kopkind prefigured not only the itinerary of Peretz from fashionable rad to rabid neocon but the later mime of that shift, embodied in the rise of the Democratic Leadership Council which was born in 1985. The favored vehicle of ambitious Southern and Western Democrats like Bill Clinton, Bruce Babbitt, John Breaux and Al Gore, a founding member, the DLC was designed to extract money and

19

political endorsements from corporate bigwigs while selling to ever-receptive pundits the notion that here at last was an outfit prepared to do battle with the hated "special interests", otherwise known as the base of the Democratic Party—people in unions, blacks, Hispanics, Greens and so on.

By 1968 Peretz was telling the late Blair Clark that "I have been in love only three times in my life. I was in love with my college roommate. I am in love with the state of Israel and I love Gene McCarthy." Peretz imparted at least two of those passions to Gore, who returned in the summer of 1968 to Tennessee to work for Gene. But Gore's energies were quickly transferred to his party's eventual nominee. On election night, he told a Harvard friend, he was praying for Hubert Humphrey's victory.

Not long after, Peretz was describing himself as "the great disenchanter" of radical enthusiasm at Harvard. In 1969 he and Gore watched in disapproval as students occupied University Hall. Harvard President Nathan Pusey summoned the state police and the students were beaten and arrested in large numbers, among them many of Gore's dorm mates at Dunster House. Gore said later he only attended a few antiwar rallies before he got turned off by the radicalism of his fellow students: "I remember going to a meeting when somebody proposed to destroy a railroad switching point with explosives. I said, 'Wait a minute, whoa, that's crazy. I don't want to hear any more about that.'"

A few years later Peretz bought *The New Republic* from Gil Harrison and fashioned its politics in accord with the neoconservative paradigm that has always been the political tropism of Peretz's protégé, Gore. As Jefferson Morley, a *New Republic* contributor in the 1980s, put it: "In cartoon form *The*

New Republic was about not being easy on blacks, not being easy on Communists, and not being tough on Jews. The magazine was self-consciously evolving out of its liberal past."

Down the years Peretz would always be on the alert for bright young men to bring into his and his magazine's orbit, sometimes interviewing them in his suite in the Sherry Netherlands Hotel in New York, ensconcing them on a white fur sofa as he probed their outlooks. Among Peretz's epigones was the briefly high-flying Michael Kinsley (later to end up in the Siberia of the Gates Gulag in Redmond, Washington, editing the online magazine *Slate*), and a clutch of writers who subsequently fled to *The New Yorker*: Hendrik Hertzberg, Lewis Menand and Sidney Blumenthal. Later still came Peretz's gay *Wunderkind*, Andrew Sullivan, who, like Michael Kelly, was ultimately run out of *The New Republic*'s editorial chair.

It was Sullivan who, in 1993, described *The New Republic*'s politics at the onset of Clinton time: "We live in the ruins of liberalism and conservatism. Our real problems, we see, are spiritual and psychological." This, as it happens, is an eerily faithful echo of Gore's reflexive habit of casting his personal biography and his prescriptive politics in the idiom of therapy and of America's larger travails. In Gore's life every episode is cast as crisis, epiphany, another turning point on the Damascus Road.

Gore's other main intellectual mentor at Harvard was Richard Neustadt, author of *Presidential Power* and a Kennedy man. Neustadt had as opportunistic an eye for useful contacts as did Peretz, and he lost no time in persuading Gore to abandon his English major (and plans to write a Faulknerian saga about life in Carthage) in favor of government studies. One of Neustadt's pedagogical stunts was to have his students play out the roles of JFK and his senior advisers during the Cuban Missile Crisis of 1963. Neustadt handed Gore the choice role of the President, though he did remark of Gore later, that the future Vice President was "a wimpy moderate". Neustadt's TA in this class was Graham Allison, who later advised Gore on nuclear issues in the Senate and in the White House.

Under Neustadt's tutelage Gore wrote his honors thesis on the role of television in the conduct of the presidency from 1947 to 1969. This was no cloistered foray in communications history. As befitted the son of a prominent Senator, Gore established many useful future contacts, interviewing Arthur Schlesinger Jr., James Reston, Bill Moyers and that emissary of Hollywood and all its millions, Jack Valenti.

Like most young American males in 1968, Al Gore also had to face the fact that he might get drafted. Lyndon Johnson had announced an end to the graduate school deferments. At Oxford, Bill Clinton began his intricate maneuvers to avoid going to Vietnam without, as he famously put it, compromising his "viability within the system".

Connoisseurs of Al Gore learn to recognize the note of histrionic unctuousness when he is reinventing some important moment in his life, such as his decision to go to Vietnam, his emotions at his sister's death bed, the soul searching after his son's traumatic injury, his decision to back the war on Iraq. The way he tells it, his decision to go to Vietnam was an act of the purest altruism: "I came from a small town where I knew my contemporaries. I knew how the quota system worked, and I realized that if I decided not to go and figured out some way to get out of it that would mean somebody else from my hometown would go instead of me. I thought about that a lot. I felt that would outweigh my own personal calculations of rights and wrongs about the country's policy."

Before different audiences Gore has a variant on this self-serving account, to the effect that he enlisted in order to protect his father's Senate seat, burnishing this rationale with the claim that he thus hoped to ensure that his father, a well-known opponent of the war, would survive his 1970 re-election battle and return to bring the war to a speedy close.

Albert Sr., it seems, would have been happy for his son to stay home. Pauline, having a keener eye to her son's political future, left him under no illusions about her own views that he should enlist – although she later claimed she would have supported him if he'd dodged the draft by heading north to Canada. Gore's two academic patrons were united in their pragmatic counsel. Neustadt told Gore bluntly that if he wanted to go into politics he had no choice but to go to Vietnam; "it would stand him in very good stead, both because of what he would learn about people, and because of the legitimacy it would convey".

The one person who didn't have much say in this was Tipper, to whom Gore had just proposed marriage. As always, it was Tipper's fate to have been well back in the line of people with whom Al discussed important decisions. After he got back from Vietnam, when the couple was living in Nashville, Tipper was embarking on a promising career as a photographer for *The Tennessean*. Her husband duly confronted her with his decision, already charted out with his father and *The Tennessean*'s editor, John Siegenthaler, to make a run for Congress.

In 1988, when Tipper had just started a tour to promote her book *Raising PG Kids in an X-Rated Society*, Al suddenly dumped the news on her that, after consultation with Democratic Party money man Nathan Landow, pollster Pat

23

Caddell and his father, he was going to run for the presidency. That ended the tour, and Tipper later said ruefully that it cost her 250,000 book sales. Psychically it evidently cost her a lot more, piled on top of running an essentially single-parent household, raising three kids with a husband on the Hill or otherwise absent on political duty.

In 1991, with Tipper at home still distraught about the serious injuries their little son Al III suffered in a traffic accident, Al II elected to cloister himself in the Fairfax apartment writing *Earth in the Balance*. A year later, having vowed to spend more time with his family, he accepted Bill's beckoning finger to be on the democratic ticket. By the time Tipper became Second Lady she was suffering serious bouts of clinical depression, a malady the Clinton-Gore Administration parlayed into a Tipper-led campaign to promulgate the use of Prozac, an antidepressant made by the Lilly pharmaceutical company, whose sales force now counted the Second Lady as one of its most effective crusaders.

One of Gore's biographers, Bill Turque, cites an obviously well-informed though unnamed source who describes a series of meetings he had with 22-year-old Al Gore in Washington, in which they discussed how Al could serve in the army while simultaneously satisfying the political requirement of self-sacrifice and the personal desire to take no untoward risks. This informant, a distant relative on Gore's mother's side, says that Gore told him he was about to enlist, didn't want to get killed but feared that since his father was a prominent opponent of the war he might get "rat-fucked"—that is, put in dangerous situations for political reasons.

Gore's relative, who was both rich and connected, duly contacted a person well placed to give useful counsel, none other than Gen. William Westmoreland, at that time Chief of Staff of the US army. After further parleys, Westmoreland was informed that Gore wanted to be an army journalist. The general advised the intermediary that if Gore went ahead and enlisted he "will be watched, will be cared for".

The way Gore tells the story, he enlisted in New Jersey. After Gore studied an aptitude test, completed an application form in which he elevated his position as intern at *The New York Times* to the dignity of "newspaper trainee" and spoke of his passion for writing poetry, an officer supposedly said, "We think you'd make a good reporter". In fact, Westmoreland had been as good as his word and set everything up.

While still a student at Harvard, Gore had written a letter to his father—naturally disowned in later years—in which he wrote, "We do have inveterate antipathy for communism—or paranoia, as I like to put it. My own belief is that this form of psychological ailment—in this case a national madness—leads the victim to actually create the thing which is feared most. It strikes me that this is precisely what the US has been doing. Creating—and if not creating, energetically supporting—fascist, totalitarian regimes in the name of fighting totalitarianism. Greece, South Vietnam, a good deal of Latin America. For me, the best example of all is the US Army."

But no sooner had political exigency put him in this same Army than Gore became a good soldier, indeed being named "soldier of the month" at Fort Rucker, Alabama, the army's helicopter training base. In an interview with *Military Times* in the spring of 2000, Gore looked back on his times with Tipper there as an idyll. "We moved into a trailer in Daleville, Alabama, just outside the gates of Fort Rucker. Often our clothes on the clothes line were blown full of red clay by the helicopters trying to land right next to the trailer park. We had great memories of those wonderful times." Tipper remembered differently, more as a season in purgatory. She recalled being repelled by the small, filthy trailer that was infested with cockroaches.

Gore's high-level connection became overt when Westmoreland came to Rucker on an official visit, plucked Private Gore from the parade ground and conferred with the young man while senior officers looked on with distaste at the colloquy. In this conversation Westmoreland told Gore that he would be making a grave error if he didn't go to Vietnam.

The advice found its mark. In short order Gore put in his papers for transfer to Vietnam and married Tipper, in the National Cathedral in Washington, causing some offense to his army colleagues by appearing in dress blues, normally worn by officers, not privates. The photographs have been standard issue in Gore campaigns ever since.

Gore has always claimed that Nixon's dirty tricksters held up his departure for Vietnam in 1970 to ensure that in that year's congressional elections Albert Sr. would not be able to make rhetorical flourishes in Tennessee about his son doing his duty on the front lines. Albert Sr. needed all the rhetorical ammunition he could muster, since he was now locked in a desperate campaign to save his Senate seat from capture by the Republican challenger, Bill Brock, heir to a candy fortune. As a longtime opponent of the Vietnam War, Albert Sr. felt that his opposition would undermine his re-election chances.

He was right. He was doomed, for mostly respectable reasons: his antiwar stance, his refusal to sign Strom Thurmond's Southern Manifesto, his votes against Nixon's Supreme Court nominees, Haynesworth and Carswell, both Southerners. There was also the burden of his long years in Washington, provoking the usual charges that he'd gone metro and forgotten the folks back home. Overall, it was a hard time for southern senate liberals. In Texas, Ralph Yarborough, a very decent antiwar progressive, had been fatally savaged in the Democratic primary by Lloyd Bentsen, who went after the old veteran with charges that he was an integrationist, soft on student radicals and against the military. The brutal Bentsen campaign became a model for Brock; meanwhile, cartloads of undercover cash from a Nixon slush fund known as the Townhouse Operation buried Albert Sr.'s always scrawny fundraising abilities.

Even so, in late October it looked as though Albert Sr. might pull it out of the fire. He'd drawn level, even a nose ahead. Then, in the last week, Brock threw the issue of school prayer at him, and it was all over. As the sun set on Albert Sr.'s public life and he prepared to enter what he frankly described as "the tall grass" of a corporate sinecure from the oil tycoon Armand Hammer, he shouted out to the cameras and the microphones in his concession speech, "The truth shall rise again." No one had any doubt of the dynastic implications of that cry. Sons are not inclined to forget their fathers' humiliations, and Al Jr. certainly never forgot what happened to his father. He was never going to get caught exposed as a liberal, or as a dove. And he was never going to be short of cash either.

Before he took off for Vietnam, Gore returned to Cambridge for one last session with Peretz and Neustadt. During his 1988 bid for the presidency Gore told reporters that in this trip he found himself heckled by antiwar students: "My hair was cut short and I wore a uniform. I walked through the streets of Cambridge and I became so angry at the presumption of those who instantly shouted epithets and sneered."

Those students had the right instincts, of course, about a

child of privilege who'd been against the war not long before, who was making a demonstration trip to Vietnam for political reasons, while using his family's influence to get the army Chief of Staff to make sure he wouldn't be in danger.

Gore arrived at the vast Bien Hoa army base outside Saigon in January 1971. He was assigned to the 20th Engineers Brigade as an army reporter, extolling their activities for the *Castle Courier*. Campaigning in 1988, Gore boasted, "I was shot at. I spent most of my time in the field. I carried an M-16. I pulled my turn on the perimeter at night and walked through elephant grass, and I was fired upon. Something would move. We'd fire first and ask questions later." As part of his campaign literature Gore put out a photo of himself carrying an M-16.

Gore's army buddies remember it all rather differently. Alan Leo probably spent as much time as anyone did with Gore in Vietnam. Indeed, he later described himself as "Gore's security escort". Leo says that he was ordered to shepherd Gore through his tour in Vietnam, making sure he never got into any dangerous situations. The man who gave these orders was Brig. Gen. K.B. Cooper. "It blew me away", Leo said in the spring of 2000. "I was to make sure he didn't get into a situation he could not get out of. They didn't want him to get into trouble. So we went into the field after the fact and that limited his exposure to any hazards."

To some friends at the time Gore portrayed his service as a descent into the heart of darkness, an experience so shattering that he vowed, "I'm going to divinity school to atone for my sins." To others he offered a robust account, saying his only regret was that he wouldn't be returning to Vietnam for a second tour. Another version had him acquiring post-radical enlightenment. "Before I went over I never really had an emotional appreciation for the fact that there were people in South Vietnam who desperately wanted the US to win and to keep them away from this loss of freedom."

Against this we have what sounds like a pretty realistic account of Gore's tour from another army colleague, Bob Delabar. He described merry nights spent drinking Budweiser, smoking high-powered dope and playing basketball. "I think he'd say he had a lot of fun in Vietnam." Of course, that's the one thing Gore has never fessed up to.

Back on the home front Tipper most definitely was not having fun. Parked with her in-laws on the farm, with Albert Sr. brooding over his defeat, the natural worries of a newlywed about her absent warrior-mate were compounded by the old tendencies to insecurity and depression. Fortunately there was a supportive couple in Nashville, in the form of John Warnecke and his wife, Nancy, both working at *The Tennessean*. Warnecke was the son of a socially prominent architect, who designed the Kennedy Center. In respites from the rigors of the farm, Tipper would stay with the Warneckes in downtown Nashville, where the texture of life would markedly improve. For one thing the Warneckes had a comfortable relationship with drugs, ranging from marijuana to Thai sticks—marijuana coated with opium—to mescalin.

John Warnecke later went through some difficult years of depression, drug abuse and marital upheaval before putting his life together again. When the question of Gore's possible use of drugs came up during the 1998 primaries, Warnecke was the only friend who conceded that he'd seen Gore using marijuana, falsely adding that it had been a one-time thing, right after his return from Vietnam. Gore and his chief aide, Peter Knight, had pressured Warnecke strongly to deny everything; when he did make this one, entirely harmless admission, they never spoke to him again. It was a wrong move, because Warnecke gradually became more and more forthright, finally telling reporters that in the mid-1970s Gore had "smoked as much as anybody I knew down there and loved it". He also described Gore's enjoyment of Thai sticks and hashish, and jaunts to Memphis. In contrast to Tipper, he said, Gore was paranoid and would close the curtains before lighting up.

Warnecke has also spoken about Tipper's increasingly fragile state during Al's absence in Vietnam. "She had a breakdown", Warnecke recalled. "She was scared to even get out of bed, and I gave her Valium. She was shaking, crying. At one point, I had to hold her like a father, all night." Valium wasn't the only substance ingested by Tipper at that time. Warnecke describes an evening spent with Tipper after they'd dropped mescalin, a hallucinogen. "We were up all night watching a fundraiser with country music singers on TV. The effects of the drug made the singers look like freaks coming out of the TV. Tipper was into it. I remember us all laughing hilariously."

Imagine how much time in jail he and Tipper would have risked if they'd been average people and had been caught then; how much risk the same activities would involve now if they were black. No need to imagine Gore's vindictive support for harsh penalties for use of illegal drugs now. They're a matter of record.

3 ONLY FIVE YEARS A PRIVATE MAN

Three bad books shape Gore's environmental philosophy; he goes to work at The Tennessean where our hero colludes with cops and prosecutors to set up a black councilman. The Gores do Whitewater right. We meet Armand Hammer, friend of Lenin and Daddy Rabbit to the Gores. A congressional seat opens up. Tipper weeps as Al leaps. His political style.

Al Gore has always had it pretty easy, which perhaps explains why he has always gone to such preposterous lengths to exaggerate his own spiritual tribulations and travails, setting them forth always in the context of planetary crisis. Consider the five years separating his return from Vietnam and his departure to Washington as a young Congressman.

First there was the matter of what Gore billed later as the spiritual trauma of a man returning from the front. If we are to believe Warnecke such uncertainties did not seem to weigh particularly on the young man. Nor did he embark on any unduly demanding journey in examination of the higher things. He did, it's true, enlist in Vanderbilt's Divinity School in 1971, where his course of study—extremely relaxed, as we know from the fact that he failed five of his eight classes—was underwritten by a grant from the Rockefeller Foundation.

His parents had been pushing for their son to take a more traditional step toward political life, by going to law school, and Al Jr. presents his preference for divinity studies as a straightforward rejection of that career. "I felt politics was the absolute last thing I would ever do." But Donna Armistead remembers her erstwhile boyfriend visiting her grandmother in late 1971 and saying otherwise. The grandmother had been a mentor for Al down the years and now she was near death from cancer. At that last encounter, Donna says, Gore told her grandmother that he planned to enter political life.

The one class at Divinity School for which Gore displayed enthusiasm was run by Eugene TeSelle and called Theology and the Natural Sciences. Here Gore seized enthusiastically on three classics of neo-Malthusian environmentalism that would profoundly shape his environmental outlook.

The first was Fairfield Osborn's *Our Plundered Planet*, which by that point had sold more than three million copies since its publication in 1948. Fairfield Osborn, president of the Bronx Zoo, was the son of Henry Fairfield Osborn, founder of the American Museum of Natural History and an appalling anti-Semite. The elder Osborn had been one of the prime exponents of eugenics, eagerly embraced by American progressives of the period. These scientific racists promoted eugenic sterilization and supported the US immigration laws of 1924, much admired by Hitler for their categorization of "undesirable races". The Nazis honored Osborn with an honorary doctorate of science at the University of Frankfurt in 1934, and the recipient made what he described as "an enthusiastic trip" to pick up the honor.

In intellectual outlook Fairfield Osborn was unlike his awful father. Chastened by the horrors of the death camps, he was keen on constructive social actions designed to alleviate human want. He praised the TVA. But when he settled down to write *Our Plundered Planet* at the age of 61, Osborn sought counsel from men whose outlook was wholly malign. Influenced by Guy Irving Burch (co-author of *Human Breeding and Survival*) and also by William Vogt, of whom more below, *Our Plundered Planet* became an ignorant paean to the necessity for population control.

Fear of excessive population has always been a feature of American environmentalism. The conservation movement at the turn of the century had a visceral hatred of the polluting masses. The scientific racists of the time combined genetic fantasies with brusque demands that the world's poor be swiftly reduced in number. Typical was William Hornaday, director of the New York Zoological Society. In his 1913 jeremiad, *Our Vanishing Wildlife: Its Extermination and Preservation*, Hornaday warned that "members of the lower classes of southern Europe constitute a dangerous menace to our wildlife". These same lower classes are "spreading, spreading, spreading".

After Auschwitz had been opened to the eyes of the world, genetic racism fell temporarily into disrepute, though immediately after World War II liberal icons like Margaret Sanger were still pushing for sterilization plans. Fairfield Osborn's book helped powerfully to revive the old fears and fantasies of his father's generation. In the closing paragraph of *Our Plundered Planet*, Osborn declared, "The tide of the earth's population is rising, the reservoir of the earth's living resources is falling....Man must recognize the necessity of cooperating with nature." In other words, there could be no conservation without the stringent control of human population.

To see that outlook set forth in concrete terms we must turn to the second book that the young Al adopted as a guidebook to the relationship between population growth and the environment. This was William Vogt's *The Road to Survival*, another hugely influential and popular tome.

33

But why were Osborn and Vogt's books the staples of a Divinity School course? The answer comes swiftly enough in the material assistance furnished to the Divinity School. Through its scholarship program, the Rockefeller Foundation was not only paying for Al Jr.'s spiritual refreshment and edification, it was financing a lot of the other divinity students as well. Vogt himself was the president of Planned Parenthood, an outcrop of the Rockefeller Foundation; he was also the director of the Conservation Foundation, created and funded by Laurence Rockefeller.

Vogt saw the world in harshly Malthusian terms. Modern sanitation and naive doctors were conspiring to preserve poor people who should properly be dead: "Through medical care and improved sanitation they [doctors] are responsible for more millions living more years in increasing misery." Vogt's pages were sprinkled with vividly inaccurate predictions: Russia was not only "certainly overpopulated" but "its mounting population pressure" made it into the "major threat in Asia". Vogt argued that a population explosion across the thirty years after 1948 would cause a devastating famine in Great Britain: "Unless we are willing to place fifty million British feet beneath our dining-room table, we may well see the famine once more stalking the streets of London."

Elsewhere in *The Road to Survival*, Vogt drew up the game plan for foundation-financed American environmentalism over the next fifty years: "The question of how to solve our forest problems opens up a wide, grim vista of ecological incompetence. The Jukes and the Kallikaks at least who are obtrusively incompetent — we support as public charges. We do the same with the senile, the incurables, the insane, the paupers, and those who might be called the ecological incompetents, such as the subsidized stockmen and the sheepherders."

Like Margaret Sanger, Vogt was keen on sterilization bonuses, arguing that these would have a favorable selective influence, since they would appeal most to the world's shiftless: "From the point of view of society, it would certainly be preferable to pay permanently indigent individuals, many of whom would be physically and psychologically marginal, $50 or $100 rather than support their hordes of offspring that both by genetic and social inheritance would tend to perpetuate their fecklessness."

As Allen Chase put it in his *Legacy of Malthus*, "for the next three decades, every argument, every concept, every recommendation made in *The Road to Survival* would become integral to the conventional wisdom of the post-Hiroshima generation of educated Americans.... The neo-Malthusianisms, from [Vogt's] updating of Malthus' denunciations of doctors who healed the sick ... to his twentieth-century version of the Malthusian food and population growth hoax, would for decades to come be repeated, and restated, and incorporated again and again into streams of books, articles, television commentaries, speeches, propaganda tracts, posters, and even lapel buttons."

Among the book's descendants was the Zero Population Group movement, founded by Paul Ehrlich and run in its early years by Carl Pope. In 1973, Pope was telling *The New York Times* that now that America had reached ZPG, the next target must be immigration, which "is a sentimental symbol whose day is long past". He became a top lobbyist for the Sierra Club, in which capacity he struck up a firm friendship with Al Gore. Gore later wrote an introduction to a book by Pope on toxic waste, and when Pope rose to become executive director of the Sierra Club, in the early 1990s, he was Gore's most untiring apologist to the environmental movement.

The third tract to influence young Gore was *The Limits of Growth*, put together by a group of businessmen who dignified themselves with the sonorous name The Club of Rome. Resources were limited, they sermonized, and while the arrangements that had made their class rich and others poor should not be excessively disturbed, the conditions that had led to their good fortune no longer existed. In essence, they called for a freeze on economic development in the poorer parts of the world, once again, relying upon an MIT computer model as rickety as those later used by Gore for his predictions of global warming. The Club traced the world's problems to excessive population and predicted, even more wildly than had Vogt, that by the year 2020 untrammeled population growth and industrialization would "cause the end of civilization enjoyed by today's contented consumer".

TeSelle, a man who probably did more than anyone else to shape Gore's brand of environmentalism, stayed close to him as an adviser for another decade. Alas, he didn't impart his principled anti-interventionism to his student. TeSelle himself became a fierce opponent of US military meddling in Central America in the eighties, and finally broke off relations with Gore when the latter voted for *contra* aid in the mid-1980s. TeSelle also recoiled at Gore's starring role in the Democratic Leadership Council, the ardently pro-corporate lobby within the Democratic Party designed to redirect the party's platform and promote Southern Democrats like Clinton, Gore and John Breaux of Louisiana.

"With the DLC pandering to corporate money why should anyone be surprised at Clinton and Gore's soft money solicitations", TeSelle told Robert Zelnick, one of Gore's biographers. "My bridges with Al have gotten pretty well burned." Nevertheless, TeSelle's intellectual input colored *Earth in the Balance* and helped shape the Clinton/Gore Administration's global population initiatives and immigration strategy. At the Cairo conference on population in September of 1994, Gore addressed the delegates with these words:

"It is becoming increasingly clear that our margin for error is shrinking as the rapid growth of population is combined with huge and unsustainable levels of consumption in the developed countries, powerful new tools for exploiting the earth and each other, and a willful refusal to take responsibility for the future consequences of the choices we make.

"Economically, rapid population growth often contributes to the challenge of addressing persistent low wages, poverty and economic disparity. Population trends also challenge the ability of societies, economies and governments to make the investments they need in both human capital and infrastructure. At the level of the family, demographic trends have kept the world's investment in its children, especially girls, unacceptably low. For individuals, population growth and high fertility are closely linked to the poor health and diminished opportunities of millions upon millions of women, infants, and children. And population pressures often put strains on hopes for stability at the national and international levels."

In sum, population pressure is the cause of environmental destruction, poverty, poor health, oppression of women and children, and political instability in the developing world. Vogt and Osborn would have been delighted.

Gore once boasted to a *New Yorker* writer that his favored trio of philosophers, to whom he'd been introduced at Vanderbilt, were Niebuhr, Husserl and Merleau-Ponty. The role played by those men is open to debate, but the footprints of

AL GORE

Vogt, Osborn and the Clubmen are plain to see in Gore's
political credo.

In the midst of these intellectual divagations at divinity
school, Gore was also working at *The Tennessean*, the state's
premier liberal paper, at that time edited by John Siegenthaler.
It wouldn't have required much political calculation to have
reckoned that a stint at *The Tennessean* would do a future
political career no harm. The paper had supported Albert Sr.
for years, although there was an estrangement at the
Democratic convention in Chicago in 1956, when Albert Sr. was
seized with the idea that he could become Adlai Stevenson's
vice presidential nominee. LBJ's aide George Reedy
remembers, "A man came running up to us. His eyes were
glittering. He was mumbling something that sounded like
'Where is Lyndon, where is Lyndon? Adlai's thrown this open,
and I think I've got a chance for it if I can only get Texas." That
man was Albert Gore Sr. "I have never seen before or since such
a complete, total example of a man so completely and
absolutely wild with ambition. It had literally changed his
features."

Albert Sr. had badly miscalculated. The powers that be in
Tennessee had the vice presidential slot lined up for the state's
senior Senator, Estes Kefauver. In Reedy's words, Silliman
Evans Jr., the publisher of *The Tennesssean*, pulled Gore aside
and told him "*The Tennessean* wouldn't support him for
dogcatcher if he didn't get out of the race." Albert Gore's
frenzies abruptly subsided and he slunk off, releasing his votes
to Kefauver. Pauline held a grudge for years and even tried,
vainly, to get her friend Katharine Graham to bring *The
Tennessean* into her *Washington Post* empire.

Siegenthaler remained an impenitent New Frontiersman

38

and diligently kept his lines open to the Eastern elites. Under his editorial wing in Nashville, a fairly hick town in those days, was Robert Kennedy's son, David (later to die from a heroin overdose), Arthur Schlesinger Jr.'s son Andrew, John Warnecke, whose architect father, John Carl, had designed the Kennedy gravesite and been a lover of Jackie Kennedy after the assassination. Also there was the son of Judge John Sirica, of Watergate fame. The kids of top executives at NBC and the Newhouse papers graced the newsroom, as did Bill Kovac, Fred Graham and David Halberstam.

Al Gore got in touch with Siegenthaler almost as soon as he returned from Vietnam, and was hired forthwith. *"The Tennessean* practiced 'celebrity nepotism'," a colleague told Myra MacPherson of *The Washington Post* years later, "but Al was the only one of the lot good enough to have gotten the job without his father. Al is so calculating I wouldn't even put it past him to have weighed the political benefits in knowing the newspaper business from the inside. He sure knows how to package himself for the press."

Gore started working nights, covering police calls, confiding thereafter to a fellow reporter that he wanted to be a cop. The first story of significance he did was a good one, a friendly portrait of The Farm, a famous hippie commune in central Tennessee run by Steve Gaskin, espouser of a New Age mix of organic food, sex, dope smoking and UFOlogy. Gaskin's *Cannabis Spirituality* was on many a bookshelf or orange crate lamp stand across hippie USA, and, who knows, perhaps even nestled next to Merleau-Ponty's *Phenomenology of Perception* in Al and Tipper's love den.

In 1988, Gore boasted that as a journalist he'd written a series of exposes that had "put a few people in jail". Typically, the boast provoked investigation, and typically, it turned out to be untrue. The most famous episode in Gore's journalistic career shows Al Jr. in an extremely poor light.

Gore had been called in 1974 by Gilbert Cohen, a developer/contractor putting up a large office tower in downtown Nashville. Cohen needed Metro Council permission to take an alley out of commission. He told Gore that he was having a tough time getting the city's approval and thought he was running into roadblocks as part of an extortion scheme run by a black councilman, Maurice Haddox.

Gore talked the story over with Siegenthaler, and then, bizarrely, instead of pushing forward with the story, they contacted the District Attorney, Tom Shriver, who had formerly worked on *The Tennessean*. The three began to concoct a sting operation.

The way they set it up, *The Tennessean* gave Cohen money to offer Haddox in return for a Metro Council okay to close the alley. The rendezvous spot for the transfer was visible from the office of *The Tennessean*'s lawyer, and photographers deployed there used telephoto lenses to snap pictures of the money being handed over. Cohen was wired by the Tennessee Bureau of Investigation, and Gore was able to monitor the conversation.

After Cohen had given Haddox a preliminary payment of $300, Haddox introduced a bill to close the alley, and the Metro Council agreed. Later that day Gore transcribed the tape in the DA's office and, before he published any story, testified before a secret grand jury. Immediately following his testimony, the grand jury voted to indict Haddox.

Collusion between the DA, *The Tennessean* and the police didn't stop there. Later on in the day of the indictment, Haddox was holding a public session of the Metro Council's ethics committee. The police entered the council chambers and arrested Haddox before the cameras of *The Tennessean*, which ran Gore's big story the next day. Across the next few weeks Gore continued to milk the story.

All of this leaves a very bad taste in the mouth. Certainly a journalistic probe of Haddox was legitimate, but collusion with the DA and the police, not to mention testimony before a grand jury by a reporter actively engaged in a story, would be deemed outrageous by most editors and reporters then and now. There was much indignation in Nashville, particularly in the black community, which thought Haddox had been set up— as indeed he had. Two juries deciding Haddox's fate took the same view. After listening to testimony, including that of reporter Gore, the first jury was hung and the second voted to acquit. Haddox was ably represented. Addressing the jury, William Wilson called the sting "a prearranged plan born in the office of the Nashville *Tennessean*.... Thank God the day has arrived when a black man can hold his head high and be elected to public office in this community. Thank God the day has arrived when the word nigger has disappeared from this language."

Gore was crushed. In the agony of disappointment he did not pause to question his own conduct or that of his newspaper but immediately called into question the probity of the courts and the integrity of the law. No longer did he feel that journalism could accomplish the high civic goals he envisaged. He put away his reporter's notebook and headed off to his mother's alma mater, Vanderbilt Law School. Looking back on Haddox's trials, he told *The Washington Post* years later, "It was an outcome that amazed me. I felt intensely frustrated about policies and decisions I was writing about because I felt they were often dead wrong. But as a journalist I could do nothing about them."

41

When Al Gore threw his hat into the Congressional ring in 1976, he billed himself as a Nashville homebuilder. It's another fairly typical example of the stretch between imagination and reality in Gore's autobiographical claims.

Albert Sr. had set up a company, Tanglewood Homebuilders and made Al Jr. president, nominally in charge of a development designed to turn 300 acres of agricultural land into a middle-class subdivision. Al Jr. didn't actually do much on the project except turn up on an occasional weekend. The gritty business of overseeing construction, wage packets and the like was undertaken by Walter King Robinson, a friend of Albert Sr.'s and a future political benefactor of Al Jr. According to Al's cousin Gore Vidal, part of the money underwriting Gore's excursions in the real estate business came in the form of a loan from the Federal Farm Credit Bureau, whose mission is to loan farmers money to keep going as farmers, not to sink the cash into real estate speculations. Three years later another young couple a few hundred miles further west borrowed money for investment in a middle-class development called Whitewater, and misapplied funds in kindred fashion. But, unlike Bill and Hillary, the Gores came out well in the Tanglewood deal.

Gore used his slice to buy a farm across the Caney Fork River from his parents' place. This property speedily became the most important underpinning of Al and Tipper's financial security, courtesy of a man of great significance to the entire family, Armand Hammer.

Hammer, who died at the age of 92 in 1990, was one of the riper adventurers of the twentieth century. Born in New York of leftist parents, he traveled to the Soviet Union in the early days of the revolution, became friends with Lenin and was soon using his family company, Allied Drug and Chemical, as a pipeline for arms and medicine into the Soviet state, with czarist treasures shuttled the other way.

Hammer left Moscow in 1929. The Soviet Union no longer needed him to secretly fund its agents and sympathizers abroad. Nor did it need to showcase its relationship to a successful foreign capitalist—Lenin's motive for giving him the concession to an asbestos mine in the Urals. Hammer had briefly owned a profitable pencil factory, but ultimately he lost money in the young Soviet Union. His one remaining role was to act as agent for selling art treasures now owned by the Soviet state. Even this was not quite what it seemed. His first attempted sale was of a painting called *The Circumcision of Christ*, which was supposed to have been a lost Rembrandt but turned out to be a fake of recent origin.

Hammer returned to Moscow in 1961. As a US Senator, Albert Sr. arranged semi-official sponsorship of his trip by the US Commerce Department. Hammer met with Nikita Khrushchev, then Soviet leader, but it wasn't until ten years later that he began to do serious business once again in the Soviet Union. His method of cultivating the Soviet hierarchy differed little from his approach to political leaders in the US. In Moscow he became a friend of Yakaterina Furtseva, the well-connected Minister of Culture. Soon thereafter, Furtseva began to build a luxurious holiday home for herself. She died in Moscow in 1974 after coming under investigation for corruption. A former associate of Hammer later testified in the US that Hammer paid her a bribe of $100,000 for various services. During the same period Hammer also arranged for $54,000 in laundered $100 bills to be paid to the Nixon White House to help finance the Watergate cover-up.

Despite the corruption of officials the Soviet Union got more than its money's worth from Hammer. He genuinely wanted to be seen as an architect of detente, pouring enormous sums from his corporate coffers into hopelessly uneconomic projects in the Soviet Union. A vast and ugly trade center that he built still rises beside the Moskva River in central Moscow.

The US security services regarded Hammer almost from the start as a Soviet asset—an accurate surmise, as disclosed by Soviet archival material which surfaced after the collapse of the Soviet Union. J. Edgar Hoover wanted to prosecute him as a Soviet agent but soon acknowledged that his target had cultivated too many influential friends in Congress. Hammer was wont to boast that he had a senator in his back pocket. The senator thus ensconced was Albert Sr.

Hammer had bought Occidental Petroleum in 1956 and began to shoulder and bribe his way into the top tier of American tycoons. Around the same time he went into business with Albert Sr., as a way of paying off the latter for services rendered. Senator Gore had a Black Angus herd on his Tennessee farm, and held periodic auctions of the stock. These auctions were mandatory events for lobbyists and corporate chieftains with business pending before committees on which Albert Sr. sat in Congress.

The cattle were of prime stock, courtesy of the semen provided by prize Black Angus bulls owned by Hammer. Even so, the bidding would rise to absurd heights, as the tycoons and lobbyists vied with one another to secure Albert Sr.'s gratitude. On one glorious day Albert Sr. pocketed $80,000 on an auction, writing a tremulous note of thanks immediately thereafter. On another, a would-be caterer from Virginia hoping for lucrative contracts with the Pentagon enlisted the services of Joe DiMaggio to visit Gore Farms and to put up a bid. DiMaggio promptly secured a lot of ten calves. At each auction the take from the sale of one cow would be reserved for Al Jr., salted away in his Harvard education fund.

Hammer and Albert Sr. dissolved the Black Angus partnership in 1964, but this was far from the end of their relationship. In 1967, Hammer engineered a one-million-dollar bribe to Libyan officials to secure a Libyan oil concession for Occidental. Albert Sr. massaged the US government to countenance the deal, and then traveled with his corporate patron to Libya to celebrate the dedication of Occidental's oil wells. Overnight, Hammer joined the first rank of American tycoons.

In 1969, Hammer acquired the Hooker Chemical Company, later infamous as the poisoner of Love Canal in Niagara Falls. As the takeover was in progress, he sold Albert Sr. 1,000 shares of Hooker stock for $150 a share, far less than the stock's value would be when news of the prospective merger became public. Albert Sr. made a major killing. The stink from Hammer's various transactions was bad enough to attract the attention of Gore's old rival Representative Hale Boggs, who accused Hammer of insider trading and vainly urged the SEC to take action.

Following his defeat in 1970, Albert Sr. said, "Since the voters of Tennessee have chosen to put me out to pasture I intend to graze in the tall grass." Courtesy of Hammer he soon was consoling himself in a particularly nutritious patch of herbage. Hammer made him an executive vice president of Occidental Petroleum and the CEO of the Island Coal Company, the nation's third-largest coal firm and one with an appalling environmental record. Gore's salary was $500,000 a year, a hefty sum in those pre-NASDAQ days.

Hammer had further dispensations. The Gores lived in Smith County, noted for its zinc deposits. A subsidiary of Occidental called Occidental Minerals had bought up mining rights to many properties in the county, including the sub-surface rights on Albert Sr.'s farm, for which the Gore family got $6,000 a year. But the largest deposits were on a farm directly across the river from the Gore home. Despite intense cajolery, the elderly woman holding the property didn't want mining on her land and adamantly refused to sell to Hammer. Eventually she died, leaving her beloved farm to the local Baptist church. It was not long before Albert Sr. was pressing the church elders to ignore the old lady's stipulations and to sell to Hammer. The men of God did so. Occidental then sold the farm to Albert Sr., who, on the very same day, sold it to his son.

Al and Tipper had a new home in the Congressional district he hoped to capture once again for the Gore name, with the meaty lagniappe of a $20,000-a-year lease payment from Occidental Minerals. A tidy sum, especially considering that, in the thirteen years Occidental Minerals held the subsurface mining rights, the company never broke soil. Finally, Oxy Minerals sold the rights to Union Zinc, from whom Al Jr. extracted the same lease agreement. Mining began in the late 1980s. The lease became the largest single source of Al and Tipper's income, all courtesy of Armand Hammer.

Gore has always taken care to leave the impression that he found his father's Hammer connection somewhat embarrassing—ancient business that he had nothing to do with. The impression is false. As a strategic investor Hammer took a keen interest in Al Jr.'s political career, ordering his executives to pony up campaign contributions and offering the candidate use of his private jet. He also arranged for the young congressman to visit the Soviet Union and meet with high officials. In 1988 one of Gore's rivals in the race for the Democratic nomination was Senator Paul Simon of Illinois. A few weeks before the Illinois primary, Hammer called Simon and said that if he would drop out of the race and endorse Gore, Hammer would ensure that President Gore would give Simon a Cabinet position.

While Al was making his way in journalism, real estate, phenomenology and neo-Malthusianism, Tipper was finding her feet. She'd got an undergraduate degree in psychology at Boston University, given birth to Karenna, in August of 1973, and completed a masters in psychology, in 1975, from George Peabody College in Nashville. Then her friend Nancy Warnecke, a photographer at *The Tennessean*, began to teach Tipper the rudiments of the trade. Tipper started at *The Tennessean* as a lowly tech assistant in the darkroom, then worked her way up. Released at last from the in-laws' farm outside Carthage, she was living in Nashville with Karenna and Al, while the latter was going to law school and writing occasional editorials for *The Tennessean*. As a photographer Tipper was, by all accounts, very good. Frank Ritter, a Metro desk editor at the paper, said later that he thought if she'd been able to stay in the profession, she might have ended up winning a Pulitzer.

On February 26, 1976, Tipper's hopes of an independent career came to an end, when Al called her to announce that he was in the race for Congress. Of course, he demanded that she give up her job on *The Tennessean* and return to Smith County to undertake that uniquely depressing role, the political wife. Ahead of Tipper lay tedious hours on the campaign trail, with boisterous locals asking her to name all twenty-nine counties in the fourth district of Tennessee; beyond, the arid rounds of Washington society. In this, as in many other respects, Gore's behavior compares poorly with that of Bill Clinton, who, even as he made untiring attempts to seduce every woman in Arkansas, smiled on the idea of Hillary's professional career, supported her wish to stick with her maiden name in his early races, and seems to have been a distinctly better dad.

Perhaps because he could not possibly compete against the prodigious gallivanter of Little Rock, there has never been much curiosity about possible cavortings by Gore. In the interest of balance we should note the remark of one of Gore's female colleagues on *The Tennessean* when it first became known that Tipper was pregnant with Karenna. This was at the time Al was spending his weekdays alone in the efficiency apartment in Nashville. The female colleague, who had often partied with Gore, confided to Katherine Boo of *The Washington Post*, "I remember being shocked when I heard Tipper was having her first child. Lord, I hadn't even known he was married." Boo quoted Gore as saying, "I loved that time. The freedom..."

Gore managed the same sort of rigid compartmentalization when in all the years of his romance with Donna Armistead he never once invited her to Washington or mentioned to his pals at St. Albans that he had a girlfriend back in Tennessee.

About Gore's entry into politics, the legend put about by his mother, Pauline, has it that he woke up that February day still pondering a career in law or maybe journalism, got the call from Siegenthaler telling him that Representative Joe Evins was retiring, that it was now or never, and only then decided to take the plunge. He put down the phone, dropped to the floor and did fifty push-ups as advertisement of his resolve.

But Gore, his parents and patrons like Siegenthaler had been awaiting the moment for his entry into politics. Indeed, *The Tennessean* was Gore's political godmother, having been instrumental in persuading Evins that it was time for him to put his feet up and bask in the tall grass himself. When Siegenthaler made the call, he made it clear to Gore that timing required that the same edition of *The Tennessean* that trumpeted Evins's retirement would also let the world know that the son of Senator Albert Gore was ready to take up the reins.

Al Jr. faced a tough race. The favorite was a well-heeled, well-prepared State Rep, Stanley Rogers, who had served as house majority leader in the Tennessee Assembly and had the backing of a popular governor, Ned McWherter. Labor was backing another well-known Tennessee character, T. Tommy Cutrer, radio announcer for the Grand Ole Opry. A populist judge, Ben Hall McFarlin, also had a following. There were five more candidates for the Democratic primary, which would in effect choose the person to go to Congress, since the Republicans didn't even bother to contest the seat.

The crowded field was a decisive factor in Gore's victory, because all of them whittled away support for the favorite, Rogers. Gore spent $188,560—a very large sum at that time. Of this amount, he put up $75,000 in cash of his own, and another $50,000 in loans. He out-campaigned his competitors, dashing across pasture and building site to grasp the hand of every potential supporter. Gore told his father to stay out of things, and put it forth that he didn't want to be elected as Albert Gore's son, to which high-minded sentiment Walter King Robinson, a longtime political backer of Albert Sr.'s, remarked caustically, "Son, that's probably the only reason they will vote for you."

Financially, Gore was more than willing to use his father's patrons, picking up lavish contributions from Armand Hammer and Occidental Petroleum's CEO, William

McSweeney. Tipper's father, Jack Aitcheson, ponied up, as did numerous staffers at *The Tennessean*. Gore's top money raiser was Johnny Hayes, an insurance executive from Henderson, Tennessee, who has continued in that capacity to this day. Hayes, a good old boy, has always been the Gores' dowsing rod in their home state, connecting them to the realities of the politics back home.

Gore's campaign staff included Ken Jost, a fellow student at Harvard, then a reporter on *The Tennessean*. Jost served as campaign press secretary and went on to serve Rep Gore in the same capacity. Roy Neel, formerly a Tennessee sports reporter, became one of Gore's closest aides over the rest of his political career, first as chief Congressional aide, then as chief of staff when Gore became Vice President. From Greenville, Mississippi, came Nancy Gore's husband, Frank Hunger, who worked as a corporate trial lawyer, defending insurance and oil companies. Hunger mobilized supporters from Albert Sr.'s address book and, in return, ultimately got a high-level job in the Justice Department.

In the end, Gore got 32 percent of the vote and beat Rogers by a little less than 3,500 votes, out of 115,000 cast. Only then was Albert Sr. allowed out of the shadows to stand on the victory podium with his son.

Across the country in that year of 1976 some of the more liberal Democrats of the next generation were also launching successful Congressional bids: David Bonior in Michigan, Tim Wirth in Colorado, George Miller in California, Tom Downey in New York, Ed Markey in Massachusetts, and Gore's longtime rival, Dick Gephardt, in Missouri. In the 4th District of Tennessee conditions may have been propitious for liberalism, but no one was betting on it. One of the fiercer contenders in that district campaigned on the following planks: against handgun registration; for the fetus's "right to life"; against homosexuality, called "abnormal sexual behavior"; for mandatory minimum sentencing for criminals; for arms-spending hikes; for a sunset law to phase out federal agencies; and, it goes without saying, full-bore for tobacco.

Those were the positions set forth by Al Gore in this first race, in which he referred to himself as a "raging moderate". There's a myth that the death knell for liberalism as the dominant strain in the Democratic Party came with the crushing of Walter Mondale by Ronald Reagan, in 1984. That disaster supposedly engineered the "moderate" takeover. A year later the Democratic Leadership Council was formed, with Gore applying his old journalistic skills to write its inaugural press release.

But the real progenitors of the "moderate" Democratic Anschluss were Richard Nixon and Kevin Phillips in 1968, devisers of the Republican Southern Strategy, which proved that an updated appeal to God, guns, states rights and racism could secure the south. It was that strategy that finished off Albert Sr., stigmatized by Bill Brock as an effete Yankee liberal, the "third senator from Massachusetts", anti-God, anti-military, pro-bussing. In his very first campaign Al Jr. took the Southern Strategy for himself, and it remained his political roadmap in the campaigns that followed. Gore won his first and, indeed, only seriously contested race as a Tennessee politician campaigning against Democrats, and that's how he has continued to define himself.

4 SNAIL DARTER SOUP

*Gore's unpopularity with colleagues on Hill; Prince
Albert becomes the Sun King. Learns skills of faux-
populist grandstanding for tv camera, but takes a
dive on radiation experiments on kids at Oak Ridge.
Poster boy for NRA, hammer of the gays, contends
life begins at conception. Invents God Squad to
destroy minnow. Tries to save breeder reactor and
forms alliance with "B-1 Bob" Dornan to protect
racist schools.*

Read any biography or profile of Al Gore and there are
always the childhood sources in Carthage or St. Albans, the
classmates at Harvard, the fellow soldiers in Vietnam, the
colleagues on *The Tennessean*. But, aside from Tom Downey,
rarely on the record does one find any kindly remarks from the
representatives or senators with whom Gore worked on the Hill
for sixteen years. What one does find are fellow Democrats
taking swipes at him. The consensus seems to have formed
early that he was a grandstander, a loner, a backstabber,
someone who would use his pedigree to get favored committee
assignments from the men who ruled the House: Dan
Rostenkowski, Tip O'Neill, Jim Wright and John Dingell.
Iowa's Senator Tom Harkin used to call him "Prince Albert".

When Gore was hit by the Buddhist temple campaign
fund scandal after the 1996 election the White House cast
about desperately for a Democrat in Congress to go on the
morning shows and defend the vice president. No one stepped

forward. Finally the person most closely resembling a friend in the Senate, John Breaux, explained to a reporter, "Warm and fuzzy he's not." Another Democrat told Gore Vidal, "Around here he's what we call 'a glory boy'. He gets to the House and he starts running for the Senate. He gets to the Senate and start running for the White House. There's no time left to do any of the real work the rest of us have to do."

Gore's style was to pick out safe issues on which to cut a posture. He'd digested the lessons of his own masters' thesis, that television had shifted the balance of power from the Congress to the Executive branch. Mindful of appearances and remembering JFK's tan, Gore began taking a sunlamp with him on his travels. He became a zealous promoter of TV cameras in Congress and contrived matters so that he was the first to speak to those cameras from the House floor. Characteristically his premier message concerned the therapeutic value of filming House proceedings on a day-to-day basis: "It is a solution for the lack of confidence in government." Anyone who has watched C-Span for the past twenty years would surely come to precisely the opposite conclusion.

Gore would seize on an issue that could be easily exported to the Sunday talk shows, such as children's nightwear treated with Tris, a flame retardant that turned out to be carcinogenic. Those particular hearings in May of 1977 were the first to bring young Rep Gore onto the network news shows, and he made full use of the opportunity. "Did it trouble you," he howled theatrically at one industry executive, "that the children of this country might have tumors, carcinogenic or otherwise, produced by the chemical that would be used in all this sleepwear?"

From perilous nightwear he turned his attention to infant formula, another sure-fire TV grabber, where he and the shapely Tipper discoursed on the virtues of breastfeeding. On the heels of fiery sermons against Nestle for its infant formula came Gore's efforts to enact a national organ transplant database. This talent for converting minor issues into major TV opportunities was no doubt what prompted Gore's enthusiasm for Clinton's pollster Dick Morris when the latter arrived to bail out the Clinton White House in 1995 and 1996.

The legislative venue for Gore's grandstanding was the House Commerce Committee's subcommittee on oversight and investigation. Gore had lobbied strongly to be appointed to this subcommittee, correctly assaying its screen-time potential. In short order he developed an inquisitorial style, matched off the floor by his mercilessly abusive treatment of his staff. His sponsor was the powerful Michigan Democrat John Dingell, the auto industry's greatest friend on Capitol Hill and later the most virulent opponent of clean air legislation. Dingell can himself be a pitiless interrogator and evidently saw Gore's potential. Gore would describe himself later as Dingell's spear carrier.

Gore's skills at self-promotion carried his name into the news and afforded him a certain national reputation as a crusading liberal. But a colleague in the House described Gore's posturing to *The Washington Post* as a brand of faux populism: "When you're investigating Love Canal there isn't anyone who is rooting for Hooker Chemical. Yeah, he was a fighter for the working men and women of this country when it involved notoriously bad actors. But if it's an important corporate interest he was a little less decisive."

One example of this prudence came in 1981 when a case was brought to the attention of Rep Gore, by now chairman of the subcommittee, about allegations that children dying of leukaemia had been the subject of radiation experiments at a lab in the Oak Ridge complex in the late 1960s. One such child was Dwayne Sexton, who'd spent some of his final days being subjected to major doses of radiation in a room which also housed 50 cages of mice undergoing the same treatment. Reports of the course of the radiation doses were secretly remitted to NASA, which was interested in the possible effects of solar flares on its astronauts.

But when Gore finally held a hearing on this appalling breach of medical ethics, the proceedings were markedly more demure than the robust grandstanding against perilous nightwear. On one side was only Mary Sue Sexton, Dwayne's working-class mother. On the other was a brigade of Oak Ridge doctors and high-ups. Congressman Gore, well aware of the weight of Oak Ridge in the political economy of Tennessee, was extremely meek, sparing the doctors his usual pitiless interrogations. The hearing was brief and went nowhere. Mrs Sexton continued to write to Gore, asking for justice. He never replied. In 1994, amid a new Department of Energy investigation into the radiation experiments, *60 Minutes* ran a segment on Dwayne Sexton and 19 other children, noting the failure of Gore to answer Mrs Sexton's letters. Vice President Gore declined *60 Minutes'* request for an interview or statement.

But at the substantive legislative level Gore remained emphatically on the center-right. Take the issue that perhaps defines the Democratic Party's social mission more than any other: labor rights. In the dawn of the Carter presidency, with Democrats controlling both houses, a bill came before the House aimed at expanding unions' picketing rights. Famously in America, one has the right to strike (barely) but not the right to win, because picketing—a vital component of any serious strike—is so circumscribed by legal restrictions as to be effectively useless in many cases as a coercive tool in a fight with employers. So this vote was a big one. The AFL-CIO felt confident of victory, but it missed the fact that newly arrived Democrats like Gore felt no loyalty to labor and were intent on advertising that disposition to their business contributors. Gore provided one of the crucial votes that turned back labor's bill.

As a House member Gore was virtually a poster boy for the National Rifle Association. In 1978 he voted to block funding for the implementation of new federal handgun regulations, explaining many years later that "when I represented a rural farm district in the House of Representatives there wasn't a problem [with handguns] perceived by my constituents". In 1985, after he had moved from representing the crackers in the 4th District to being the junior senator for all the people of Tennessee, he voted for what the NRA called "the most significant pro-gunners' bill in the last quarter-century", which struck down impediments to the interstate sale of handguns.

As a Congressman, Gore spoke of his belief in "the fetus's right to life". He was a relentless supporter of the Hyde amendment, which banned federal funding for abortions for poor women. In one early version of Hyde's bill there was language allowing exceptions to the ban in the case of rape. Gore voted against that.

The most far reaching of all the measures dreamed up by the conservative right to undercut *Roe v Wade* was an amendment put forward by a Michigan Republican, Mark Siljander, in 1984. It carried a one-two punch. First, it defined the fetus as a person from the moment of conception. Second, it denied federal funding to any hospital or clinic that performed an abortion. Gearing up for his Senate run that year, Gore was one of seventy-four Democrats to vote for Siljander's ultimately unsuccessful measure.

Those votes returned to haunt Gore as his political ambitions went national and he was bidding for more support than he ever needed in the 4th District or even the entire Volunteer State. By 1988 he was brazenly rewriting his political biography. He and his staff were well aware that his votes against choice of only four years earlier would be brought up by his opponents. "Since there's a record of that vote", an aide told *US News & World Report* in March of 1988, "in effect what we have to do is deny, deny, deny."

The problem returned briefly in 1992 and again in the Democratic primaries in 2000, when Bill Bradley, challenging Gore for the nomination, used the occasion of a debate in the Apollo Theater in Harlem, to flourish and then read out a letter Gore had written to a Tennessee constituent in 1984, in which he had stated: "It is my deep personal conviction that abortion is wrong. I hope that some day we will see the current outrageously large number of abortions drop sharply. Let me assure you that I share your belief that innocent human life must be protected and I have an open mind on how to further this goal."

When confronted with contradictions between his pretensions and his deeds, Gore reflexively performs a ritual of numbed incantation. "I believe a woman ought to have the right to choose", he kept repeating to his interlocutors in 1992, and he did the same thing at the Apollo in 2000. Someone less rigid could have immediately said, "Look, I've evolved." In fact, he did eventually arrive at that position, after the Apollo when the lie was so flagrant and Bradley pushing so hard to get women's group support that Gore's backers in NARAL and elsewhere were embarrassed as they were pressed to explain their candidate's contortions. Then suddenly all the talk was about his "evolving", and Gore pounced on the phrase, adding his gloss about going through psychic travail before coming to his present position. His NARAL backers then turned this flip-flop into a moral victory, saying it takes a big man to admit he was wrong, to "evolve" as he has. They never bothered to explain why he was preferable to Bradley, who had been consistently pro-choice. But Gore, the perfect child of demanding parents, finds it enormously hard to admit error, even in retrospect. In 1988, even as both Al and Tipper issued their fabrications about their use of marijuana, Tipper said, "It was either admit it or lie, and we would never lie."

One unlovely hoof-print after another tracks its way across Gore's legislative voting record. In 1980, when the IRS proposed new regulations denying tax-exempt status to private schools that barred black students, Gore was among those in Congress supporting Robert (B-1 Bob) Dornan of California who put up a bill trying to undermine the regulations. In the same year Gore voted for an amendment prohibiting the Legal Services Corporation from assisting homosexuals whose rights were denied because of their sexual orientation. As a member of the US Senate Gore backed three anti-homosexual measures put up by his colleague, and on this issue, comrade in arms, Jesse Helms. In August 1986 Gore voted for a Jesse Helms amendment forcing the District of Columbia to overturn its law prohibiting health, life and disability insurance corporations from using the new HIV test to reject applicants for insurance. A year later Gore voted for a Helms amendment requiring HIV testing for immigrants, effectively prohibiting HIV+ people from settling in the US.. In August 1988 he voted for another Helms amendment, this time the "Fair Housing Bill". The amendment prohibited the bill's anti-discrimination section from protecting "an individual solely because that individual is a transvestite." During the anti-gay, pro-censorship hysteria surrounding a Robert Maplethorpe exhibit in September 1989, Gore joined his fellow Senators in unanimously approving a Jesse Helms bill attacking the National Endowment for the Arts for its funding for the exhibit. *Gay Weekly* from Gore's home state summed up the matter quite well: "Even our own Tennessee Senators, Jim Sasser and Albert Gore, Jr., did nothing to try to stop the vicious North Carolinian's bigoted, dangerous foolishness."

Likewise, in Gore's supposed devotion to the environment there has always been a vast rift between stirring proclamation and legislative reality. Back in the late 1970s two of the hottest environmental battles concerned the Clinch River Breeder Reactor and the Tellico Dam, both within the purview of the TVA. As planned, the Clinch River reactor not only was a $3 billion boondoggle of the first water but was also destabilizing in terms of the arms race, since it was scheduled to produce weapons-grade plutonium. The Congressional battle over the planned reactor stretched from the mid-1970s to 1983, when, amid growing national disquiet about nuclear power, it went down to defeat.

Gore was a fanatic defender of the reactor, the most ardent of all in the Tennessee House delegation. When the Republicans briefly captured the Senate in 1981 the senior Senator from Tennessee, Howard Baker, became majority leader and made protection of the Clinch River project one of his prime tasks. He and Gore kept the fight going until the end. Arkansas's Senator Dale Bumpers gave an entertaining account in a speech in 1997: "I remember in 1981, Republicans took over this place and Howard Baker, the senator from Tennessee and one of the finest men ever to serve in this body, became majority leader. I was trying to keep any additional nuclear plants from being licensed—and it was not a tough chore. A lot of people had made up their minds at that point that the nuclear option was not a good one. I fought for about four years to kill the Clinch River Breeder. But I was up against the majority leader. And as everybody here knows, as the old revenuer said, when they announced United States versus Jones, he turned to his lawyer and said, 'Them don't sound like very fair odds to me.' And it was not very fair odds to go up against the majority leader on the Clinch River Breeder, which was going to be built in his beloved Tennessee. Howard Baker could always just pull out that one extra vote he needed. The vote was always close, but you are majority leader, you know, you can just call somebody over and say, 'I need your vote', and you usually get it. Finally, one year I was ahead by about six or seven votes as the votes were being cast, and I think Senator Baker decided that he was done for, and he turned everybody loose that had committed to him who did not really like the idea of the Clinch River Breeder Reactor and only voted for it to accommodate him. He turned them loose, and I think we won that day by about 70 to 30. Happily, that was the end of the Clinch River Breeder." In 1984, Al Gore took Baker's Senate seat and over the next eight years voted for the nuclear lobby 55 percent of the time. As vice president and author of *Earth in the Balance* (which stays fairly mute on the topic of nuclear power) Gore, along with his former staffer Energy Department Assistant Secretary Thomas Grumbly, tried to bring the Clinch River scheme to life again as the Fast Flux Test Facility in the Hanford nuclear reservation in the State of Washington. One sales pitch the DoE used was that the plutonium could be used in medical research looking for ways to cure AIDS.

Then there was the Tellico Dam, the first big test of

America's greatest environmental law, the Endangered Species Act, passed in 1973 during the Nixon presidency, which also saw the creation of the Environmental Protection Agency. The dam, on the Little Tennessee River, was 95 percent complete when biologists discovered the imperiled snail darter species still clinging on in the stretches of the river that were to become the reservoir behind the dam. Environmentalists brought suit against the dam project, and eventually the Supreme Court ruled that the Endangered Species Act required that the dam not be completed.

The Little Tennessee was one of the few wild rivers left in the state unmolested by the TVA. The dam wasn't needed for flood control and wouldn't generate power. All it would do was store water and divert it to another dam nearby. The recreation benefits were negative, since the Little Tennessee was a famous trout stream and popular with canoeists. In fact, the only purposes of the dam were to line the pockets of the cement producers and construction nabobs of Tennessee and to afford an amenity for the "Timberlake" community being planned by Boeing. As Marc Reisner puts it in his book *Cadillac Desert*, "It was like deciding to put a 50,000 seat Superdome in the middle of Wyoming and then building a city of 150,000 around it to justify its existence."

Shocked that the Act could threaten huge pork barrel projects, the very lifeblood of Congress, the legislators set up the so-called God Squad, which would pass judgement on species-endangering schemes, using cost-benefit analysis as the standard. In the case of the snail darter the God Squad, led by economist Charles Schultze, did its homework. "Here is a project that is 95 percent complete", Schultze concluded, "and if one takes just the cost of finishing it against the benefits, it doesn't pay."

The fight over the snail darter was fierce and bitter because the stakes were so high. If the pro-dam forces could win a waiver of the Endangered Species Act here, then such a waiver would inevitably be the first of many. Gore was among the leaders in the effort to get this waiver, and in the end Congress exempted the dam from compliance and overturned the Supreme Court's injunction. As the defenders of the snail darter predicted, the path to destruction of the Endangered Species Act now lay open, and first down that path had been none other than Al Gore.

After he and the other pork-barrelers got the vote that exempted the dam, Gore announced triumphantly, "It was unfortunate that the controversy over the snail darter was used to delay completion of the dam after it was virtually finished. I am glad the Congress has now ended this controversy once and for all."

How Gore, Howard Baker and James Duncan (the Republican Congressman in whose district the dam was located) consummated their awful victory was vividly described by Representative Bob Edgar, a Democrat from suburban Philadelphia. Edgar recounts how on June 18, 1979, Gore and his colleague Duncan pushed through, as a rider to the appropriations bill, a measure allowing the Tellico Dam to go forward. "Duncan walked in waving a piece of paper. He said, 'Mr. Speaker! Mr. Speaker! I have an amendment to offer to the public works appropriation bill. Tom Bevill and John Myers [two dreadful reps] of the Appropriations Committee both happened to be there. I wonder why. Bevill says, 'I've seen the amendment. It's good.' Myers says, 'I've seen the amendment. It's a good one.' And that was that. It was approved by voice vote! No one even knew what they were voting for! They were voting to exempt Tellico Dam from all laws! They punched a loophole big enough to shove a $100 million dam through it, and then they scattered threats all through Congress so that we couldn't muster the votes to shove it back out. I tried—lots of people tried—but we couldn't get that rider out of the bill. The speeches I heard on the floor were the angriest I've heard in elective office. They got their dam. That is the democratic process at work."

The foes of the dam had one last hope, that President Jimmy Carter would veto the bill. But Carter too was bushwhacked. The Baker-Gore forces threatened to withhold support for the Panama Canal Treaty, which Carter was fighting for at the time.

Gore supported a scheme to transplant some of the snail darters to the nearby Hiwassee and Holston rivers, where they survived. But the larger damage was done. As David Brower, America's greatest environmentalist, said in retrospect, "This was the beginning of the end of the Endangered Species Act." After the snail darter came other species and other waivers, the most notorious of them engineered under the auspices of Vice President Gore. In the Pacific Northwest the spotted owl and marbled murrelet, in the Southeast the red-cockaded woodpecker, in Southern California the gnatcatcher—all were as chaff under the chariot wheels of the timber and real estate industries, who successfully lobbied the vice president and his minions for the all-important waivers. Like refugees in wartime, imperiled species were assigned one holding pen after another, issued temporary "safe" passes, while Gore's people in the Interior Department and the Council on Environmental Quality felt the heat from developers and timber barons and crumbled.

The way American politics works, it took a reputed environmentalist to destroy America's best environmental law.

In 1981 there wasn't a major environmental group in the country that didn't bugle its frantic alarums at the approach of the Reaganauts and that Beelzebub of the greens, James Watt, Reagan's Interior Secretary. The Sierra Club, the Wilderness Society, National Audubon, the Natural Resources Defense Council, all raised millions of dollars on the spectre of Watt and the havoc he would wreak on environmental regulations. In fact, the pathetic and maladroit Watt never stood a chance. He set back the cause of environmental pillage by at least a decade.

But when Watt was gone and Reagan was gone and Bush was gone, the Democratic "greens" came back to power, and they engineered assaults on nature that the Republicans had never dared dream possible. Gore, who had reinvented himself as an environmentalist largely on the basis of *Earth in the Balance*, was embraced by the Big Green organizations. They used his largely mythical green credentials as a way of getting their membership to overlook Bill Clinton's own adversarial relationship with nature while he was governor of Arkansas.

Yet consider Gore's record by the big groups' own criteria. Like all the major environmental organizations, the League of Conservation Voters functions as an outrider for the Democratic National Committee, and its annual ratings of members of Congress are notoriously skewed against Republicans. Gore's lifetime rating from the League is 64 percent, meaning he was in sync with the League's positions two-thirds of the time. This is not much when you look at such green stars of the League as Patrick Leahy of Vermont, Tim Wirth of Colorado, George Miller of California or even a Republican like the late John Chafee of Rhode Island, all of whom were consistently in the 90s. The League's rating of Gore in his House years ran at an average of about 55 percent, with one year seeing him down to 30 percent, putting him in harness with such world-class predators as Don Young of Alaska.

Gore didn't make many friends in the House, but his propensity to techno-flatulence (e.g., "The government is like a big software program") soon prompted him to sniff out a kindred soul in the form of a pudgy young Congressman from suburban Atlanta with a marvelous facility for rotund phrase-making on any issue to hand. From the time he was first elected, in 1978, Newt Gingrich was positioning himself with precisely the same blend of opportunism, albeit at a noisier level, as Al Gore.

The two consecrated their amity in a group called the Congressional Clearing House on the Future. They met monthly, published a newsletter and hosted lectures by futurists and pop scientists including Carl Sagan and Alvin Toffler. But these monthly klatsches were not enough to satiate the passions of Gore and Gingrich for heady chat about meta-technical trends, artificial intelligence, the population bomb and extraterrestrial life (Gore believes ardently that We Are Not Alone). The two would meet for dinner at each other's houses. Poor Tipper, hoping for a romantic candle-lit evening with her spouse, would open the door to see the beaming, porcine features of the rising Republican star from Georgia on the doorstep. The relationship didn't end when Gore reached the Senate. In fact, in 1985 he and Gingrich co-authored a bill titled the Critical Trends Assessment Act. The legislation called for the creation of a White House Office on Futurism (WHOOF) to "study the effects of government policies on critical trends and alternative futures". In his career in Congress, Gore was rarely the principal author of a bill. This was an exception, albeit a doomed one. Although the two battled for WHOOF strenuously, it never went anywhere.

Soon after his arrival in Congress, Gore formed the Vietnam Veterans Caucus with John Murtaugh, Jim Jones and Les Aspin. For Gore the caucus opened up a useful avenue into hawkish Democratic circles, where men like Aspin and Sam Nunn were doing the Pentagon's work, proclaiming that "Vietnam Syndrome" was sabotaging the nation's vital sinews. Gore picked up the lingo quickly enough: "I think it is important to realize that we do have interests in the world that are important enough to defend, to stand up for. And we should not be so burned by the tragedy of Vietnam that we fail to recognize an interest that requires the assertion of force."

With such language, Gore established himself early on as "safe" from the point of view of the Pentagon and the national security complex. Safety meant never straying off the reservation on such issues as America's right to intervene anywhere it chooses. Gore backed Reagan's disastrous deployment of the US Marines in Lebanon in 1983. He supported the invasion of that puissant Caribbean threat to the United States (population 260 million), Grenada (population 80,000). He later chided his 1988 Democratic opponents for their failure to embrace this noble enterprise. At a time when many Democrats wanted to restrict the CIA's ability to undertake covert actions, Gore said he wouldn't "hesitate to overthrow a government with covert actions", a posture he ratified with his approval of the CIA's secret war in Afghanistan. This, the largest covert operation in the Agency's history, ultimately saddled Afghanistan with the Taliban fundamentalists, destroyers of cities, stoners of women and overseers of that country's rise in status to the eminence of world's largest exporter of opium and heroin to the United States and Europe.

5 SHABBES GOY

*("The gentile who is asked on the Sabbath by
Orthodox Jews to light the fire, put out candles,
perform a chore – all of which are forbidden the
devout on the holy sabbath". Leo Rosten, The Joys of
Yiddish.)*

On issues affecting Israel, even in a Congress almost
entirely deferential to the demands of the Israeli lobby, Gore
has always stood out as fanatical in his fealty: "Israel is our
strongest ally and best friend, not only in the Middle East but
anywhere else in the world", he declared in 1992. But it could
have been any other year. Gore has always been a steady
fixture at functions of the American-Israeli Public Affairs
Committee (AIPAC), whose leaders tend to be far more
hawkish than the Israelis themselves. In 1993 the vice
president of AIPAC, Harvey Friedman, was forced to resign
after calling Israel's deputy foreign minister, Yossi Beilin, a
"little slime ball". Friedman was responding to Beilin's
suggestion that Israel should return land on the West Bank
and Gaza Strip to the Palestinians. Tom Dine, AIPAC's head
until 1993, was another extreme hard-liner. He, too, had to step
down after making unpalatable remarks describing some
Orthodox Jews as "smelly" and "low-class".

AIPAC's influence in terms of US Middle Eastern policy is
extreme. Back in February of 1991, amid the Gulf War, Saudi
Arabia requested that the United States sell it seventy-two
F-15E war planes. Immense opposition to the sale immediately

arose, coordinated by AIPAC. Faced with sure defeat—-sixty-seven senators, including Gore, delivered a letter of opposition to the Saudi deal to Bush—the president backed off. The deal finally went through the following year, but only after AIPAC acceded to the transaction.

According to a report by the Project on Demilitarization and Democracy, many proponents of the deal, especially weapons manufacturers, "insist that the campaign's success was due primarily to its private side: an effort to gain Israeli acquiescence by promising Israel additional US military technology, including its own F-15E". Few political analysts would dispute a Senate staffer's claim that "only active opposition from Israel and the US Jewish community can block sales to Arab nations". The report says that McDonnell Douglas, maker of the F-15E, hired Dov Zakheim, a former Pentagon official, to talk with Jewish groups to determine how to win their approval for the deal: "Supporters of the sale worked energetically behind the scenes within the administration to win for Israel promises of new weapons and continued US government grants to pay for those weapons. Those promises were apparently made in late August when Israeli Prime Minister Yitzhak Rabin publicly said he did not object to the sale. At that point AIPAC, which had been organizing against the sale with arms control groups, stopped its active opposition and signaled that it would not expect its congressional supporters to block the sale."

Some of what is written about the power of the Israeli lobby in Washington lurches toward paranoia. If the Jewish state had been founded in Timbuktu, as Republican Congressman Hamilton Fish Sr. publicly recommended in the 1930s, it is extremely doubtful that $4 billion a year would now be furnished to that nation isolated in the oil-free Sahara. All the same, it's fair to rate the lobby as one of the capital's most effective, and one of the most lavish in its donations to its favored representatives and senators. Seventy pro-Israel PACs distribute more than $4 million each election cycle.

Gore has been a notable favorite for such money. Cautious after the Buddhist temple funding scandal, Gore pledged not to take PAC money directly. However, people associated with just one Israeli PAC, the National Jewish Democratic Council, had given Gore $52,250 by May of 2000, making them the eighth-largest contributor to his presidential campaign.

AIPAC has only to ask, and Gore is on board, later boasting of same. In May of 2000 he addressed AIPAC in these terms: "I stood against the efforts of two previous administrations to pressure Israel to take stands against its own view of what was in Israel's best interest. When a friend's survival is potentially at stake, you don't pressure that friend to take steps that it believes are clearly contrary to what is in that friend's best interest." He then lashed at one of President George Bush's few courageous initiatives in foreign policy, the withholding of $10 billion in US loan guarantees in order to induce the obdurate Prime Minister Yitzhak Shamir, of the Likud Party, into parleys on the matter of Palestinian rights.

"I vividly remember standing up against a group of Bush Administration foreign policy advisers who promoted the insulting concept of linkage, which tried to use loan guarantees as a stick to bully Israel", Gore intoned. "I stood with you, and together we defeated them." The concept of no-strings-attached aid—Israel is, along with Egypt, the largest recipient of US foreign aid—would have interested Winston Churchill, who knew very well that the US lend-lease money, which saved the empire, had strings attached, in the form of all-important British imperial assets transferred to the US when World War

II was over. No one of sound mind has ever suggested that Israel was in as much danger as the UK in the darkest days of the war. In 1988 the columnist Mary McGrory quoted a New York politician leaving a Gore speech as saying that Gore had taken a position "to the right of Likud on Jewish settlements".

Even today, when public education on issues in the Middle East and on Palestinian rights is certainly improved from the awful racism and scare-mongering of ten years ago, Gore is as unreconstructed an errand boy of the Israeli lobby as he was in 1988, when he toured New York in the company of Mayor Ed Koch, donning a yarmulke, baiting Jesse Jackson for meeting with Yasir Arafat, haranguing blacks and making Israel the litmus test issue in the primary. In Koch's company Gore boasted to one Hasidic family in Brooklyn, "I have a 100 percent voting record for Israel, even though there wasn't one synagogue in my congressional district."

In 1999 Vice President Gore addressed the Washington Institute for Near East Policy, yet another pro-Israeli outpost in DC: "The United States must continue to maintain a strong military presence in the region to help deter aggression and defend our friends and allies. We must keep our word. We must stand by our commitments. This is not charity; it is national security.... I was privileged to meet several times in July [1999] with Prime Minister Barak. I had the privilege of speaking with him about what he called 'an historic opportunity for peace.' For my part I assured him that, of course, we will continue to stand by Israel as it takes risks for peace. I assured him that we will continue to help ensure that Israel maintains a qualitative military edge that is essential to its security."

What always has lent a particularly sharp edge to Gore's delirious grandstanding toward Israel and the Israeli lobby is undoubtedly Gore's lifelong association with Martin Peretz, a man hysterical well beyond the point of unbalance on the topic of Israel and the innate vileness of Arabs. Politician that he is, Gore knows perfectly well that the bonds of more than thirty years of friendship would count as nothing if, in Peretz's eyes, he erred in the matter of Israel. *The New Republic*, which has done so much to inflate Gore as a national figure, would turn on him in an instant, and he would be the topic of harsh rebuke from one of Peretz's hoplites, maybe Leon Wieseltier, perhaps even General Peretz himself.

An intimation of what could happen occurred in 1993 and again in 1995. Richard Marius, a native of Tennessee and a lecturer at Harvard, was also a friend of Roy Neel, Gore's chief of staff at the time. Marius volunteered his services to Neel, who tapped him from time to time as an unpaid speechwriter for Gore. In March of 1993, Gore's office asked Marius to write a speech for the vice president to deliver at Madison Square Garden commemorating the fiftieth anniversary of the Warsaw Ghetto Uprising against the Nazis. Marius went to work and read his draft to Gore and his national security aide, Leon Fuerth. Both men were reduced to tears by Marius's eloquence. Indeed, Fuerth had to leave the room to compose himself. But a few days later Marius got a call from Gore's press secretary, Marla Romash. She told him that Gore's office had received an angry call from Martin Peretz, accusing Marius of being an anti-Semite and warning Gore's staff that they shouldn't allow Marius to write speeches, particularly on this subject. Peretz then told Romash that he himself had written a draft on the Warsaw uprising for the vice president.

What provoked this sudden call from Peretz? It emerged that Marius had written a review for *Harvard Magazine* of Helen Winternitz's *A Season of Stones: Living in a Palestinian Village*, a book chronicling the Israeli occupation of the West

71

Bank and Gaza. In his review Marius had the temerity to compare the brutal tactics of Israel's secret police, the Shin Bet, toward Palestinians in the *intifada* to the activities of the Gestapo. Marius behaved with dignity, telling Gore's people, "I've never had an anti-Semitic thought in my life. That's the only thing I've ever written against Israel. I certainly have never written anything anti-Semitic. I won't defend myself against the charge. If the vice president thinks I'm an anti-Semite, I won't write for him again." In the end Gore's staff backed down, using Marius's draft with one paragraph from Peretz thrown in.

In the early summer of 1995, Tipper and Al ran into Marius at their daughter Karenna's graduation from Harvard. Marius says that Gore was so excited by the encounter that he "practically fell all over me", and that the Second Couple told him, "You're our savior". The following week Marius says that he took Gore up on an invitation to come aboard the '96 campaign staff as a speechwriter. Marius was offered $70,000 a year to join the team. He had been director of the Harvard undergraduate writing program, had lectured on the Reformation and had also written two highly praised books on Sir Thomas More and Martin Luther. He and his wife, Lanier Smythe, herself a distinguished academic, rented out their house, and Marius signed on.

An early assignment found him in Nashville, writing a speech for Tipper on family values. Early on a Sunday morning he got a call from Lorraine Voles, Gore's communications director. Marius later recalled Voles as saying, "Richard, I have some very bad news for you. As you know, we have very close relations with the Jewish community." She went on to say that Gore's office had received angry calls protesting Marius's appointment. She also told Marius that Gore had now studied his book review. "The vice president read it, agonized for three days and decided he cannot have you in Washington." Marius insisted once again that there was not an anti-Semitic bone in his body, concluding, "I thought the whole issue of that review was behind me. I have been very careful not to touch those buttons again."

Maybe he could write for Gore on a piece-work basis, Voles said. She also told him, 'We'll expect you to say that this was your own decision. You can say you changed your mind and we'll say the same thing." Marius wouldn't bite. He gave up the job and went public with the exchange. He later wrote, "It sounded something like this. 'Hey, I'm not going to marry you after all. Some important friends of mine think you're wicked and evil and malicious and I can't afford to be seen with you in public or to acknowledge you in any way, although I know you're none of those things, but hey babe! You give me great sex. So let me pay you now for what you've been giving to me for nothing. Just keep it secret.' Well, alas, I don't lie, and I don't have a red light hanging in front of my computer or my yellow pad. And I don't give a good god damn if people attack me when I'm right on a moral issue."

Voles told Marius that "someone" had given Gore the review of Winternitz's book. Marius concluded that this "someone" was Peretz. Gore biographer Robert Zelnick, who himself lost his job at ABC-TV for writing a book critical of Gore, quotes a member of Gore's staff as saying, "Marty Peretz put the death sentence on the Marius appointment. Peretz gloated about the matter to *The Washington Post*: "I never talk about what I say to the vice president. What I will say is that there were many people who were upset by the impending appointment and there were many people who made their views heard, including within the staff. It's a very simple matter. What Richard Marius wrote did not go unnoticed in Cambridge and beyond, because it was in the Harvard alumni magazine. When you make the Nazi analogy it cannot be tossed off as 'Oh, how silly of me to have done this.' When you write that you believe it. So, once the vice president knew, he had to figure out if he wanted someone who believed that on his staff." Marius never did back down on the comparison, and called the criticism of his review "a little extreme".

Marius died from cancer on November 5, 1999. By that time comparisons of the Shin Bet with the Gestapo had been made by more than a few commentators, amid detailed descriptions of the torture techniques used by Sin Bet on Palestinians. The descriptions surfaced as a consequence of the Israeli attorney general finally barring Shin Bet from torturing suspects. Previously such torture had been legal. A last word from Marius: "I despise these Republicans crawling to Pat Robertson. But, honest to God, I don't see any difference between crawling to Pat Robertson and crawling to Marty Peretz."

Peretz's editors at *The New Republic* serve very much at the king's pleasure, and when one of them, Michael Kelly, took to writing harsh assessments of Al Gore at the time of the campaign finance scandal, Peretz was incensed. Peretz's line in *The New Republic* was that Gore inhabited a moral altitude far superior to that of the president. His lieutenant, Leon Wieseltier, apostrophized the vice president thus: "Gore is too good to waste on Bill Clinton." So when the insubordinate Kelly persisted in criticizing Gore, it was not long before he was shown the door. Peretz told *The New York Times* that he considered Kelly's writings on Gore's funding scandals "a little obsessive". For his part Kelly summed up, "I think that he probably saw that I was going to continue writing... on the soft money scandals, since I had made something of a cause out of it. And he made it clear to me that he didn't like that and that this is a subject area that is obviously increasingly involving Al Gore. As long as Marty Peretz has the involvement with Al Gore and with the magazine to the degree that he does, I think the job of editor is structurally impossible." A *New Republic* staffer told *The Washington Post*, "People feel they can't write about Gore. If they write pro-Gore pieces, they look like Marty tools. If they write anti-Gore pieces they'll face Marty's anger. A lot of us feel it's an unacceptable way for the political magazine to be run."

6 MIDGETMAN

Epiphany in Murfreesboro and a terrible nightmare;
Gore meets Leon Fuerth, his Kissinger; they play
nuclear wargames and give birth to a lovechild,
Midgetman. Night of the duped Owls. Gore ends up
as pawn of Reagan's MX boosters. He makes the bold
leap from "raging moderate" to "centrist realist".
Iraq, and Gore cries "war".

Typically, Gore has presented his maneuvers toward
establishing himself as a national security expert as, in origin,
yet another personal awakening. For this particular moral
reveille he recruits the young women of Tennessee, who, in
1980 happened to be mustered for a statewide political
convention in the town of Murfreesboro. Congressman Gore,
now facing a trouble-free election to a third term, was there
giving a humdrum talk on national affairs. One girl asked him
what he proposed to do to prevent nuclear war. As he later told
the story (many times and in many different versions) Gore was
at a loss, because he apparently hadn't given the matter much
thought. This is telling, since nuclear war was one of his
father's prime concerns, both in the Senate, where he was an
architect of the ABM Treaty (which his son is intent on
undoing) and in retirement, where he headed the strongly anti-
nuke Council for a Livable World. So Gore parried, asking the
hall how many of them thought they would see a nuclear war
in their lifetime. Almost all raised their hands. How many of
you, Gore then inquired, believe that we can change things if

we try? Only two or three sheepishly optimistic hands went up.

Gore says he headed home that night deeply shaken. In bed he tossed and turned, prey to nightmares, one of which had him feverishly trying to disarm a nuclear device under the bleachers at the Carthage High School gymnasium. Realizing he lacked the technical knowledge, he raced home to find some disarm-it-yourself manual. As he was searching, a terrible flash was followed by a mushroom cloud. He decided forthwith to master the dark mysteries of the nuclear balance of terror, inflect government policy and prove to those pessimistic teenagers at the Murfreesboro conference that they were wrong.

As a matter of practical reality, any ambitious young politician aiming at the higher rungs finds it useful to demonstrate some sophistication on national security issues. Perhaps because his credibility as a warrior had been gravely impaired, and because he came out of a governor's mansion, Bill Clinton was a refreshing exception here. His indifference to foreign policy was probably a factor in his popularity, and allowed Gore to be a major force for the worse in the wars, bombings and embargoes of the Clinton era.

Whether or not driven by the Murfreesboro moral crisis, Gore moved adroitly. Using his family connections with Speaker of the House Tip O'Neill, Gore wheedled himself a seat on the House Select Committee on Intelligence and then began to set himself up as an authority on arms control.

In these post cold war days it may be difficult to recall the arms-control industry at its height, with think tanks and experts of varied hue churning out reports and proposals on how to live with nuclear weapons. Politicians and policy wonks who would be hard put to fix a bicycle discoursed glibly about "throw-weight" "CEP ratios" megatonnage, silo-busting and other arcana. The mooring lines attaching these speculations to reality were frayed to nonexistent. In the entire history of US nuclear testing there had been only four attempts to launch from a silo. Factors such as unpredictable gravitational forces and wind along the (untested) path of an ICBM heading from the US to the Soviet Union made assumptions of 100-foot radius accuracy absurd, as Secretary of Defense James Schlesinger once admitted. Nonetheless, the nuclear priesthood continued to spin fantasies of accuracy and deterrence, and devise new "safe systems", all of which had one certain effect—the continuance of America's nuclear testing programs, and the laboratories at Livermore, Los Alamos and Oak Ridge, and the well-being of the aerospace and nuclear manufactories.

At the start of the 1980s the nuclear establishment was in a state of particular commotion. On the one hand newly elected President Reagan had pledged to push through the Pentagon's favored new missile deployment plan—-the MX, a rocket carrying ten separate warheads. President Carter's scheme had been to deploy the MX on a vast railway system in the interior West, with the missiles constantly on the move to elude possible Soviet attack. After that scheme had been subjected to merciless and successful abuse, Reagan's advisers came up with "Densepack", whereby MX missiles, renamed Peacekeepers, would be grouped inside super-hardened silos, on the theory that even after a sneak Soviet attack, enough missiles would survive to launch a devastating counterattack.

Meanwhile, the nuclear freeze movement was gathering force, articulating the popular position that the best way to reduce the threat of nuclear weapons was to stop building new ones, which in turn meant to stop billions of dollars flowing into R&D accounts at the nuclear labs. In April of 1982 polls were showing that 82 percent of Americans favored a freeze. In the

1982 midterm elections, freeze ballot initiatives were approved in nine states and the District of Columbia. On July 12, 1982, an anti-nuke rally in New York's Central Park drew a million people. Just a year earlier, as Reagan ambled into the White House, a poll had reported that only 30 percent of Americans favored the elimination of nuclear weapons. By 1983, four out of five favored elimination.

Al Gore's political antennae told him this popular mood cried out for exploitation. He went methodically to work. Gore has always been an assiduous student of the briefing book and the expert background memo. He looked for a tutor on the nuclear mysteries and found one in Leon Fuerth, a man of whom Strobe Talbott, deputy secretary of state, said in 1998, "Fuerth has iron-clad control over the foreign policy and national security agenda of the vice president. Nobody gets between him and Al Gore."

In origin, Fuerth was Gore's polar opposite: born in Brooklyn, son of an ice-cream vendor who died when Leon was 8, mother working at a dry cleaner; educated at Brooklyn Technical School, then at New York University. Under the ROTC program, he enlisted in the US Air Force, spent three years at Keesler Air Force Base in Mississippi and avoided service in Vietnam, returning thereafter to NYU, where he pursued a doctorate (though did not complete his dissertation) in Russian diplomatic history. Short on money and with two kids, he joined the US State Department, where he spent eleven years. His one overseas posting was in Zagreb, the capital of what was then the Yugoslav province of Croatia. Years later he and Gore were the prime voices for sterner military action against Yugoslavia, and by the same token in favor of Croatia.

Self-confessedly ambitious to become a player in

intelligence and policy-making circles, Fuerth seized on an opening in the State Department's bureau of intelligence and research, and subsequently went to the Department's politico-military affairs division. He finally wound up in what he later described as "a place that nobody really knew about, the Office of Strategic Analysis, which was a four-person outfit. [It is] the place where the Department of State is connected with the rest of the intelligence community on strategic intelligence matters." It was during this period that Fuerth developed his obsessive penchant for secrecy, which he later defined as a desire to remain "nameless, faceless and odorless."

In 1979 Fuerth caught the eye of Les Aspin, a Wisconsin Congressman who was in the process of re-engineering himself from Vietnam dove and Pentagon critic to supple supervisor of the interests of the military-industrial complex. Aspin persuaded Fuerth to quit State and join the staff of the House Intelligence Committee, which Aspin chaired.

When Gore landed his seat on the Intelligence Committee in 1981, he soon singled out Fuerth as a reliable guide through the labyrinth of intelligence and arms control policy. Keeping their encounters secret from the rest of his staff, Gore met Fuerth for regular Friday afternoon tutorials, recalling later that "we spent thirteen months studying, probably eight hours a week, every aspect of the nuclear arms race".

The fruits of those protracted studies were not flattering to either man. Seldom has so much cramming yielded so little. This was at a time when some veterans of the Vietnam-era Defense Department had formed the Military Reform Caucus and were holding seminars to instruct interested members of Congress and their staffs in the realities of weapons procurement, military efficiency and cost effectiveness in the cause of national defense. Among the principals in those sessions were the late Col. John Boyd and Pierre Sprey, a man who infuriated the Air Force by designing the F-16 and A-10 planes, both conceived to be relatively cheap and simple, and therefore anathema to the procurement lobbies.

Sprey remembers Gore in that period as a "total nuclear nut", pumped up by his staff to remember everything he'd been given to study. "He was totally mindless. He had no ideas or interest in what we were saying about conventional weapons. I found him quite unintelligent. Gore was a grind student spouting staff briefings stuff [i.e., the lessons of Fuerth] about the arms race and nuclear exchanges. He was deep into arms limitation in the way of somebody who has been reading a crib sheet. He had no interest in real defense issues, the defense budget, or the fact that people are more important than hardware."

Sprey's perception was correct. Gore and Fuerth were now heavily into nuclear war-gaming, an entirely meretricious exercise deployed most famously by Herman Kahn in his demented book *On Thermonuclear War*, which he wrote while working at the RAND Corporation and consorting with men like Bernard Brodie. Brodie, who was undergoing psychoanalysis at the time, had written a paper for private circulation among his colleagues comparing war plans with sex. Brodie equated the Strategic Air Command's plan for an all-out nuclear assault on the Soviet Union with "going all the way". He likened the tactic of avoiding cities and "withholding" full nuclear assault to withdrawal before ejaculation. Kahn ridiculed the SAC target scheme as being not "a war plan" but "a war orgasm" and devised a ladder with no less than forty-four rungs of escalation, ranging from "Ostensible Crisis" to "Spasm, or Insensate War", Brodie's G-spot. Fuerth claimed that his own interest in nuclear-war-gaming was provoked by

Kahn's escalatory ladder, which prompted him to try to devise a war-fighting scenario that did not inevitably entail mutual assured destruction.

Gore and Fuerth then recruited James Woolsey, a rising player in national security circles. Woolsey had moved nimbly from being a supporter of Eugene McCarthy in 1968 to chief counsel for the notorious cold war hawk and whore for Boeing, Senator Henry "Scoop" Jackson. Woolsey had gone on from Jackson's office to the law firm of Shea and Gardner, where he represented arms contractors as well as CIA/NSC operatives who had got themselves into trouble. In 1977, President Carter tapped him to be undersecretary of the navy, overseeing intelligence operations. Seeing which way the wind was blowing in 1979, Woolsey quit and returned to his law practice to avoid contamination from the coming Carter debacle and to await fresh opportunity. It duly arrived, in the form of Gore and Fuerth.

The duo summoned Woolsey to a hideaway in the Rayburn Building to explicate a nuclear war game model that he had developed as a Pentagon analyst in the 1960s, known as Code 50. Woolsey later described the scene thus: "Here was Gore, who looked about 25, and Leon sitting next to him in the grubbiest congressional office you've ever seen, and they both had these big computer run sheets. I remember thinking, This is an interesting team. This is not the common way of doing business in this town."

Brimming with mutual esteem, this trio pored over Code 50 and emerged from their deliberations with the Gore Plan, hyped as a mid-course between the imperatives of the Pentagon hawks and the hopes of the doves of the freeze movement. Gore and his associates announced they were pioneering a third way, and dubbed themselves The Owls. They envisaged the development of a single-warhead intercontinental ballistic missile, or ICBM, which soon became known as the Midgetman. Five hundred of these would be built and placed on mobile launchers, which would move around the Western desert. Under this plan the Pentagon would be given the go-ahead to continue with R&D on the MX missile.

As can be easily appreciated, the plan offered no twig on which a dove might perch, and Gore devoted a portion of his speech launching the plan to harsh denunciation of the naivete of the freeze movement. Indeed, pleasing doves had never been the intention of these parlor strategists. Their entire aim was to mark themselves as Democratic hawks, true heirs of Scoop Jackson. Intentions aside, Gore's Midgetman plan actually functioned to offer cover for the Reagan White House, then intent on deploying the MX, which was on the ropes.

In short order, the following sequence unfolded. Gore's Midgetman, sinking into obscurity amid indifference from fellow Democrats, was hauled from the trashcan by none other than Henry Kissinger, who hailed it in a column in *Time* magazine. Thus given the Kissingerian imprimatur, Midgetman became a topic of conversation in the Reagan White House, where it was assayed as a possible life preserver for the MX. A blue-ribbon panel was duly convened to scrutinize Midgetman, said panel being chaired by Air Force Gen. Brent Scowcroft, its final report being drafted by James Woolsey. The prime recommendation was that 100 MX missiles be built and deployed. Midgetman was also given a green light, with the pledge to deploy 500 by the mid-1990s. What this had to do with arms control was never satisfactorily explained, unless one accepts that the operative rule of arms control was—-and for that matter is—the orderly regulation of arms production.

The Princeton-based nuclear physicist Frank von Hippel

gives a withering retrospective on Midgetman and Gore's role: "The one exchange that I have ever had with Gore was in that period. I asked him why we needed 500 new single-warhead missiles [the Midgetman] if we already had 500 single-warhead missiles: the Minuteman II. His answer as I recall was, 'The Air Force wants a new missile.' That was certainly true. But the Air Force wanted the MX very much more than the Midgetman."

The Reagan White House played The Owls with cynical skill. Gore, Aspin, Sam Nunn and Norman Dicks (successor to Scoop Jackson as Boeing's local rep on the Hill) were invited to dinner and given talking points for the all-important mission of persuading fellow Democrats that support of Midgetman would absolve them on charges, particularly in the South, that the party was run by liberal wimps and crypto commies. The price tag for this absolution was MX. Gore and the others rose to the challenge. By a vote of 239-186 in November of 1983 the House of Representatives gave the kiss of life to the MX, limited to fifty missiles, and approved the development of Midgetman. When the dust finally settled a few years later, fifty MX missiles had actually been built but no Midgetman was ever deployed. George Bush finally killed off Midgetman in 1992, and Al Gore raced to California to campaign on the cancellation, pledging aerospace workers that under Clinton-Gore they would not be treated with such contumely.

One of the most ardent Congressional supporters of the freeze in those days was the Oregon Democratic rep Les AuCoin, who was miffed at Gore's efforts to bring reluctant Democrats on board the MX/Midgetman bandwagon with heady promises of outfoxing the Reagan team. AuCoin quipped: "I'm glad they weren't negotiating with the Soviets."

Others were less forgiving. "Gore was fucked", a

Democratic staffer on the House Armed Services Committee told us. "The question is whether he knew it or not. His apologists describe him as gullible, naïve, credulous. But with Fuerth and Woolsey behind the scenes, this excuse seems absurd. They knew what they were doing. They were willing pawns of the Reaganauts, determined to screw over the freeze movement in order to advance Gore's political career."

The whole pirouette of Midgetman was indeed precisely that, and Gore cashed in his hawkish credentials as hard currency in his 1984 bid for the US Senate seat vacated by Republican Howard Baker. Gore's only credible opponent would have been Lamar Alexander, then a popular Tennessee governor, but the Midgetman caper—a thoroughgoing betrayal of all Albert Sr.'s deepest held convictions about arms control— served Gore well, giving him the useful status of statesman-strategist. Despite personal pleas from Reagan and Baker, Alexander declined the race, and Gore was home, crushing his Republican opponent.

Gore described himself at the time as a "centrist realist". It's long been his habit to yoke a compliant duet of words in self-characterization. In the late seventies he was a "raging moderate", the term surrendering in the early eighties to "centrist realist". In the early nineties the torch was picked up by his call to "practical idealism", which endured until the millennial turnover, when Gore again reinvented himself as a practitioner of "forward engagement" and "pragmatic progressivism".

Gore took Fuerth with him to the Senate, where they continued to refine the foreign policy stance devised in the House. They entered the Senate with the same airs that had so irritated Gore's House colleagues, prompting the always sharp-tongued Ernest Hollings of South Carolina to remark, "That young know-it-all takes some getting used to."

In his first Senate term Gore supported both the B-1 and B-2 bombers, and the development of nuclear-powered aircraft carriers which were opposed by most Democrats. He backed the 1986 bombing of Libya, although he said it probably wouldn't be enough to stop the Libyans' export of terrorism. In that same year Gore voted against an amendment to the defense appropriations bill that would have prohibited the production of nerve gas. He argued that such a ban would create a nerve gas gap, encouraging the Soviet Union to step up its own gas production. He then voted to fund the development of a new nerve gas missile called Big Eye. He justified that vote by saying that the new technology would actually result in a safer bomb than the old material in the arsenal. Gore held one of the decisive votes here, bringing the tally to 49-49. Vice President Bush cast the tie-breaker, then shame-facedly asked Reagan to call his mother, Dorothy, in Hobe Sound to explain why her son had felt it necessary to vote in favor of this terrifying weapon.

At the start of his second Senate term, in 1991, Gore voted for the Pentagon on three hotly contested measures to cut back on various outrageous military boondoggles. The first was a budget amendment offered by Senator Paul Simon of Illinois to cut military spending by 2 percent in fiscal 1992. Next, Gore denounced as imprudent a measure offered by Senator Tom Harkin of Iowa to transfer $3.1 billion from the military budget to Head Start and other domestic programs. Finally, he voted against a resolution put up by Senator Bill Bradley calling for the Pentagon to develop a plan on how it would achieve an $80 billion reduction in the military budget over the next five years.

It should be recalled that these were the years in which the Soviet threat had imploded; in which, for the first time since 1945, political grandstanding on the Communist threat no longer was fungible currency. Many Democrats were talking about a peace dividend. Not Gore. Never for a moment did he abandon servility to Pentagon programs, earning his campaign treasury handsome subventions from arms manufacturers such as Lockheed. Nor did it lessen his zeal to detect new threats to the national security of either the United States or Israel, whose interests he has always regarded as identical.

Amidst the collapse of the Pentagon budget's best friend—the Soviet Union—the hunt for a new enemy was urgent business. Already in the mid-eighties, Reaganite publicists Clare Sterling and Constantine Menges (known familiarly as Menges Khan) were touting "rogue nations" as the true threat. In their fevered forecasts Libya, Cuba, North Korea, Iran, Nicaragua and even mighty Grenada stood ever ready to pounce on an enfeebled United States and wreak their worst. Gore and Fuerth leapt on the "rogue" threat and ran with it for the rest of the century and into the new one. Fuerth referred to the "rogue states" as "giant zits on the body of the world".

Gore was also one of the few Democrats to favor the reflagging of Kuwaiti oil tankers, making them US registered, so that any threat against them by Iran would be taken as a gauntlet thrown at the feet of Uncle Sam. Reflagging also led to deployment of US Navy ships in the Persian Gulf, eventually becoming the largest naval armada since World War II.

Looking back through the 1980s, one finds that on every issue, whether it was supporting the *contras* (of which more later), shilling for the Pentagon's latest weapons systems, backing the Reagan-Bush position on NATO deployments in Europe, Gore's hawkishness was unflagging. Thus it's all the more surprising that his most significant vote of the early

87

1990s, backing George Bush and the war on Iraq, should have been transmuted by the Gore myth-factory into yet another "agonizing decision", yet another distraught night on the Damascus Road.

Gore went over the top on this one, even by his own standards of self-inflation. On the Senate floor on January 12, 1991, he told his colleagues of his "heavy burden of conscience" and the lonely weeks spent "questioning, probing, searching for the truth". "My decision today", he said, "is the product of an intense, may I say excruciating, effort to find my way to a place as close to a sense of the ultimate truth in this matter as I am capable of getting. I have struggled to confront this issue in its bare essence: to separate what I think is fact, or at least highly probable, from what I think is false, or at least highly improbable; to strike a balance and to take my stand."

But any fool could have guessed which way Gore, with Fuerth and Peretz looming over each shoulder, was going to jump. He had always taken the hard line on Iraq, pushing for the imposition of sanctions against it as early as 1988.

In the twenty-minute preface to his pro-war vote Gore drew from his trusty trunk of melodrama. Once again the "men and women of my hometown of Carthage" were ushered onto the stage of Gore's rhetoric, "leaving their loved ones, saying goodbye to husbands, wives, children and parents". He evinced concern for all those living in the region where 520,000 US troops had massed for war, "including not only those who are with us: but our enemies as well".

He promoted himself as the voice of studious rationality, wedging his position between the chest-thumping of the Bush crowd and the skittishness of the Democratic Party. "As I searched on this issue over the last few days with special intensity...I found myself feeling that if I voted for the Mitchell-

Nunn resolution [to forestall war and continue sanctions] I would do so hoping that it would not prevail. I found myself feeling, even late last night, that since it now appears that there is a majority in favor of the other point of view, that it would pass and will pass, regardless of how I vote. I found myself pulled, once again, to support the Mitchell-Nunn resolution, speaking only of the process I had gone through. But, Mr. President, I feel I owe it to those who are there in Saudi Arabia prepared to make the ultimate sacrifice, to give the best judgement of my head and my heart on what this nation should now do. I cannot reconcile myself to a point of view and a vote that says, in effect, we will let this deadline come and go, and try the sanctions, perhaps until the next window, next August, when military operations would again become feasible."

In his oration Gore never once spoke of the real reason for the war: oil. The topic had to have been on his mind, since he was at that moment in the midst of writing his 700-page manuscript describing the internal combustion engine and fossil fuel consumption as the greatest threat to the planet. Instead, he launched into an Owlish sermon on the destabilizing influences of rogue nations. Saddam, he lectured, was "a threat to regional and even global security.... [T]he threat he represents is so severe that responding with force is not only legitimate but could be unavoidable." He grossly inflated the power of the bedraggled Iraqi army. "Saddam Hussein has more troops than Hitler did in the early years of World War II.... [H]e is using weapons of mass destruction. He is threatening to continue his march throughout the region. His nature has been clear to us for quite a long time. He is seeking to acquire ballistic missiles and nuclear weapons...it is only a matter of time."

By this time, Democratic Senate majority leader George Mitchell was boiling with rage, since Gore had bluffed him into thinking he would vote No on war. Gore's biographer Bill Turque, politely skeptical about most of Gore's claims, writes portentously of the political courage of this particular vote: "Gore's advisers were alarmed—'apoplectic,' as one put it—at the prospect of Gore casting a vote to support Bush on the Gulf war. It risked incalculable damage to his chances for the 1992 Democratic nomination." It did nothing of the sort. Gore, already polling furiously on the possibility of contending for the nomination, would have inevitably positioned himself—as he did in 1988—as the war-fighting realist amid a flock of doves.

Gore later spoke of this vote as his finest hour in the Senate. There is another, less flattering way of looking at his conduct that day. Senator Alan Simpson of Wyoming, Republican whip in the Senate at the time, subsequently charged that Gore shopped his vote to both the Republican and Democratic leadership in order to secure the most favorable slot before the network cameras, massed to televise the debate. The morning before the debate, Simpson said, Gore came to him and Bob Dole, then the Senate majority leader, in the Senate cloakroom. "How much time will you give me?" Gore asked Dole. "How much time will you get from the other side?" Dole asked. "Seven minutes", Gore said, to which Dole replied, "I'll give you fifteen." Then Simpson offered Gore an additional five minutes. Later Simpson derisively referred to Gore as "Prime Time Al", adding, "If you're talking about who people are, and about their character, I never saw such a thing happen with anybody else."

Looking back on the vote, a well-informed staff member on the Senate Foreign Relations Committee puts it this way: "I didn't think there was ever any real question as to how Gore would vote. He was merely feigning indecision to get the optimum attention. This was the vote he'd been waiting his entire career to cast."

Of course, it turned out that those voting No on war, like Sam Nunn, had some political explaining to do, and Al Gore reaped nothing but political capital. But this was only the first time that Gore voted for a mode of warfare whose end consequence was the remote-control destruction of economic and social infrastructures. He hailed this again in Iraq, and later in Yugoslavia, Sudan and Afghanistan.

The US and its allies destroyed Iraq's water, sewage and water-purification systems and its electrical grid. Nearly every bridge across the Tigris and Euphrates was demolished. They damaged twenty-eight hospitals and destroyed thirty-eight schools. They hit all eight of Iraq's large hydropower dams. They attacked grain storage silos and irrigation systems. Farmlands near Basra were inundated with saltwater from allied attacks. More than 95 percent of Iraq's poultry farms were destroyed, as were 3.5 million sheep and more than 2 million cows. They bombed textile plants, cement factories and oil refineries, pipelines and storage facilities, all of which contributed to a long-term environmental nightmare.

When confronted by the press with the sight of Iraqi women carting home buckets of filthy water from the Tigris, itself contaminated with raw sewage from the destroyed treatment plants, an American general shrugged his shoulders and said: "People say, 'You didn't recognize that it [the bombing] was going to have an effect on water and sewage.' Well, what were we trying to do with sanctions—help out the Iraqi people? What we were doing with the attacks on the infrastructure was to accelerate the effect of the sanctions." In others words, maximize the misery of Iraqi citizens.

Since the Geneva conventions of the 1940s forbid war on civilian populations, all of these bombardments properly come under the category of war crimes, just as kindred acts against Serbia did eight years later. Saddam survived, as did his high command. Those who perished or starved or died of disease or saw their children waste away for want of decent drinking water or a shot of penicillin were mostly very poor civilians or impressed conscripts. There is another part of the Geneva conventions that outlaws wars where the one-sidedness is extreme, where war is being waged against an essentially defenseless population. This was certainly the case in the bombing campaigns against Iraq and later Serbia. In the former, after 110,000 sorties across forty-four days, the US lost only thirty-eight airplanes, most of them due to accidents or mechanical failure. On the ground in Iraq, the US lost 148 soldiers, of whom at least thirty-eight fell from friendly fire. There's no reliable estimate of how many Iraqi soldiers died; many certainly deserted long before the final offensive. But this grotesquely unbalanced form of conflict became the standard during the Clinton-Gore years, with Gore the most vehement and enthusiastic advocate. Gore was also rabid in his support of these wars' peacetime twin—sanctions, both against Iraq and Serbia. Bush imposed the sanctions on Iraq, but their frightful effect became fully apparent in the long years that the Clinton Administration tightened and refined them.

Gore managed to mend fences with his Democratic colleagues. Nunn and others had come under fire from the Republicans for their antiwar stance. Phil Gramm, the repellent senior senator from Texas, had proclaimed, "Democrats cannot be trusted to define the destiny of America; they can't be trusted to make America a world leader." Gore's dining partner and fellow futurist Newt Gingrich had said, "If Norm Schwartzkopf had had to report to the Democratic Congress, we'd still be unloading the first five tanks and debating which way they should point." Gore deployed himself to the well of the Senate and issued a stately rebuke, announcing with a straight face that the Republicans were "manipulating votes of conscience into political tools". Then he opened fire on Bush for failing to restrain these Republican critics.

By now Gore was reading polls telling him that, despite 87 percent approval ratings for the president, Bush had an Achilles heel. Americans were mad at him for not having finished off Saddam. Gore staked out his ground on the opinion page of *The New York Times*. "We can no more look forward to a constructive relationship with Saddam Hussein than we could hope to housebreak a cobra." Then he set forth a position on Iraq that would, a couple of years down the road, fuel the Clinton Administration's unrelenting sanctions policy. Saddam Hussein, Gore wrote, "is not an acceptable part of the landscape" and "his Ba'athist regime must be dismantled as well". He followed this up with an appearance on CNN's *Larry King Live*, where he put the argument in even stronger terms: "We should have bent every policy—and we should do it now—to overthrow that regime and make sure than Saddam Hussein is removed from power." Even for Gore this was an upping of the ante, since in January of 1991 he had spoken in favor of a resolution declaring that the removal of Iraqi troops from Kuwait would be enough to warrant a suspension of military operations.

Gore surely knew through Fuerth and Woolsey's contacts in the intelligence world that the CIA was mounting more than

93

one effort to topple Saddam's regime, but this didn't prevent him from publicly excoriating Bush for namby-pambyism toward the Iraqi leader. Gore's posture on Iraq had a lot to do with his selection as Clinton's vice president the following summer. Among those scouting out the credentials of likely running mates for the Arkansas governor were Warren Christopher and Mickey Kantor, both California lawyers. Dismissing contenders such as Mario Cuomo and Sam Nunn because of their positions against the war, they plumped strongly for Gore as the best person to buttress a candidate whose own views on the war had been cast in entrancing equivocation: "I would have voted with the majority", Clinton had said, "if it was a close vote, but I agree with the arguments of the minority."

7 THE SOUND OF DIRTY MUSIC

A nasty experience for Tipper and daughter. They listen to Prince and are shocked at the M word. Parents Music Resource Center is soon on its way. Digression on earlier campaigns against dirty music. PMRC's day in Congress. Tipper pushes for a blacklist, allies with racists and anti-Semites. Record industry cowed. A reality check: Al needs campaign cash from Hollywood, whither they journey to make amends.

Put the name Gore in a poll in the mid-eighties and, on the recognition factor, Tipper would have won handily over Al, at that time in the piedmont of his Senate career and already cocking an ear to his father's urgings that he make a run for the White House.

When we last encountered Tipper in this narrative she was entertaining Newt Gingrich, bringing up Karenna, Kristin and Sarah, and striving for a male heir. Friends of the Gores would recall in later years the duo's unsparing descriptions at dinner parties of the precise sexual maneuvers decreed under the Shettles Method to produce a male. Two cups of coffee first thing in the morning as preface to rear entry sex, Gore would intone triumphantly to guests such as Michael Cardoso, a DC lawyer married to the daughter of one of Gore's money men, Nate Landow. Under optimum circumstance for the production of a male, the woman should be the first to achieve orgasm. In due course Tipper gave birth to Albert III, in October of 1982, and the proud father would buttonhole people to outline for them the efficacy of Shettles.

Maybe it was these descriptions that aroused Tipper's interest in sexual lyrics. At all events she embarked on a campaign that would bring her to national attention. In later years she would claim, with some justice, that when Dan Quayle talked up "family values" in the presidential election of 1992 and when Bill Clinton took care to insult the rap singer Sister Souljah as a way of distancing himself from Jesse Jackson in that same election, they were both following a trail she blazed seven years earlier.

As is so often the case with the Gores, the way Tipper tells it her campaign had its origins in a family crisis. It was December 1984. Tipper went to a record store and bought Prince's album *Purple Rain* for her daughter Karenna, who was 11 years old. "We brought the album home, put it on the stereo, and listened to it together, we heard the words to...'Darling Nikki': 'I knew a girl named Nikki/ guess you could say she was a sex fiend/ I met her in a hotel lobby/ masturbating with a magazine.' The song went on and on, I couldn't believe my ears! The vulgar lyrics embarrassed both of us. At first, I was stunned—then I got mad! Millions of Americans were buying *Purple Rain* with no idea what to expect. Thousands of parents were giving the album to their children—many even younger than my daughter."

There are some minor puzzles in this distraught, albeit well-honed, reminiscence. Amid the furore of the censorship drive she launched shortly after this epiphany, she told Dave Marsh, editor of the newsletter *Rock 'n Rap Confidential*, that she had bought *Purple Rain* because the Gore family had heard and liked Prince's single, "Let's Go Crazy", which was included on the album. It is conceivable that the word "masturbation" is what so inflamed the born-again Baptist (Al and Tipper took Jesus into their lives in 1977) and her daughter, but it's odd that these sensitive souls were in no way perturbed by "Let's Go Crazy", that indeed they reveled in a song whose lyrics include the lines, 'U see, I called my old lady / 4 a friendly word/ she just picked up the phone/ dropped it on the floor/ sex, sex is all I heard."

Again, that Tipper should have been shocked that Prince was singing about sex demands a certain credulity. *Purple Rain* had already caused a major public fuss, particularly among liberal women like Tipper. It would be like someone buying the books of Henry Miller in the mid-sixties and being startled by descriptions of intercourse.

Nevertheless, Tipper was on her way. The domestic tedium of a Congressional wife was dispelled in a series of phone conferences that soon minted an alliance with Susan Baker, wife of James Baker, Reagan's Treasury Secretary. (In 1992, when Baker was Secretary of State, Al would call him the only "man of honor" in the Bush Administration.) Susan Baker had had her own terrible rendezvous with the youth culture, courtesy of Madonna. Baker had heard her 7-year-old child singing "Like a Virgin", prompting her to exclaim furiously that Madonna was teaching girls "how to act like a porn queen in heat".

There were two other well-connected co-founders of Tipper's campaign: Pam Howar, a fixture of the Washington social scene and a woman scarcely prudish in her public demeanor. Howar had been aurally affronted at her aerobics class, when the sound system had belched out some unspecified gobbet of raunch. The fourth musketeer was the somewhat more austere Sally Nevius, dean of admissions at Mount Vernon College and the wife of the former chairman of the DC

City Council.

Marketing themselves as just another group of concerned moms, this high-powered coven formed the Parents Music Resource Center. They eventually set up shop in Alexandria, Virginia, courtesy of a donation from the Coors family. Coors wasn't their only patron. The PMRC also pulled in money from 7-UP, Dow Chemical and the Mary Reynolds Babcock Foundation, one of the philanthropies of the R.J. Reynolds tobacco fortune.

Baker took their crusade against "porn rock" to pundits such as George Will, who dashed off a column praising the women's courage in confronting the "de-moralizing" nature of rock and rap. Tipper worked the liberal side of the tracks, recruiting prissy pieces from *The New Republic*'s Charles Krauthammer and the *Boston Globe*'s Ellen Goodman, who complained that "the lyrics drift, like cigarette smoke, polluting everyone within range, doing the worst to the youngest".

Assaults on popular music are nothing new. In the 1920s jazz was held up for public censure as a degenerate music form, tempting youths to booze, sex, racial mingling and spiritual delinquency. In the August 1921 edition of the *Ladies Home Journal*, Anne Faulkner Shaw, head of the General Federation of Women's Clubs, warned American parents to shield their children from this corrupting music, describing it as "the accompaniment of the voodoo dancer, stimulating the half-crazed barbarian to the vilest deeds".

Faulkner Shaw's racist diatribe found a sympathetic ear in Harry Anslinger, head of the Federal Bureau of Narcotics. Anslinger believed that jazz and rhythm and blues were a mainline to drugs and subversive behavior. He ordered his agents to keep files on the activities of jazz musicians, including Louis Armstrong, Thelonius Monk, Count Basie, Cab Calloway,

Duke Ellington, Dizzy Gillespie, and Lionel Hampton. In the late 1940s Anslinger sent this memo to his agents: "Because of the increasing volume of reports indicating that many musicians of the swing band type are responsible for the spread of the marijuana smoking vice, I should like you to give the problem some special attention in your district. If possible, I should like you to develop a number of cases in which arrest would be withheld so as to synchronize these with arrests to be made in other districts."

In 1948, Anslinger appeared before the House Ways and Means Committee to denounce popular music. "We have been running into a lot of [drug] traffic among these jazz musicians," Anslinger testified, "and I'm not talking about the good musicians, but the jazz type." Three years later, Anslinger prevailed upon the State Department to deny visas to musicians he suspected of being dope-smokers (and Communists), singling out Thelonius Monk as a particularly suspicious character.

By the mid-1950s Southern preachers and segregationists were fulminating about the dangers of rock 'n roll, which was variously described as promoting a "pagan way of life", a Communist plan to make "a generation of American youth mentally ill" and a plot to degrade white kids "down to the level of the Negro".

In early June of 1985, the PMRC sent a letter of demands to Stanley Gortikov, president of the Recording Industry Association of America. The letter was signed by the four initiators of the PMRC, plus some newfound conscripts to the censorship cause, the wives of fifteen members of Congress. To ratchet up the intimidation factor, the women signed themselves in their husbands' names: Mrs. Tom Downey, Mrs. Guy Vander Jagt, Mrs. Richard Schulze, Mrs. James Jones,

Mrs. Bill Frenzel, Mrs. John Heinz, Mrs. David Durenburger, Mrs. Paul Simon, Mrs. Ernest Hollings, Mrs. Strom Thurmond, Mrs. Richard Armey, Mrs. John Danforth, Mrs. Bob Packwood and Mrs. Al Gore, in sum the wives of nine senators and six representatives, plus the wife of the Secretary of the Treasury, probably the most influential member of the Reagan Cabinet.

The PMRC set forth a list of demands, starting with a ratings code. The group called for an "X" to be slapped on songs that contained profanity, violence, suicide and sexually explicit lyrics, "including topics of fornication, sado-masochism, incest, homosexuality, bestiality and necrophilia". The inclusion of homosexuality in this list of verboten topics harked back to Al's comment in 1976 that he considered homosexuality "abnormal" sexual behavior.

The group wanted music that "glorifies" drug use stamped with a "D/A". This begs the question as to what Tipper would have done with those arch-promoters of illicit drugs, the Grateful Dead. Tipper fancied herself one of the Dead's most devoted fans, a "true Deadhead", as she boasted in 1996. In 1993 she invited the band to her DC office and took her entire staff to see them perform at RFK Stadium. A couple of years later, Jerry Garcia died, his body pickled in heroin and alcohol.

Any music deemed to promote the occult, the PMRC letter said, must be marked with an "O". This last demand was a clear assault not only on free speech and artistic rights but on religious freedom. In similar vein, the group demanded that the record industry ban the practice of "backward masking", a curious obsession of the religious right concerning the supposed Satanic habit with putting everything back to front.

Soon Tipper, Pam Howar, Susan Baker and Peatsy Hollings convened a meeting with Gortikov in which they reiterated their demands. The meeting took place in Al's

Washington office. The quartet announced that not only did they want the industry to adopt the labeling scheme but they also wanted to ban children from attending concerts where "vulgarities" might be sung or dramatized on stage. As the clincher, Tipper and Baker called for the record labels to drop acts that wouldn't go along with these prescriptions. The PMRC wrote in a memo that it wanted the record labels to "reassess contracting artists who engage in violence, substance abuse and/or explicit behaviour in concerts where minors are admitted".

In other words, these latter-day Comstocks were calling for a blacklist. As Phyllis Pollack, a leader of the music anti-censorship coalition and a publicist for several rap and rap groups targeted by the PMRC put it, "They came on like Joe McCarthy in drag". The only question was who would be on the blacklist: Madonna, Prince, Motley Crue, Black Sabbath, Ozzy Osbourn, Slayer, Venom, WASP and the Dead Kennedys were favorite targets, the rock equivalent of Al's hated "rogue nations". But Tipper and her cohort also cited supposedly deviant songs by the Jacksons, Cyndi Lauper, Tom Petty, Pink Floyd and The Who. Working-class hero Bruce Springsteen was excoriated for his songs "I'm on Fire", interpreted by PMRC researchers as an ode to incest, and "Dancing in the Dark", which allegedly offered Satanic incantations when played backward. "Even Bruce isn't clean", Howar excitedly told a reporter. This may have discountenanced George Will, who once tried to purge his dweeb reputation by writing ecstatically of a visit to a Springsteen concert, palavering with the Boss in his dressing room.

The Rolling Stones came in for a lashing for their song "Tie Me Up," condemned as an endorsement of the sexual tastes of the Marquis de Sade. This was quite an about-face for

Tipper, who at the age of 15 sent a pre-Al boyfriend a copy of the band's single "Get Off of My Cloud", signing it "Rolling Stones Forever! Love, Tipper."

Eventually, of course, the attention of the freelance censors would zero in on black groups, NWA, 2Live Crew, Public Enemy and the notorious Ice-T. Rap was cited for being misogynistic, drug-promoting and violent. "Tipper Gore has been against black people and our music", said Luther Campbell, leader of 2Live Crew. "You expect to find her at the door of Tower Records demanding that all rap music be removed." Campbell wasn't far from the truth, as the Recording Industry Association of America soon demonstrated.

In the face of threats from PMRC, it didn't take Gortikov long to fold. In a notebook he wrote of being lectured on the social evils of rock music, stating that Tipper and Baker had told him that "the practices heard and seen by children constitute secondary child abuse". Two days after his session with "the Washington Wives" (Frank Zappa's term) the record industry's top lobbyist sent off a memo to his clients, the heads of the major record labels. His recommendation: a strategy of appeasement. Gortikov suggested that the industry compromise by putting warning labels on recordings that contained explicit lyrics. If the battle got any hotter, Gortikov warned, it could put some of the industry's most cherished legislative goals at risk: copyright, anti-piracy enforcement and the blank-tape tax. "Non-response by companies can have serious negative backlash effects. Our legislation and national/international anti-piracy projects can be diluted or jeopardized."

Gortikov was even willing to acquiesce to the most outrageous of the PMRC's demands, the dropping of controversial artists. "It is impossible to justify publicly some of the blatant and extreme recording examples protested by the parent groups", he counseled his clients. "I recommend that a renewed policy of sensitivity, discretion and reasonableness be applied in recording and releasing practices.... Artist contracts, new and old, might be examined to assure that future content allows such company discretion." Tipper would later refer to Gortikov as her "secret ally".

With Gortikov and the industry association thus cowed, the PMRC pressed ahead, engineering one of the most raucous and raunchy oversight hearings in the history of the Senate. On September 19, 1985, the Senate Commerce Committee convened to hear testimony from the ladies of the PMRC, their hired gun, Jeff Ling (a rocker turned minister), sociologists and psychologists, and musicians Frank Zappa, John Denver and Dee Snyder, lead singer of Twisted Sister. It was a show-trial, held before a jam-packed audience.

The hearing was chaired by Senator John "St. Jack" Danforth, the Missouri minister and Purina dog food heir, who later shepherded his friend Clarence Thomas through tumultuous confirmation hearings. Aside from Danforth and Gore, the Commerce Committee included three other husbands of PMRC members, Bob Packwood, Ernest Hollings and Paul Trible. "The reason for this hearing is not to promote any legislation", Danforth announced, "but simply to provide a forum for airing the issue itself, for ventilating the issue, for bringing it out into the public domain...so that the whole issue can be brought to the attention of the American people."

The hearing was designed to censor through intimidation, not legislation. As a way to cast herself as a guardian of the First Amendment, Tipper repeatedly claimed that they preferred "voluntary compliance" over a federal labeling law. "It is important to note that there is a difference between wanting to restrain and wanting to suppress and censor", Tipper proclaimed. "The deviant slowly becomes the normal if the apathy of the middle allows it to be so." Dick Morris would have been proud of this particularly fine example of triangulation politics applied to the cultural playing field.

Still, Tipper thought that Danforth might have tipped his hand too soon. In her book *Raising PG Kids in an X-Rated Society*, Tipper refers to a secret source inside the record industry: "In his view, it would take congressional attention to make the record industry budge. His only regret was that Senator Danforth let the executives know in advance that no legislation would come out of it."

Danforth didn't want legislation, but others did. No sooner had Danforth given this assurance than Fritz Hollings rose to denounce "outrageous filth" and "music interspersed with pornography". Hollings said he might propose legislation. "To be perfectly candid with you, I would look for regulations or some kind of legislation, if it could be constitutionally accomplished", he said.

A similar sentiment was expressed by another Democrat, James Exon of Nebraska. Exon was perplexed. While he thanked the "ladies for coming here and testifying on [their] concerns", he couldn't understand why the Senate was wasting its time if no action was planned. "Can anyone answer that?" Exon asked. "I did not schedule these hearings." Still, he noted that if legislation was contemplated, he'd get behind it. "I simply want to say to you that I suspect that, unless the industry 'cleans up their act'—-and I use that in quotes again— there is likely to be legislation." (In 1996, Exon authored the Communications Decency Act, an amendment to the telecommunications bill, outlawing the distribution of pornography on the Internet. The measure, backed by Al Gore, was struck down by a federal court as unconstitutional.)

When it came time for Tipper to testify, she deplored everything from sexually explicit album covers to violent lyrics that she said debase women, glorify rape and lure children toward Satanism. Introducing a theme that Tipper would reiterate over the next few years, she suggested that rock music was responsible for "an epidemic" of teen pregnancies and suicides. She and the other PMRC ladies were treated deferentially by the panel, including Al Gore, who touchingly asked his wife a series of questions regarding explicit album cover art.

The inquisitors weren't nearly as respectful of Frank Zappa, the avant-garde guitarist and songwriter, who served as point man for the rockers at the hearing. Zappa didn't mince words, calling the PMRC a band of sexually repressed cultural terrorists. "The PMRC's proposal is an ill-conceived piece of nonsense which fails to deliver any real benefits to children, and infringes on the civil liberties of people who are not children," Zappa said. "The PMRC's demands are the equivalent of treating dandruff by decapitation...[they read] like an instruction manual for some sinister kind of 'toilet training program' to housebreak all composers and performers because of the lyrics of a few. Ladies, how dare you?"

Then Zappa zeroed in on one of his key points: the hearing, which Senator Paul Trible had ludicrously dubbed "the most important of the year", was a distraction from serious matters of state, namely the looting of the federal treasury with another Reagan tax measure. "While the wife of the Secretary of the Treasury recites, 'Gonna drahve mah love insahde you', and Senator Gore's wife talks about 'b-b-bondage' and oral sex at gunpoint, on the CBS Evening News, people in high places work on a tax bill that is so ridiculous the only way to sneak it through is to keep the public's mind on something else: porn rock."

Senator Exon called Zappa's suggestion outlandish and conspiratorial. Senator Paula Hawkins, the Florida Republican, suggested that Zappa neglected his own children and sought to dismiss his testimony because he made "a profit off of the sales of rock songs".

When it came time for Gore to question Zappa, Al sought to portray himself as something of a groupie and chided Exon for never having heard of the Mothers of Invention. "Let me say, although I disagree with some of the statements that you make, and have made on other occasions," Gore told Zappa unctuously, "I have been a fan of your music, believe it or not, and I respect you as a true original and tremendously talented musician." As such a fan, Gore must have been familiar with one of Zappa's few pop hits, the 1974 scatological parody of parental admonition, titled "Don't Eat Yellow Snow." Or perhaps it was Zappa's 1976 song "Ms. Pinky" that Al Gore was so fond of, with the robust lyrics: "I got a girl with a little rubber head/ rinse her out every night just before I go to bed/ she never talked back like a lady might do/ and she looks like she loves it every time I get through/ and her name is P-I-N-K-Y... Her eyes all shut in an ecstasy face/ you can cram it down her throat, people, any old place/ throw a little switch on her battery pack/ you can poot it, you can shoot it till your wife gets back."

Soon after the hearings Ronald Reagan himself endorsed the group's mission, mumbling that the music industry was exploiting children and indoctrinating them with the "glorification of drugs and violence and perversity". Reagan's culture czar, Bill Bennett, appeared in a PMRC video. The surgeon general, Dr. C. Everett Koop, spoke to a PMRC gathering, railing against music videos, "as a combination of senseless violence and senseless pornography to the beat of rock music."

Raising PG Kids in an X-Rated Society was published in 1987 by Abingdon Press, a Nashville-based religious publisher whose catalogue included *Preaching in American History*, primers on church fundraising, and tax preparation guides for ministers. The book reprised many of Tipper's greatest hits, including her obsession with "moral decline", "social evils", "throbbing chords" and "sadistic sex". But the book's rhetoric also evinced a more political flavor, linking her fears about the influence of raunchy rock lyrics with the issues that her husband was using to advance his career in the Senate.

"Just as it is imperative that we work intelligently to defuse the nuclear threat," Tipper wrote, "so must we come to terms with the unfettered commercial exploitation of violence and violent messages through our culture." Having thus linked rock porn with nuclear Armageddon, Tipper called for a "new environmental movement. This movement would mobilize citizens concerned with the degradation of the physical environment to also turn their attention to the cultural environment." (All the evidence anyone would ever need that Al and Tipper have never encountered an Earth First!er.)

Tipper's book was in part the product of the editorial labors of an old Gore friend and political media specialist, Carter Eskew, who helped her develop the idea. Eskew is one of those hired guns that flit in and out of Al Gore's life, working for him in election seasons and then going on to gorge himself in the private sector on the spoils of victory. In 1995, Eskew joined BSMG Worldwide, a pr firm. There this former advocate of children's well-being oversaw big tobacco's $40 million campaign to kill off anti-tobacco legislation in the Senate in 1998.

Later in 1987, their sights set on a bid for the White House, Al and Tipper went to Hollywood to sue for peace and to beg for money. A meeting between music industry executives was arranged by Gore's intimate, Mickey Kantor, then one of LA's most wired-in attorneys. In attendance were Irving Azoff, head of MCA's music division; Danny Goldberg, president of Gold Mountain Records; Lenny Waronker of Warner Bros. Records; and musician Don Henley.

Azoff didn't waste time letting the Gores know what he thought of their crusade against rock music. "I blame you for all of it", Azoff told Tipper. The Gores demurred. Al claimed that the 1985 Senate hearings were "not a good idea". Tipper agreed, calling the hearings "a mistake...that sent the wrong message". Gore said he didn't "ask for" and "was not in favor of" the hearings, implying that they were pressed upon him by Senator Danforth. All of this was secretly taped and then handed over to *Daily Variety*, which ran an article on the Gores' backpedaling before powerful Hollywood donors.

The record entirely contradicts Gore's contention that he was an innocent bystander. Most senators fluttered in and out, but Gore stayed for the duration, questioning every witness. After listening to one set of ribald lyrics, Gore shook his head and exclaimed that record labels were being "really irresponsible in promoting suicide and all the other things we have heard about here".

During the hearings Gore even railed at the record industry execs for failing to show up. "I am told that every single one of the chief executive officers invited to participate chose to decline. I want to note that fact for the record, and I think that they should take a look at themselves as human beings, whether or not this is the way they want to spend their lives, if this is the way they want to earn a living, if this is the kind of contribution they want to make to the society in which we live." Then he went further, suggesting that the execs be compelled to testify. "It seems to me that we have the right to ask them, whether or not they wish to answer the question."

From the start the PMRC worked hand in hand with right-wing fundamentalist Christian groups. It endorsed the endeavors of Dan and Steve Peters and their book *Why Knock Rock*. The Peters brothers, both ministers from Minnesota, preached that "rock music appears to be one of Satan's grandest schemes". Their solution would have made Torquemada proud: public bonfires. They have boasted that their record burning ceremonies have destroyed more than $10 million worth of music. PMRC's Sally Nevius credits the Peters brothers with adding some zest to the new crusade: "It was guys like them who got the rock 'n roll wrecking ball swinging in the right direction."

In her book Tipper recommends the Fullerton, California, Back-in-Control Center as a resource for parents worried about the influence of rock music on their teenagers. The Back-in-Control Center, run by two former parole officers, was a deprogamming operation that treated rockers as if they were victims of cults. The programs, used as sentencing options by juvenile courts, featured "de-metalling" and "de-punking" sessions. Both mind-cleansing regimes called for complete isolation from rock music, friends who listen to rock, and clothing associated with rock, including t-shirts, black boots and silver jewelry. Convalescence no doubt included mandatory immersion in the songs of Pat Boone. The Center's handbook for parents and law enforcement listed various ways to determine if teens were succumbing to malevolent musical forces. One such sign is the "six-pointed star representing the

Jewish Star of David", which was interpreted as a Satanic icon. The Center circulated pictures of Paul Stanley, lead singer of the glam-rock band KISS, wearing a Star of David, as if this were proof of devil worship.The Center made the absurd claim that KISS was an acronym for Knights in Satan's Service. It didn't note that Stanley is Jewish or that the parents of the group's bassist, Gene Simmons, had barely survived the Holocaust. Tipper, in a statement released through Al's press secretary, said that the Center's views on the Star of David were "a mistake".

This was not the only group touted by the PMRC. Take The Missouri Rock Project, an outfit run by an associate of Phyllis Schlafly, which distributed information packets prepared by the Victory Christian Church of St. Charles, Missouri, claiming that the Holocaust was overblown, that Hitler didn't write *Mein Kampf* and that Hollywood shamelessly advocates race-mixing. The slain civil rights leader, whose memory is so often invoked by Al Gore, is referred to as "Martin Lucifer King".

Much of the material circulated by the anti-rock brigades was racist in outlook, but perhaps none was so rabid as the writings of David Noebel, author of *Rhythm, Riots and Revolution*. "The full truth is that it [i.e., the origin of rock] goes still deeper— to the heart of Africa, where it was used to incite warriors to such a frenzy that by nightfall neighbors were cooked in carnage pots! The music is a designed reversion to savagery!" The PMRC's newsletter plugged Noebel's work as a useful resource.

The group also reached out to the Rev. James Dobson, whom the ACLU's Barry Lynn called the "most powerful fundamentalist in the country". Dobson, a minister and pediatrician, ran Focus on the Family, which employed 500 people in the late eighties and brought in more than $57 million a year. Dobson, who argued that serial killer Ted Bundy had been driven to murder by an addiction to pornography, was tapped to serve on Attorney General Ed Meese's 1985 commission to eradicate smut. The Meese commission's agenda, remarkably similar to the work of the PMRC, was to overturn the conclusion of a Nixon-era presidential panel that there was no causal link between pornography and criminal behavior.

In its newsletter, *Citizen*, alongside articles praising antiabortion zealot Randall Terry and attacking the teaching of evolution in public schools, Focus on the Family faithfully distributed PMRC materials to its hundreds of thousands of adherents. This was scarcely surprising, since one of Dobson's board members during this time was Susan Baker. One of the Reverend Dobson's top advisers back then was Bob DeMoss, who worked for Focus on the Family as "a youth culture specialist". DeMoss also toiled for the PMRC, producing its hysterical 1988 video, *Rising to the Challenge*, a slickly produced companion to Tipper's book which accused rock music of promoting suicide, teen pregnancy, youth violence and drug abuse. The film included a statement by Bruce Springsteen (formerly on the PMRC's watch list), decrying the trend toward degenerate rock lyrics. The only problem: the quote was entirely fictitious.

The PMRC got caught fabricating support for its cause on several occasions. In a 1989 interview with the *Harvard Political Review*, Tipper suggested that the ACLU backed the PMRC's drive to label recordings. "ACLU president Norman Dorsen and the National Coalition Against Censorship co-chair Harriet Pilpel both had praise for the [album stickering] approach I advocated", Tipper claimed. "They mentioned that it

111

respected First Amendment rights, while at the same [time] it respected the rights of parents in the marketplace. So while it wasn't an out and out endorsement, they definitely had warm remarks and praise for this approach, and said that it was a perfectly legitimate approach to make."

Not true, said Barry Lynn, then the ACLU's chief legislative counsel, who publicly disputed Tipper's statement and accused her of twisting Dorsen's comments to suit her purposes. "We have unequivocally opposed ratings systems", Lynn said. "We don't like the Motion Picture Association of America's or any music industry ratings because they inhibit artistic freedom." Lynn noted that labeling could amount to a form of censorship, citing decisions by major retail chains to restrict the sale of stickered music to minors. Lynn's fears came true when Wal-Mart, the nation's largest music retailer, capitulated to the pressure of the censors and decided not to stock stickered music at its 2,300 outlets. Sitting on Wal-Mart's board at the time: Hillary Rodham Clinton.

Another blunder by the PMRC came in June of 1989, when the group used an op-ed piece for *Billboard* to invoke the name of Paul McCartney in the cause of cleaning up rock music. This didn't set well with the former Beatle, who instructed his manager, Richard Ogden, to set the record straight. "Whilst Paul does believe that in extreme cases there may be cause for individual parental concerns, Paul would like to put on the record that he is totally opposed to censorship of any art form for any reason and disassociates himself entirely from the policies of the PMRC", Ogden said.

That summer of 1989, PMRC consultant Bob DeMoss wrote an article for the *Citizen* attacking the Los Angeles rap group NWA's song "F—- tha Police." DeMoss's article, headlined "Rap Group NWA Says 'Kill Police", called on readers to "alert police to the dangers they may face in the wake of this record release". Within a few weeks police across the country began receiving faxes about NWA.

Then in August the FBI got into the act. FBI assistant director Milt Ahlerich sent a letter on FBI stationery to NWA's label, Priority Records. The three-paragraph letter demonstrates how high-powered "private" censors can work in sync with federal law enforcement:

"A song recorded by the rap group NWA on their album entitled 'Straight Out of Compton' encourages violence against and disrespect for the law enforcement officer and has been brought to my attention. I understand your company recorded and distributed this album, and I am writing to share my thoughts and concerns with you.

"Advocating violence and assault is wrong, and we in the law enforcement community take exception to such action. Violent crime, a major problem in our country, reached an unprecedented high in 1988. Seventy-eight law enforcement officers were feloniously slain in the line of duty during 1988, four more than in 1987. Law enforcement officers dedicate their lives to the protection of our citizens, and recordings such as the one from NWA are both discouraging and degrading of these brave, dedicated officers.

"Music plays a significant role in society, and I wanted you to be aware of the FBI's position relative to this song and its message. I believe my views reflect the opinion of the entire law enforcement community."

Ahlerich said that his letter was not a personal note but reflected the "official position" of the FBI. The ACLU's Lynn remarked on the chilling effect of the FBI letter. "It would not violate the First Amendment for an individual working for the

FBI to personally write such a letter. But it's incredible for the FBI to send this kind of official letter to a person in the creative community."

NWA was repeatedly harassed by local police as they toured the country, most notably in Detroit, where cops rushed the stage when they tried to perform "F— tha Police" and detained them in their hotel room. "Maybe next they'll send the CIA after me, arrest me for treason," quipped NWA's Ice Cube.

Of course people in the ghettoes were experiencing on a daily basis a large amount of police brutality, but such conduct wasn't as well known among the respectable element as it became after the Rodney King beating. Even so, in the spring of 2000, when Bruce Springstein wrote and performed a song, "41 shots" that obliquely criticized the police for the killing of Amadou Diallo, the police raised a storm of outrage in New York.

Tipper lashed out at rapper Ice-T for his songs, especially "Cop Killer". In an op-ed in *The Washington Post*, Tipper wrote, "Cultural economics were a poor excuse for the South's continuation of slavery. Ice-T's financial success cannot excuse the vileness of his message.... Hitler's anti-Semitism sold in Nazi Germany. That didn't make it right." Once again the police got into the act. The Houston police association sent a letter warning Warner Bros. Records that, combined with "the summer, the violence and a little drugs", Ice-T's songs "are going to unleash a reign of terror on communities all across this country". The reign of terror didn't materialize, except for the one unleashed by the police, particularly in Los Angeles. Even so, Ice-T voluntarily pulled the song from his album *Body Count* and soon left his record company.

Contrary to Tipper's repeated suggestion that the PMRC wanted to act only as an agent of consumer information, the rock "porn" crusade quickly transmuted into a spate of legal proposals and criminal trials of musicians, songwriters and record retailers. In Maryland, a bill that would have made it a crime to sell "obscene" music to minors was only narrowly defeated. Similar measures were proposed in eighteen other states. Mandatory labeling bills were introduced in twenty-two states. In 1990, a labeling bill was passed by the Louisiana legislature but was vetoed by the governor. A Washington State measure to criminalize "erotic" music was also vetoed.

In her book Tipper lavishes special praise upon the "courageous" initiative of San Antonio's Mayor Henry Cisneros prohibiting children under 14 from attending concerts with "lewd or violent" performances. In an ironic twist typical of the fate of many such moral grandstanders, Cisneros, later Secretary of Housing and Urban Development in the Clinton-Gore Administration, was forced to resign under a cloud, chased by an independent counsel investigation. He ultimately plead quilty to a misdemeanor for lying to the FBI during a background check about how much money he had paid to his mistress while he was mayor of San Antonio. After leaving HUD, Cisneros went on to serve as CEO for Univision, the Spanish-language television network, known for its racy talk shows and louche music videos. Media critic Jill Stewart describes Univision's programming under Cisneros as a form of "Mexploitation" which feeds "Southern California's Mexican-American population a steady diet of the dumbest, cheapest, most prurient TV programming imaginable".

It must have been a point of pride for Tipper that her ladies' crusade was taken so seriously as to prompt police actions. When, in 1986, Jello Biafra, lead singer of the anarcho-punk band Dead Kennedys, was charged with producing "material harmful to minors", she applauded the prosecution and lamented that she hadn't personally been responsible for the charges being brought. Biafra's crime? For Tipper the band's "tastelessly styled" name may have been enough, and the reasoning of the Los Angeles DA's office wasn't much more advanced than that. Inside the band's *Frankenchrist* album, Biafra had included a poster by German artist H.R. Geiger titled *Penis Landscape*, depicting, as Tipper excitedly put it, "multiple erect penises penetrating vaginas". Ultimately, Biafra was acquitted, but the ordeal contributed to the break-up of the band.

In the late 1980s and early 1990s, the rap group 2LiveCrew was hounded by police, arrested several times and convicted of producing an obscene recording ("Nasty As You Wanna Be") by a Miami judge. The conviction was overturned on appeal. In New York City, a group was arrested for performing a couple of 2LiveCrew's songs at an adults-only club. In addition, six record store owners (in Alabama, Texas and Florida) were arrested for selling the album. In several other states, store owners were warned by police and local prosecutors to remove the album from the shelves or face arrest.

In 1990 the heavy metal band GWAR was arrested in Charlotte, North Carolina, after simulating anal intercourse with a plastic fish/penis on a doll representing a judge who had outlawed lewd rock music. The band was fined and banned from playing in North Carolina for a year.

Efforts to stigmatize and criminalize music have continued into the present. In 1998, George W. Bush signed into law a measure prohibiting the State of Texas from investing money in any private entity that owns more than 10 percent of a corporation producing music that "describes, glamorizes, or advocates violence, drug abuse or sexual activity". Early in the summer of 2000, the *Los Angeles Times* printed a rambling column by one of its reporters, Anna Valdes-Rodriquez, that made a connection between rap music by "dark-skinned men" filled with hatred for women and the sexual assault on a group of women in the aftermath of New York's Puerto Rican Day parade. "The idiots who ripped the clothes off the women in Central Park were raised on gangsta rap and aggro-rock," Valdes-Rodgriguez wrote. "It did not reflect their world view, it formed it."

In 1988, Tipper told the *Chattanooga Times* that her wars against rock music were reflective of the new Southern strategy on cultural values, promoted by her husband and his political advisers, and designed to capitalize on the Super Tuesday primaries, dominated by Southern states. "We have not dealt with this kind of a political landscape before, where the South is going to have a lot more power, frankly, and influence over the eventual nominee", Tipper said. "I personally think that is healthy, because it is time to put the values of the New South on the national agenda."

One sector of the recording industry that escaped scrutiny by Tipper, Al and the PMRC was country music, despite its mournful catalogue of despair, drinking, adultery, suicide and revenge. Gore himself was fond of singing to the press on his campaign plane a song about serial marriage, "All My Exes Live in Texas, But I Hang My Hat in Tennessee". Tipper said such music wasn't worthy of censorship because "kids don't listen to it." This might have come as a surprise to country teen idols such as Tanya Tucker, Garth Brooks and Wynona Judd—or even Dolly Parton, builder of DollyWorld, a country music theme park for kids in Pigeon Forge, Tennessee.

Phyllis Pollack gives an energetic retrospect on Tipper: "She's such a hypocrite! For example, while condemning rappers like Tone-Loc, who Tipper's PMRC blamed for the proliferation of marijuana use, she also leaked her own dope-smoking past and just can't draw enough attention to herself doing photo ops with members of the Grateful Dead.[Gore staffers in 1988 leaked to the Washington Post the news that they were happy to let stories of Tipper's marijuana smoking get out, in order to loosen up her image.] While desperately pretending to be "hip" (a word she has used in the press to describe herself) in order to get the "youth vote" for her husband, she gives credit in her own book to sources that include conservatives who hold record album burning bonfires. After signing a letter sent to the RIAA demanding an "X" on records that "glorify" homosexuality, she can't wait to do photo ops to help Al's campaigning with gays who are celebrities. The constant face-lift that Tipper has to give herself to serve her own need for desperate attention and to help Al's political campaigns never seems to end. It requires never-ending damage control, lies and re-writing history in order to cover up whatever it was she said or did the day before."

In 2000, Al Gore defended his wife's actions: "She was early and she was right."

8 AIMING HIGH, AIMING LOW

An ill-fated bid for the 88 nomination. Thrashed, Gore stays in the race as party's hitman against Jesse Jackson. He brings Willie Horton to the attention of George Bush, communes with shrinks, ponders Meaning of Life. Albert III has a nasty accident. Gore in crisis. Promptly writes book about Earth in crisis. Off to Rio! A fateful phone call from Bill Clinton.

In 1988, Al Gore offered himself as the youngest presidential candidate since William Jennings Bryan. If elected he would have been 40. But in his own mind he'd been a suitable aspirant for the Oval Office at the age of 36. In 1984 he actually hesitated between a race for the US Senate and an early bid for the Democratic nomination, won that year by Walter Mondale. Gore went out to Hollywood and checked out the fundraising possibilities. Whence this hubris? It surely had something to do with the overall Gore family project of winning the presidency. Old Albert Sr. would wander around fantasizing that the vice presidential nomination had been his for the asking in 1956, and Al Jr., at that time best known as the husband of Tipper Gore, had already mentally ensconced himself in the White House.

Gore's bid for the Democratic presidential nomination in 1988 remains the greatest political humiliation of his life thus far. Nor could he take from his defeat even the consoling morsel of being a plucky underdog. He displayed himself as a mean-spirited and graceless campaigner whose two achievements were entirely negative. He served as the political assassin whistled up by the Democratic powers to destroy another contender for the nomination, Jesse Jackson, and his oppo research team picked up the story of Willie Horton. The manner in which Gore set about those tasks was the prototype for the famously racist campaign designed by Lee Atwater for George Bush in his victory over Michael Dukakis.

Two weeks after New York governor Mario Cuomo took himself out of contention as a candidate for the Democratic nomination, Al Gore arranged a meeting between himself and a group of big Democratic funders mustered under the working title IMPAC 88. These were largely self-made millionaires, some forty-five of them, mostly from the Democratic Party's traditional fundraising centers in New York, Florida, Texas, California, Chicago, Philadelphia, Boston and Minneapolis. One of their leaders was Nate Landow, a DC-area construction magnate who had been Walter Mondale's campaign finance manager in 1984.

Landow and the others had been for Cuomo and had also eyed Sam Nunn. Now neither of these two were available and they turned their attention to Gore, who at least did not remind them of Mondale. Gore met with Landow and the preliminary encounter proved satisfactory. Landow pledged that seventeen of the forty-five IMPAC members would raise $250,000 each to underwrite a run by Gore. This gave him $4 million, propelling him instantly into the front rank of the Democratic pack.

Landow put out the news to the political correspondents, with the message that they had made Gore a serious contender. There was another message too, and it was quickly understood. Landow said of his IMPAC group: "It's a little fraternity. If you figure this group could raise $10 million, that's a pretty important number. It certainly sends a message to those who don't get the endorsement." On April 14, Jesse Jackson released the text of an angry note he'd sent Landow, noting that he had not been invited to make his pitch to the IMPAC group, and saying that members of IMPAC 88 were waging a campaign to "question my credentials as a Democrat" and were trying to keep him out of the race. Jackson added prophetically that members of IMPAC "have indicated your goal is to magnify the influence of large contributors in presidential campaigns. Does not that activity violate the spirit of campaign law reform and principles of the Democratic Party?"

IMPAC was in the financial realm what the Democratic Leadership Council was in the political arena. The object was to push the Democratic Party to the right and to purge it as far as was humanly possible of its ties and loyalties to the "special interests", otherwise known as the working class, minorities, the poor.

There were and are various code words for such perennial forces within the Democratic Party. In the 1980s the term "moderate" enjoyed much popularity in the mainstream press. With bracing frankness William Crotty, a lawyer from Daytona, member of IMPAC and keen supporter of Gore, proclaimed, "The more and more money you make, the more likely you are to protect your interests. This group is much more moderate than our elected leaders." He said that in 1987, when the nation's leader was Ronald Reagan.

Shortly after the funders in IMPAC had settled on Gore as their man in 1988, Fred Wertheimer, then head of Common Cause, told *The New York Times*, "They appear to be interested in restoring the fat cat rich contributors to a disproportionate influence in the Democratic Party. They appear to be wealthy people trying to obtain special influence." On his next visit to

IMPAC, Gore commenced his pitch for more cash with the quip, "Where are those fat cats when I need them?"

His pockets swollen with IMPAC pledges, Gore went on the campaign with a roadmap provided by Jimmy Carter's old pollster, Pat Caddell, commissioned by IMPAC to crunch polling numbers and figure out the most opportune platform for a candidate trying to win back Democrats who had voted for Reagan in 1984. According to Caddell, this ideal candidate should be strong on defense, tough on crime, pro-choice, hawkish on the deficit, and an advocate of lean, mean government. With such a focus-group profile mostly fortifying his natural inclinations, Gore embarked on the first task of his candidacy: assailing his prime early rival, Dick Gephardt.

Gephardt, a Congressman from Missouri, was busy rehabbing himself from this same Caddell profile (he'd voted for the Reagan budget cuts of 1981) into a populist. Gore went after him as a double-talker and a hypocrite for having changed positions, and as a dimwit for now being protectionist and isolationist, two terms of abuse that sat well with the media's political correspondents, who cheered Gore as he lashed out at the liberals. When Gephardt said that the Democratic Party should not be hospitable to Dixiecrats like Strom Thurmond, the Gore camp retorted by sending forward Albert Sr. to say, "What you're seeing now is no accident. We've got to get the Dixiecrats back into the Democratic Party, and we're playing damn hardball. Later in the campaign, after he has won the nomination, people will see the other side of his record come through." Gore's hysterical attacks on Gephard enraged the Missouri rep and his staff. "Gore's like a little boy who comes into the first grade and pulls his pants down," said William Carrick, Gephardt's campaign manager. "We kept hoping he'd wake up and discover he's embarassing himself instead of just attracting attention."

Party elders begged Gore to calm down in the coming round of debates, but Gore told them to stuff it. "I don't want to do that. It's become apparent that some in our party want us to censor our remarks, especially in debates. In the days ahead, I intend to say more, not less." And so he did.

By posturing on defense, Gore missed no opportunity to distinguish himself from not only Gephardt but other contenders, including Paul Simon of Illinois and Gary Hart of Colorado. He accused them of leading the Democratic Party down a road of "complacency, doubt and retreat". The Reagan Administration had been caught using the CIA to run an illegal war in Nicaragua, and some Democratic candidates peldged to curb the CIA's covert operation. Gore denounced their pledges as "absurd and reckless". When Michael Dukakis, the Massachusetts governor who eventually won the nomination, said he would not authorize "one more penny" for the Nicaraguan *contras,* Gore charged that Dukakis was willing to accept "a Soviet client state" in America's backyard. The atttack had its effect. Dukakis hastily amended his position, meekly agreeing that the US had a perfect right to defend the Monroe doctrine.

Early in Campaign 2000, Gore shifted direction, attacking Bill Bradley for having gone the wrong way on one the biggest foreign policy issues of the 1980s—the US onslaughts on the Sandinista government of Nicaragua. Yet while Gore's position had been better than Bradley's, it was hardly principled. In 1978 the thirty-year rule of Anastasio Somoza was coming to an end. The Sandinistas were marching on Managua, and the popular tide was with them. America's attention, normally indifferent to bloodshed in Latin America, was abruptly seized when Somoza's National Guard shot dead an ABC news correspondent, Bill Stewart.

In Washington legislators abruptly cut off funds to the dictator, propped up by the US since World War II. Representative Charlie Wilson from Texas, put forward an amendment urging restoration of this money, and Gore voted with him.

In the Congressional battles of the early to mid-1980s, Gore largely followed the path blazed by his mentor on the House Intelligence Committee, Edward Boland of Massachusetts, and voted on at least two occasions to beat back efforts by the Reagan Administration to win legal approval for *contra* funding. Gore was also with the House majority that in the first days of the Sandinista government, voted for $75 million in economic assistance. But Gore also voted to ensure that long-term sabotage of the Sandinistas could be undertaken by CIA-backed *contras* operating out of Honduras. Gore voted against an effort by Tom Harkin of Iowa to forbid use of US funds to build military bases in Honduras. These bases became crucial in the *contra* campaign, and the funds were also used by the Honduran generals to launch their own dirty war against domestic dissent.

In 1985, his first year in the Senate, Gore voted against the release of "humanitarian aid" to the *contras*, but a year later he opposed an effort by Ted Kennedy to cut off all aid to the *contras*. In 1989 the Senate Appropriations Committee set a limit of $85 million on military aid to El Salvador, whose bloodstained regime and death squads had been bankrolled by US dollars and instituted with US military support. Gore joined with the Wisconsin Republican Robert Kasten in a successful effort to remove this ceiling.

Gore's hawkish maneuvers in the early moments of the 1988 campaign won him applause from the establishment, ever nervous at the spectre of populism. The imprimatur of the Permanent Government came in an April editorial in *The Washington Post*: "Mr. Gore is unlike his rivals and much of his party in the sense that he does not feel it necessary to apologize for the defense budget." But while he may have basked in this salute from Washington, Gore was finding that his hawkish posturing on the military was not playing well with the ordinary people of Iowa or of any of the other primary states.

The national nuclear freeze campaign had an Iowa branch that polled the Democratic candidates in relation to their position on a ban on ballistic missile tests. Gore denounced such ban as "an extremely irresponsible action", then had the mortification of seeing his polling numbers plummet in consequence. He then said that the other candidates had capitulated to peaceniks and that Iowa had been captured by doves. He hastily shut his field office and quit the battleground.

In New Hampshire Gore's numbers were no better, and although he stayed on the ballot, he stopped campaigning in the Granite State and headed for a last stand in the Super Tuesday series of primaries across the South and West, where he would have to make a significant showing to retain any credibility. The Gore campaign was already demoralized enough to be spinning elaborate theories of a brokered convention in which their man would somehow be picked as the compromise candidate.

In extremis Gore began to roll out some populist rhetoric, with references in the Southern states to "working men and women", which could also translate as "white folks". But he continued to project a mean-spirited posture toward his rivals that offended even Bruce Babbitt, another lovechild of the Democratic Leadership Council, who advised him in one debate to "lighten up" and drop his "intemperate use of pejorative adjectives".

Watching the results come in on Super Tuesday night, the Gores—father and son—saw that Al Jr. had won Tennessee, North Carolina, Kentucky, Arkansas, Oklahoma and Nevada. "We're on our way now", whooped Albert Sr. It was the last moment of good cheer that evening. A few hours later they watched *Nightline* with Ted Koppel. The lead story was George Bush's showing in the Republican primaries. Then came news of Michael Dukakis's big wins in Texas and Florida. The third story concerned Jesse Jackson's victory in no less than five states—Mississippi, Louisiana, Georgia, Virginia and Alabama. Only then came a brief mention of Gore's showing. It was all over. But it wasn't all over. Gore's function was now to destroy the most exciting political candidate of that year.

Jackson's populist campaign of 1988 has faded in memory now, but it was an inspiring moment in American politics. He managed to knit together the old populist coalition of industrial workers, farmers, blacks and middle-class progressives. The greatest political eloquence in decades came out of Jackson's mouth that year, and as always when a populist campaigner is sweeping all before him, Establishment America flung up the barricades. Jackson was vilified in the press. It would be only seven years till an American president welcomed Yasir Arafat into the White House, and till that same president's wife said publicly she looked forward to the creation of a Palestinian state, but Jackson was vilified for having been premature by a decade in his diplomacy.

After eight years of Reagan and the rout of the Democratic establishment candidate in 1984, conditions were ripe for a candidate of Jackson's energy, a fact that did not escape his enemies within the Democratic Party. The regulars had pinned their hopes on Mario Cuomo, the governor of New York. But in February of 1987 he bowed out, leaving Jackson as the candidate with the power and energy to set the political temperature.

Already, on the eve of the big Super Tuesday sweep of primaries, it was clear Jackson was attracting a significant measure of white support. Vermont, Maine and Minnesota were not known as having substantial black populations. There were scarcely more than a thousand blacks in Vermont, yet Jackson got 27 percent of the vote. In Minnesota, where the black population was 4 percent, Jackson got 20 percent. In Maine, Jackson came in first in the state's two big cities, Portland and Bangor, and came in second overall, with 30 percent of the vote in a state that was less than 1 percent black.

On Super Tuesday Jackson came in first in five states, second in ten more and won the popular vote overall. The *Chicago Tribune* responded by noting that many of Jackson's supporters were "politically active homosexuals". The *San Francisco Chronicle* brooded that "Jackson's vote in black districts resembled the totals that dictators pile up in no-opposition elections". The *Chronicle* didn't bother to mention that Jackson got his March 8 victories on precisely $100,000 of paid television time. Some newspapers did concede that it was okay for a black man to run for the presidency so long as his name wasn't spelled Jackson. "He would have to be a candidate," wrote a columnist in *The Boston Globe*, "with a cool, conservative style, and a message that was mainstream and not threatening to the status quo."

The moment that Jackson won the Democratic primary in Michigan was one of pure horror for the establishment. The Democratic Party had done its best to keep democracy at bay. In Flint there were normally ninety-one polling places open.

That year on caucus day, March 26, there were nine. Voting could take place only between 10 in the morning and 4 in the afternoon, when many autoworkers were on shift down in Pontiac. Even so, the turnout was much larger than expected, and some of the caucus centers in Flint had run out of ballots. Voters waited patiently, for up to two hours. Then came the preliminary results. In Flint's first ward, Jackson, 2,050; Dukakis, 67. Car horns started sounding in triumph. A black man had routed his white opponents in a state synonymous with blue-collar America. After Jackson's victory in Michigan, Gore had been obliterated and even Dukakis's lead was under challenge. The next big battle was in New York, and polls showed Jackson neck and neck with the Massachusetts governor.

Al Gore's political function in 1988 approached its denouement. Given the optimistic fantasies of political candidates it was perhaps understandable that Gore should have tried another throw in Illinois. But after a poor showing there, why would he have gone on to court further humiliation in Michigan, where, on the distant heels of the incredible win by Jackson, he managed to score only 2 percent in a depleted field? And then, after a string of abject failures and with no money left, why would Al Gore have borrowed a million dollars from Tennessee banks with ties to his father, and gone on to New York?

On this topic there's been a tactful silence and some rewriting of history. In the spring of 2000 a number of stories appeared saying Gore had somehow ended up in New York with Ed Koch elbowing his way into the campaign in a manner so embarrassing to Gore that the night it was over he phoned Jesse Jackson to distance himself from Koch's racist attacks.

That really won't wash.

The answer to the puzzle of Gore's persistence starts not with Gore's showing in Michigan but with Jackson's. The evening Jackson wiped out Dukakis and Gephardt in Michigan the air quivered with agonized appraisals, as the opinion formers took heed of the here-and-now and hurried to oppose it. While the horns were honking in Flint, a few hundred miles southeast, in Washington, the political and journalistic elites were resplendent in white ties and long dresses at the Gridiron dinner, poking decorous fun at one other. The vote in Michigan came like that finger writing its message of doom on the wall at Belshazzar's feast.

The Democratic Party faced a crisis. It looked quite possible that Jackson might make a strong showing in New York. He then could be poised to head west to California and maybe prevail there in a winner-take-all state. Jackson had to be slowed and sullied, but not by the candidate's party and the man the media establishment had agreed was the appropriate nominee, Michael Dukakis. Dukakis would need every black vote he could get, and going after Jackson in New York would scarcely help to achieve that end.

So Gore borrowed his million and headed for New York, where Mayor Koch guided him around the city amid a blizzard of invective against Jackson as an enemy of Israel. Koch was looking forward to a drive for a fourth mayoral term the following year and, as always, was organizing his constituency around racism and the perceived threat of anti-Semitism.

As the candidates arrived from the Wisconsin primary, a Marist College poll was showing that, among Jewish voters being so shamelessly courted by Gore and Koch, 10 percent supported Gore and 9 percent Jackson. "Jews would be crazy to vote for Jackson", Koch promptly declared. Party regulars joined in. Geraldine Ferraro, Mondale's running mate in 1984,

129

declared that Jackson wouldn't be a serious candidate and "wouldn't be in the race if he weren't black". Jackson reeled under this ambush by the Democratic Party, and by the New York press: "We went across the South on Super Tuesday without a single cat call or boo, without a single ugly sign at a mass meeting. It was not until we got north to New York that the litmus test of race and religion became spouted from the mouths of public officials without a significant media challenge."

One refrain in this memorably disgusting spectacle held that it was somehow racist *not* to attack Jackson. Gore was first with this line, which was then picked up by Ronald Reagan, who expressed the view that Jackson was getting a "free ride" (another refrain about this much-vilified man) because any criticism would be interpreted "as some kind of racial attack".

Destruction of Jackson wasn't Gore's only mission in New York. At that time, in the midst of the *intifada*, the Reagan Administration was making a timid effort to induce the ultra-hard-line Shamir government in Israel to make some token concessions to the Palestinians. Some thirty US senators, many of them Democrats with long records of support for Israel, had been mustered to sign a letter urging Shamir to adopt the course of reason. Urged on by Marty Peretz and the leaders of Jewish organizations, Gore lashed out at his fellow senators, also at Dukakis for somehow being soft on Palestinian terror. Gore's shameless whoring on the Israel issue—he even baited Dukakis for refusing contributions from Likud supporters even as he himself grubbed for them—infuriated those senators, who felt they'd gone out on a limb. Now Gore was sawing it off, as Stan Greenberg, later to become a pollster for Gore, put it. "It's not often that a member of the Senate does something that has the prospect of no political gain", one high-level Senate staffer said at the time. "Here, thirty of them did it; then along comes Al Gore taking a cheap shot that he knew was a cheap shot."

The heat told on Jackson, who began to backpedal on the issue of Palestinian rights with sanctimonious remarks to the effect, "We must somehow get Israel beyond the burden of occupation, and the Palestinians beyond the pain of being occupied." This did him no good with the pro-Israel crowd and merely irritated those who admired his stance on the issue. Gore scored only 10 percent in New York, in a contest where Dukakis won handily, with 51 percent. Jackson got 35 percent, but he had been slowed. All of the undecided voters drifted into the Dukakis column. Jackson went on to run second in California and to make a great showing at the Democratic convention, but the raw populist surge had gone.

Having done his job, Gore finally retired from the race. The IOUs from the Democratic Party's kingpins weren't slow in coming. His $2 million campaign debt was paid down with singular speed, using a network of top party donors that he would call on for the next twelve years. Gore dubbed this his 40/40 Club — forty donors who would each raise $40,000. If the Democratic Party had any regret it was that Gore, in his eagerness to play politics with racial themes, had brought up the spectre of Willie Horton.

Willie Horton was a convict who had taken advantage of a Massachusetts prison furlough program to travel to Maryland in June of 1986, and there attacked a couple, tying up the husband and raping and beating his wife. Previous to this crime, Horton had committed a grim murder, robbing and stabbing a 17-year-old gas station attendant called Clifford Barnes, then stuffing his body in a trash barrel. After twelve years in prison Horton had been given weekend furloughs, as were many other long-term prisoners. It was in his tenth outing that he committed the rape and beating. Originally it was a small newspaper in Massachusetts, *The Lawrenceville Eagle*, that did a series on the furlough program. It was poorly reported and hysterical, but was rewarded with a Pulitzer Prize.

Naturally, a furlough program that led to a black convict committing rape was ripe political bait in an election year, particularly one in which the man ultimately responsible for the furlough program was Governor Michael Dukakis, who also opposed the death penalty. A week before the New York primary Al Gore raised the furlough program in the course of a debate. He asked Dukakis how it was that convicted murderers in Massachusetts were thus awarded get-out-of-jail passes. Dukakis, politically tone deaf, launched into a substantively accurate but nonetheless labored explication: "Al, the difference between you and me is that I have to run a criminal justice system. You never have.... We're running a very tough, strong, well-defined furlough program in this state, which by and large has been very successful."

Although Gore didn't mention Horton's name, he was certainly intent on using the case to embarrass Dukakis. That evening of the debate his aides handed out a press packet on the case, producing exactly the result Gore had been hoping for. The press in Massachusetts began to circle round the Horton affair again, snapping at Dukakis's heels. It wasn't long before Dukakis had to sign a bill cutting off all furloughs for convicted murderers.

Because his own race was over a week later, Gore didn't have many opportunities to dwell further on the Horton affair. As it was, Paul Kirk, head of the Democratic National Committee, had already warned him publicly that he needed to tone down his rhetoric: "If one candidate has a strategy of moving hard right of center, there are things he can do without tagging others with labels that don't fit. We've got to be very careful with labels, because the Republicans can turn them into tattoos."

Kirk's warning was prescient. Readying themselves for the fall campaign against Dukakis, Republicans hastened through the door opened by Gore. First came some advertisements prepared by a right-wing millionaire named Floyd Brown, playing the race card flagrantly, with pictures of a feral-looking Horton, insinuating that when it came to homicidal blacks there was no man more forgiving or indulgent than Michael Dukakis. All fall George Bush's campaign strategists, Lee Atwater and Roger Ailes, played the theme mercilessly. "By the time we're finished", Atwater crowed as he reviewed Gore's research on Horton, "they're going to wonder whether Willie Horton is Dukakis's running mate." Indeed, Horton said later that a Republican Party worker had contacted him in prison, asking him whether he would endorse Dukakis.

The coup de grâce was delivered by a black man, Bernard Shaw of CNN. During one of the presidential debates, Shaw directed a brusque question to Dukakis. How would he feel if a murderer raped his wife? Instead of saying that he would obviously want to tear such a man apart with his bare hands but due process was still due process, Dukakis strove to change the subject by talking about education—probably the most maladroit response in national politics since Teddy Kennedy found himself unable to answer NBC's Roger Mudd as to why he wanted to be president.

Four years on, Gore's decision to play race politics with Horton was remembered fondly by the people running the Clinton-Gore campaign of 1992. Bob Beckel, a prominent

Democratic operator, said the episode had displayed Gore to advantage: "The rap on Al Gore is that he's not a very tough campaigner. That's dead wrong. He's going to be used to take on Bush and take on Quayle, to respond to what are clearly going to be an increase in Republican attacks. Let's remember about Al Gore: the first to use Willie Horton against Dukakis in 1988 was not George Bush; it was Al Gore in New York. Gore's a tough campaigner and that's going to be an important role for him."

In Campaign 2000, Bill Bradley, his back to the wall in the New York primary, charged that Gore had played the race card in 1988. "Gore introduced him into the lexicon. I wouldn't have used Willie Horton. It proved in the course of the campaign to essentially be a poster child for racial insensitivity." With bare-faced effrontery Gore piously accused Bradley of perpetrating "a negative personal attack" by raising the Horton issue, and Dukakis was wheeled out from the Kennedy School to say that it had been appropriate for Gore to raise the matter against him. Dukakis's 1988 campaign manager, Susan Estrich, contradicted her former boss: "I would never accuse Gore of being racist, but his reference to furloughs was certainly the first shot of the Willie Horton issue. Everyone understood Willie Horton to be the furlough issue."

Gore's onslaught had left a sour taste in many mouths. Greg Schneider, Babbitt's campaign manager, remarked, "the whole contest in New York—the way Gore handled Israel, the way he handled Jackson—are going to be serious things he is going to have to deal with. He had better get it right with the blacks in a hurry."

In recent accounts of his '88 campaign Gore has taken care to stress his inner disquiet, even revulsion at Koch's deportment. But this is damage control at long range. At the time Gore was unapologetic. After the pro forma call to Jackson about Koch's antics, he made no public effort at reconciliation. To the contrary, when he formally announced his withdrawal from the race his mode was defiance: "We set out to move the Democratic Party toward the center of American political thought. We also spoke out for a new Democratic foreign policy based on standing up for American principles in the world and standing by American friends." He was in the mainstream, he insisted. Dukakis and Jackson were on the margin. When he did travel to Chattanooga in his home state to appear with Jackson, the crowd booed him. It became obvious that Gore was edgy about the considerable animosity toward him entertained by blacks across the country. Even some relatively mild comments by Harold Ford, Tennessee's only black Congressman, caused Gore to snatch the offending tape from the cassette machine, throw it on the ground and exclaim that Ford was threatening him and should apologize.

Gore was also confronted with somewhat stark evidence of what his colleagues thought of his candidacy. In the US Congress only ten had endorsed Gore, and six of those were from Tennessee.

The Gores have a habit of couching the particular in terms of the universal. As he brooded on his humiliation, Al cast his abortive bid as a lost opportunity to save the world from nuclear annihilation and environmental meltdown, "a perishable window" for America. "I had just lost a presidential election, having given it everything that I had, and encountered the limits of my capacity to persuade people of policies I felt so deeply needed to be followed." The high-flown retrospect came in the course of a period of disappointed reassessment stretching across the end of the 1980s. Not well liked on the

Hill and now rejected by the electorate, Gore tried a new form of polling, this time attempting a survey of his own psychic landscape.

In the course of a meeting with a group of shrinks in Knoxville, Gore treated the group of five to a forty-five-minute monologue that more than one of them understood to be a strangled cry for help. Gore dwelled on the stressful dynamics of father-son relations ("You remember Oedipus, don't you?" Tipper exclaimed when asked about the specific relationship between Alberts Sr. and Jr.), and brooded on the poet-cum-mystagogue of male crisis, Robert Bly. Could they recommend any books that would help him come to terms with his sense of failure as a son?

Gore has always been vehement in denying these were therapeutic sessions, but before long he was having intimate colloquies with Dr. Lance Laurence, a clinical psychologist and professor at the University of Tennessee. Laurence recommended two books in particular. One was Allen Wheelis's *How People Change*, a rumination on the psychic destruction wrought by distant and over-demanding fathers, plus a ringing endorsement of the virtues of therapy. The other book was *The Drama of the Gifted Child*, an exploration by Alice Miller, a Swiss child psychologist, of the traumatic consequences of having parents whose emotional exactions may drive the child to the desired achievements but at the cost of an emotional numbing which sets up true and false selves. In the mirror of this book Gore saw himself and made haste to press Miller's book into the hands of his closest friends and top staffers. Gore also sought spiritual fortification from Paul Gorman, a theologian associated with the cathedral of St. John the Divine in New York.

Amidst these efforts at self-discovery came an accident, in

April of 1989, to Gore's son, Albert III. Al, Tipper and the 6-year-old were leaving Memorial Stadium in Baltimore, where they'd watched the Orioles play on opening day. As they prepared to cross Hillen Road, a busy four-lane thoroughfare, Albert III broke free from his father's hand, dashed across two lanes, then was struck in the third by a '77 Chevy. He was pretty badly hurt, with broken ribs, a ruptured spleen, punctured lung and a cracked shoulder blade. The Gores were fortunate that two nurses were on the scene, and looked after the boy until the ambulance arrived. Tense days for Al and Tipper at Albert III's hospital bedside followed. In the end Albert III made a full recovery.

Seldom has a nasty accident been more sedulously worked over in politico-literary rhetoric. In *Earth in the Balance*, Gore claimed that those dark days were the "catalyst" for "a life change that has caused me to be increasingly impatient with the status quo, with conventional wisdom, with the lazy assumption that we can always muddle through". In 1992, Gore used his son's travails in his vice presidential speech at the Democratic convention in New York. Delegates and a national TV audience listened to descriptions of Albert III "fly thirty feet through the air and scrape along the pavement another twenty feet until he came to rest in a gutter. I ran to his side and held him and called his name, but he was motionless, limp and still, without breath or pulse. His eyes were open with the nothingness stare of death, and we prayed, the two of us, there in the gutter, with only my voice".

At least one pair of eyes in the convention hall stayed dry. "The worst thing about Gore was that he read that heavy stuff right off the teleprompter", said Al's onetime hero, Eugene McCarthy. Responding to suggestions that Gore had gone over the top, Tipper promptly gave her husband's gross lack of taste cosmic content: "That happened to us, in public, and we dealt with it in public. We kept as much private as we could, but it's become a part of our lives and it's a part of who we are and very much a part of who Al is, and I think it was courageous of him to reveal that. He's very much a different person in many ways because of that trauma, and if you want to know him, you have to know what happened."

Now, Americans lived through the nineties hearing both Al and Tipper lecture people on the need to take responsibility for their actions, whether they be teenage mothers, rockers and rappers, or other targets for their preachments. But though Gore has claimed that his son's accident prompted a profound metamorphosis in his world view, the writing of *Earth in the Balance* and a recommitment to his role as globo-savior, in all of these interminable discourses he has never even hinted that he might have held his son's hand a little more tightly at the curb of Hillen Road. Most parents would have blamed themselves. It's a natural human tendency, and in this case evidently a justifiable one. The first duty of a father standing on the sidewalk is to make sure his child doesn't run into traffic—though why exactly Albert III should have elected to tear himself free from his dad (if indeed his dad was actually holding his hand) and run across a busy highway is another question one can ponder. But Gore's rendition of the trauma becomes a homily, anchored in melodrama, about the need to stop "muddling through". He can't even manage to mention his wife's name, and pronouns other than the one referring to himself are so vague that one cannot tell whether Tipper or Albert III are praying silently as back-up to Al's voice. The nurses, incidentally, say Albert III never lost consciousness.

At Johns Hopkins Hospital prayer alternated with therapy. Loraine Voles, a member of Gore's staff, has said that

Gore believed "the power of prayer helped to heal his son". For her part, Tipper used this crisis to persuade her husband to participate in family therapy. Gore later wrote that the accident prompted him to spend more time with Tipper and the children. He pledged both publicly and to Tipper that he would redirect his life toward the home front. When he decided in August of 1991 not to throw his hat into the presidential ring in 1992, he invoked the accident and family commitments as the prime reason. Then again, some test polls and the reception accorded trial-run speeches he gave to Democratic audiences were not encouraging to a man who had never abandoned the thought of another try for the nomination.

Gore made his pledge of good husbandry in his mother-in-law's house in Arlington, Virginia, but Tipper and the children may have had some difficulty recognizing the new stay-at-home Dad. His Senate schedule was exacting enough. David Pryor, a senator from Arkansas, remembers seeing Gore at a committee hearing summon an aide who presented him with an enormous map of Tennessee. Marked on it with flags were all the town meetings to be attended by Gore that coming weekend. Pryor remarked that the itinerary made him feel dizzy. Gore has boasted of having attended more than 2,200 such town meetings in his Congressional career, prompting incredulous Republicans to dash to their calculators and discover that Gore was claiming to have done 2.5 Tennessee town meetings a week for sixteen years.

But on top of the absences consequent upon being a senator, Gore found that his rebirth required that he write a book, which in turn required that he spend whatever free evenings he had, apart from his family, in an apartment belonging to his parents in the Methodist Building, close to Capitol Hill. There he immured himself for two years to write

139

the 700 manuscript pages of *Earth in the Balance*. Senator Howell Heflin of Alabama lived in the same building and would regularly encounter Gore late at night. "Son," the bluff judge finally cried, "You go home and see your family."

Forlorn after her son's accident and her husband's fleeting presence, Tipper fell into a deep depression, a condition she chose to reveal in 1999. The strain showed up in her public comportment. In April of 1991 her mother, Margaret, crashed into a car stopped at a traffic light, and the cop inspecting the accident noticed she smelled of booze. Margaret was combative, shouting at the officer, "Get away from me, you rookie son of a bitch." At this point Tipper came up and also started shouting: "Get your goddamn hands off her. You don't have to arrest her. That's my mother. She's on medication." Finally, the cop threatened to arrest Tipper for obstruction of justice. Margaret came out of it relatively unscathed, with only a $44 fine and, no doubt, raised insurance premiums.

Earth in the Balance finally weighed in at around 400 pages and got an enthusiastic reception in *The New York Times*, *Washington Post*, *Time* and other influential publications. With Mort Janklow, a fashionable New York literary agent, supervising the contract with Houghton Mifflin, Gore did well off the book.

Earth in the Balance is an extended essay in eco-catastrophism, of a genre that was particularly prevalent in the early 1990s. This was a time when Congressional delegations were visiting the Amazon rainforest on a regular basis. US politicians who had superintended the deforestation of their own districts with equanimity thundered their outrage to the Brazilian government at the prospect of converting Amazonia to cattle pasture or submerging it with dams underwritten by the World Bank. Great conferences on the environment, climaxing with the 1992 Earth Summit in Rio de Janeiro, were replete with mournful jeremiads, to wit, "It is almost too late, unless we act now." A constant feature of these parleys was their infatuation with the grand scale: global warming, ozone depletion, population explosion.

Earth in the Balance circles these same big issues relentlessly, linking them to the even bigger crisis of Man's spiritual alienation (for which Descartes gets a thrashing): "I believe our civilization is in effect addicted to the consumption of the earth itself." Gore likened earth-consumption, perpetrated by "addictive personalities", to drug addiction. "Our new power to work our will upon the world can bring with it a sudden rush of exhilaration." This high-flown approach has the advantage of sparing Gore, as it does others, the necessity of confronting the innumerable smaller-scale but politically more volatile environmental problems with which America is beset. A senator talking about global warming is a more robustly eloquent man than a senator being put on the spot about strip-mining in Tennessee—an environmental crisis about which the voluble Gore has remained silent.

In the book Gore theorizes that the earth and its human inhabitants are mutually undergoing a mid-life crisis. Even though he prudently berates the deep ecologists and Earth First!ers as "morally unacceptable", he shares with them a belief in Gaian eyewash. James Lovelock's "Gaia hypothesis" holds that the earth is a living organism, an extension of the older idea of the Great Chain of Being. Gore takes the Gaian metaphor as literal truth: "It cannot be accidental, one is tempted to conclude, that the percentage of salt in our bloodstreams is roughly the same as the percentage of salt in the oceans of the world." The final ingredient in this holistic stew is a pallid Christian spiritualism blended with therapeutic homilies culled from his reading of R.D. Laing, Gregory Bateson and Alice Miller, plus a sprinkling from the motivational psychologist John Bradshaw.

Earth in the Balance is the most ample representation of Gore's lifelong habit of magnifying his own problems into national or, in this case, universal nightmares. The man who had been talking to therapists about a stilted relationship with his father (as Tipper and the kids dined without Dad) wrote: "Police officers, doctors and psychologists who deal with the victims of child sexual abuse often wonder how any adult— especially a parent—could commit such a crime. How could anyone be deaf to the screams, blind to the grief, and numb to the pain their actions cause? The answer, we now know, is that a kind of psychic numbness, induced by the adult's own adaptation to the dysfunctional pattern in which they were themselves raised as children, serves to anesthetize their conscience and awareness in order to facilitate their compulsive repetition of the crime that was visited upon them." Five years later Gore was explaining to reporters that this same phenomenon of "psychic numbness" had forced him to continue to take tobacco subsidies and campaign money from tobacco companies after he had pledged to forfeit both when his sister died of lung cancer. Since Gore follows Miller in blaming this numbness on abusive parenting, it does make one wonder about the repressed matter that is swimming around in Gore's psyche.

Finally Gore ties it all together—his own crisis, his own therapy and the salvation of the earth: "But there is a way out. A pattern of dysfunctionality need not persist indefinitely, and the key to change is the harsh light of truth. Just as an addict can confront his addiction, just as a dysfunctional family can confront the unwritten rules that govern their lives, our civilization can change—must change—by confronting the unwritten rules that are driving us to destroy the earth. And, as Alice Miller and other experts have shown, the act of mourning the original loss while fully and consciously feeling the pain it has caused can heal the wound and free the victim from further enslavement.... The first step is toward mourning what we have lost, healing the damage we have done to the earth and to our civilization, and coming to terms with the new story of what it means to be a steward of the earth."

It was while Gore was down in Rio for the Earth Summit, brandishing *Earth in the Balance* (though also doing his political duty by attacking George Bush), that he received the first probing call from Warren Christopher as to whether he was interested in the vice presidential slot alongside Bill Clinton. He assured Christopher that he was. Out the window went the pledge to be a family man. Out the window went his commitment to be an Earth Warrior. Within in a few months Gore was on the campaign trail and meekly obeying the orders of the Clinton camp to tone down his environmental rhetoric. Tipper raged at him for dumping his family once more and went back to her Prozac bottle.

9 WHITEHOUSE DOPPELGANGER

Gore eyed with suspicion by Clinton aides, but he brings respectability to the ticket. Glorious victory. "The most powerful vice president in history" brings therapy to Camp David, places his people throughout the government. Asides on Peter Knight and Thomas Grumbly. Bill Clinton learns the facts of life. Sunset on the bold promise of the new regime. Gore ushers in David Gergen.

The Clinton camp that summer of 1992 was divided about Gore. In the war room men like James Carville and George Stephanopoulos actively disliked him. They remembered the '88 campaign, and Stephanopoulos had his loyalties to Gephardt. Harold Ickes didn't care for him, nor did Susan Thomasses, Hillary Clinton's closest adviser. But the highest tier esteemed Gore for precisely the reasons their subordinates despised him. Bill and Hillary saw him as a kindred soul in political philosophy, hewing to the pro-corporate, anti-union positions of the Democratic Leadership Council, which together they had founded and nurtured. In terms of age and appearance the Gores were agreeably in sync with the Clinton campaign's emphasis on youthful change. Clinton had also contemplated a run in '88 but had backed out not only for reasons of his messy private life but because Gore had jumped in ahead of him.

Earlier that spring, when Gennifer Flowers' memories of her affair with Governor Clinton were being handled in the press (with relative discretion let it be it said), Gore had robustly defended Clinton on the Larry King show, at a time when the candidate had few defenders. This stood Gore in particularly good stead with Hillary.

When Warren Christopher called Gore to sound him out about the vice-presidential spot, Clinton was third in the polls, behind not only Bush but Ross Perot. Gore would bring a number of immediate assets. As a Vietnam vet he would counter derision about Clinton the draft dodger. Furthermore, Gore's pro-war vote on Iraq would help the Clinton campaign blunt Bush's advantage there. On the issues their political DNA matched up nicely: grandstanding against crime and welfare, solid for globalism and world rule by the IMF. They were both deficit hawks.

Bush's running mate, Dan Quayle, was sermonizing on family values and attacking Hollywood, so here too the Gores, with their campaign for cultural decency on record, would add to the ticket. On the matter of family values, in contrast with the questionable moral currency in the top half of the Democratic ticket, Al's marriage with Tipper seemed solid and decorous, and had been fecund with photogenic Caucasians. Probing by the Clinton team did not dislodge any immediate skeletons from the closet.

One influential political pro, the late Bob Squier, touted Gore to Clinton, saying, "He'll never stab you in the back, even if you deserve it." At around 11 PM, July 8, 1992, Clinton made the call, and Gore instantly accepted. Tipper was vehemently opposed, hoping her husband would live up to his pledges to spend more time with the family. Then, as so often before, she bowed to the fait accompli, remarking sarcastically to Tim Wirth's wife, Wren, "Here we go, on our way to try to save the world."

The Gores flew down to Little Rock, where the news of Gore's arrival on the ticket was imparted to the press while the two couples appeared on the porch of the governor's mansion. Back in the farmhouse on the Caney Fork River, Gore's parents watched the scene on CNN. Albert Sr. exulted and then hastened to his files to prepare a memo on his ties to Armand Hammer and Occidental for the Clinton campaign, to ward off possibly embarrassing questions. Pauline was restrained in her joy. She regarded Clinton as a hick and a rogue. "Bill came up in a very provincial atmosphere", she was later quoted as saying, "and even if he went to Yale and he went to Oxford, you don't undo, or move out of that provincial atmosphere that has influenced you all your life." And now this same hick was at the top of the ticket, where, in a proper world, her boy should have been installed. (One can see why Al Gore's teen flame, Donna Armistead, was never invited to visit the Gores in Washington.)

Alex Jones of *The New York Times* asked Gore about how he weighed family commitments against his decision to run. Gore's explanation of why he'd accepted Clinton's invitation was characteristic: "I thought about it. And I reframed the question to take the personal ambition part out of it, because I didn't want to do it in that sense. I didn't expect it. I didn't seek it. When I said yes, the question to which I answered yes was, 'were you willing to give your country a better chance to change?'—not 'do you want to run for vice president?'"

Gore's first public appearance after he had given his acceptance speech at the Democratic convention was an address to the board of the League of Conservation Voters, held in the Manhattan law offices of Cravath, Swaine and Moore. If anyone was seeking a reliable signpost to the setting on Gore's political compass this was it. The League is the prime PAC of the mainstream environmental movement, a loyal buttress for Democratic candidates. Neither the League nor Gore found anything odd in having this rendezvous on the premises of a law firm that had represented notorious polluters and enemies of nature such as the Swiss-owned Ciba-Geigy, or the giant utility Con Edison, or Royal Dutch Shell, or Texaco.

The story of the 1992 campaign has been told often enough. Gore lived up to the Clintons' hopes, though his failure, in the debate with Dan Quayle, to issue ringing endorsements of Bill's character rankled, particularly with Hillary. Indeed, the match-up with Quayle threw into question Gore's reputation as a deadly debater. It took his baiting of Ross Perot a year later, hotly acclaimed in the press, to retrieve that reputation.

With an economy nose-dived into recession by Federal Reserve chairman Alan Greenspan, George Bush waged a wan campaign. Ross Perot's third party candidacy pulled 19 percent of the vote, most of it from Bush. Blessed with these strokes of fortune Clinton pulled through, with much credit being given to Al and Tipper Gore for having enhanced the ticket to an unusual degree, lending particular sinew to its moral profile. Gore had happily played the attack dog, allowing Clinton to be the glad-hander. Gore was also seen as the man who could bring the Little Rock gang the ballast of political savvy in the to-and-fro of legislative bargaining on the Hill. Fortified by polls showing his contribution to victory, Gore went into the transition period as a vice president-elect wielding clout unprecedented in American history.

Gore immediately set about consolidating this initial advantage. The historical buttress for an influential vice president was weak to nonexistent. The day after election night Gore assigned his top adviser, Peter Knight, along with his old

St. Albans schoolmate Reed Hundt (later to become head of the Federal Communications Commission), to survey vice presidents since John Adams. Their briefing was bleak. Hundt told Gore's biographer Bill Turque they had concluded you could "go back 200 years and find zero successes".

This discomfiting history lesson was darkened by another cloud across Gore's aspirations: Clinton's famous campaign pledge that the American people would get "two for the price of one"—the two being not Clinton and Gore but Bill and Hillary. The First Lady had big ambitions, even to the point of plotting to set up operations in the office traditionally reserved for the vice president.

Determined not to be sidelined, Gore shadowed the president-elect, sedulous in attending, even gate-crashing any meeting of significance. Gore had a contract drawn up and signed by Clinton. Among the stipulations: Gore's top aide, Roy Neel, would not only become the vice president's chief of staff but enjoy the title Assistant to the President, which would put him at the daily briefings that set the administration's political itinerary. His national security man, Leon Fuerth, was made a member of the Principals' Committee, the top-level foreign policy team including the secretary of state, national security adviser, the director of Central Intelligence, and other powers and plenipotentiaries. Clinton promised to have regular lunch sessions with Gore, and the vice president was given a major role in picking presidential Cabinet and staff appointees.

The man who was Gore's executive in the transition maneuvering was Peter Knight. When Gore entered Congress, in 1977, Knight, a Massachusetts native, Cornell economics major, and graduate of Georgetown Law School, was the first staffer he hired. After law school Knight had signed on to the staff of Congressman Robert Macdonald, a Massachusetts

Democrat. Macdonald died within a year. Knight went scrambling for a new job, with a special eye toward the incoming group of Democrats. Friends at Harvard's Kennedy School of Government told Knight that Gore seemed to be the cream of the crop. Knight sought out a meeting with the Congressman-elect and it was love at first sight, a meeting of "political soul mates," as one former member of Gore's staff put it.

From 1979 to 1991, Knight served as Gore's chief legislative aide, staff disciplinarian, money man, confidant and link to the dank world of DC lobbyists, lawyers and political kingmakers. Knight also handled many of Gore's personal affairs, helping to negotiate the contract for *Earth in the Balance* and heading up two family foundations. He supervised Gore's 1988 presidential campaign, and in 1989 went with Gore to Taiwan on a trade junket headed by Maria Hsia and John Huang, both later convicted in the fundraising scandals stemming from the 1996 presidential campaign. It was a fateful trip for Gore. In Taiwan, Gore visited the Fo Kuang Shan Buddhist temple, run by master Hsing Yun. The visit included a face-to-face session with the Buddhist master, who told Gore that he looked "presidential". Seven years later, Gore, again under the orchestration of Knight (now attending to fundraising matters for the 1996 campaign), attended the infamous "donor maintenance" meeting at the sect's Hsi Lai temple in Hacienda Heights, California, where monks and nuns served as pass-throughs for cheques to the Democratic National Committee.

In 1989, Knight had left Gore's paid staff and re-emerged in the shining armor of lawyer-lobbyist. First, he worked as general counsel for a drug company. Then, in 1991, through the intervention of his friend and fellow Cornell alum Ken Levine, he landed a lucrative spot at the DC law firm Wunder,

Diefenderfer, Cannon and Thelen. Brandishing his connections to Gore, Knight got special treatment, securing not only a hefty salary but also a nice bonus, when several of the firm's senior partners pitched in $7,000 each to add to his compensation package. Among the firm's prime clients were some of the most rapacious companies in the United States: asbestos-maker Johns Manville, timber giants Maxxam and Kimberly-Clark and the industry's trade group, the American Forest and Paper Association, waste-hauler Browning-Ferris Industries, Ashland Oil, Westinghouse, RJR Nabisco and Philip Morris.

Cannon Thelen operated on the "you eat what you kill" principle, meaning that the firm's partners were able to retain a large percentage of their fees. Knight's early years at the firm were lean. His billings failed to cover his salary and expenses. But in July of 1992, Gore selected him to head up the vice-presidential campaign; six months later, when Knight returned from his leave of absence, he immediately cashed in, attracting a retinue of clients eager to exploit his access to the White House inner sanctum. Through his efforts, the firm also won a four-year consulting contract with the Tennessee Valley Authority. By 1995, Knight was billing $2.9 million a year and had even won a $1 million "services fee".

Knight duly became the vice chairman in charge of personnel for the Clinton-Gore transition team, overseen by fixer extraordinaire, Vernon Jordan. His prime responsibility was to seed the administration with people loyal to Gore. Carol Browner, formerly of Gore's staff, was made director of the Environmental Protection Agency. Katie McGinty became director of first the White House Office of Environmental Policy, and later the Council on Environmental Quality. Gore's brother-in-law Frank Hunger was made head of the civil division at the Justice Department. Reed Hundt was slotted in to oversee the FCC. Gore's pal Les Aspin was nominated for secretary of defense, and James Woolsey, Gore's tutor in nuclear war games, was selected to direct the CIA. One of Gore's few allies from his days in the House, Leon Panetta, was picked for the crucial position of director of the Office of Management and Budget. Longtime friend Mickey Kantor was brought on as US trade representative. Senate colleague Tim Wirth was made assistant secretary of state overseeing environmental matters. Fellow DLC member Bruce Babbitt was tapped as interior secretary, and Gore's friend George Frampton was picked as Babbitt's top assistant. (Gore later hired Frampton as his lawyer to fend off an independent counsel investigation into his fundraising practices.) For treasury secretary, Gore and Knight successfully fought for the appointment of Lloyd Bentsen over World Bank economist Larry Summers. Gore's family friend James Galliland, a lawyer from Memphis, was named chief counsel to the Department of Agriculture. Gore's Tennessee fundraiser Johnny Hayes was given a $115,000-a-year slot on the TVA's board of directors.

But Knight's most loyal piece of jobbery concerned Thomas Grumbly, another former member of the Gore staff. Grumbly and Knight were longtime pals. Knight had hired Grumbly in 1980 to serve as staff director for the House Commerce Committee's subcommittee on investigations and oversight, which Gore chaired. Later, Knight asked Grumbly to be secretary/treasurer of the Environmental Education Foundation, the grantmaking nonprofit that Gore set up with proceeds from *Earth in the Balance*. After the 1996 election, Grumbly told Knight that he would entertain an offer for a position in either the Agriculture Department or the Office of Management and Budget. Neither offer materialized. But Knight soon called to inform Grumbly that he would be nominated as assistant secretary of energy for environmental management. In that position, Grumbly was responsible for awarding contracts for the cleanup of environmental hot spots on DOE property, such as those in Hanford, Rocky Flats and Oak Ridge. These contracts were some of the largest of their kind ever awarded by the federal government, totaling billions of dollars.

This connection greatly helped Knight when he returned to Cannon Thelen. Knight soon began recruiting clients that did business with the Energy Department. "I am very familiar with the DOE and close to Secretary Hazel O'Leary's new team", he wrote in a June 3, 1993, letter to a prospective client. His qualifications were duly noted by Lockheed Martin, Fluor Daniel and Molten Metal Technologies. All of them sought his help in setting up deals with the Department of Energy and, they did not go away disappointed.

With his people scattered throughout the government, Gore elected to exercise muscle in a somewhat bizarre way. A credulous student of management gurus and efficiency boosters such as Tom Peters and David Osborne, Gore put together a Cabinet retreat at Camp David in the very dawn of the new administration. The assembled would be put through a group therapy session, operating under the rubric of "human resource development" and run by two New Age facilitators, described by George Stephanopoulos with unusual verve as "two sensible-looking middle-aged ladies with Romper Room smiles on their faces and jumbo Magic Markers in their hands". The leader of this duo was Jane Hopkins, a Virginia psychotherapist and management consultant.

Attendance at the session was mandatory. The only adamant nay-sayer with enough seniority to stay away was

Treasury Secretary Lloyd Bentsen. Camp David was strained beyond its limits by the throng, and some senior staffers were forced to rough it in the Super 8 motel in Thurmont, Maryland. In the purlieus of the presidential retreat in the Catoctin Mountains, where Ike had fished for trout, JFK cavorted with secretaries, Nixon plotted subornation of perjury and Carter played matchmaker to Sadat and Begin, the new Clinton-Gore team hosted a "soul-baring workshop", demanding that each participant reveal to the entire group a private trauma.

The aim of the exercise was to "build trust" and "foster team solidarity". Clinton was one of the first to disclose his feelings, recounting his nasty moments as a kid, taunted for being fat. Gore launched smoothly into the well-tested waters of his sister's death and his son's accident. Lightening things up a bit, Warren Christopher admitted his enthusiasm for jazz clubs and Chardonnay. But his offering was soon buried by an avalanche of confessions by others of miseries at work or at home. Stephanopoulos described the affair as "excruciating".

The mandatory "openness" went, naturally enough, arm in arm with a profound concern for leaks. Clinton and Gore were both vivid on this topic, their stipulations being reported at once to a *Washington Post* reporter by no less than six of the participants. The press had a fine time poking fun at Gore's therapy session. Nonetheless, he remained loyal to his consultants and later put Hopkins on retainer at $3,250 a month. Hopkins' salary was channeled through the Democratic National Committee, and when this came out five years later, Senator Bob Kerrey of Nebraska sneered that rather than helping Democrats win back Congress the DNC was more interested in "paying a psychologist for sorting out the vice president's shop".

One of Hopkins' first pieces of counsel was for Gore to read *On Becoming a Leader*, by a former university president called Warren Bennis. Gore was so taken with Bennis's admonitions that he gave a copy to Clinton and told his inner circle to put it on their bedside tables, next to Alice Miller's *The Drama of the Gifted Child*.

Down the years Gore has fallen for self-help gurus with the same velocity as Clinton for Hollywood stars. By 1999 he was hiring Naomi Wolf, author of *The Beauty Myth*, part of a group of women writers on sexual politics known as the *"do-me* feminists and noted for having cried "We really are demon goddesses of lust", at a read-in organized by Erica Jong. Wolf's assignment was to convert Gore from being a "beta male" to an "alpha". Advising Gore to wear earth tones and no ties, she was compensated for these insights at an initial rate of $15,000 a month, with the money funneled through Bob Squier's political consulting firm so as to keep Wolf's name from showing up on Federal Elections Commission disclosure forms. When the story came out, Donna Brazile, Gore's campaign manager, docked Wolf's pay by $10,000 a month. Confronted with the matter by ABC's Sam Donaldson, Gore mumbled that Wolf was helping his daughter Karenna develop a website to reach out to young people, a market in which the latter was taking a keen interest. "Every ad agency in America is salivating over us", Gore's oldest daughter proclaimed at a convention of College Democrats of America. "Our consumer power moves fashion trends, dictates best-sellers, turns obscure rock bands into super stars. We should harness that power to make the highest leaders in the land accountable to our voices."

Among the first orders of business for the new team was construction of an economic plan. The campaign rhetoric had been freighted with talk about job creation, reinvestment of the "peace dividend" into civilian infrastructure and a tax cut for the middle class. But campaign rhetoric about economic change soon came into sharp collision with the realities of economic power in America—the Federal Reserve, Wall Street, the banks and IMF, the big corporations. Gore led the group insisting that Wall Street and the big institutions be placated with an onslaught on the deficit. Key here was Fed chairman Alan Greenspan, whose tweaking of interest rates in 1991 had doomed Bush in 1992. Deficit reduction meant saying goodbye to all of Clinton's populist promises on the campaign trail.

Only two weeks into the presidency Clinton had the facts of life laid out for him by Gore and Treasury Secretary Bentsen. Bentsen said he would serve as a back channel to Greenspan, but only if he could carry the pledge that the White House was committed to deficit reduction. Gore remained an implacable deficit hawk, favoring reduction over national health insurance and civilian investment. He pushed for savage cuts in entitlements, urging $40 billion more in spending cuts than those proposed by Labor Secretary Robert Reich, the most vigorous, albeit hopelessly outgunned, of those urging a more populist approach. Early in 2000, Reich attacked Gore's economics of austerity, saying it was "worse than Reaganomics, it's Coolidgeonomics".

Gore even backed a proposal by Leon Panetta to freeze cost of living adjustments for Social Security in order to save a mere $20 billion over three years. Clinton finally erupted at the complete nullification of his campaign platform. As quoted by Bob Woodward in *The Agenda*, Clinton cried, "You mean my re-election hinges on the Federal Reserve and a bunch of fucking bond traders?" Bentsen and Gore nodded. Then Bentsen said there was more bad news. The middle-class tax break was

155

toast. In fact, they were going to have to seek new taxes to meet a surge in budgetary red ink suddenly "discovered" and widely publicized by the Republicans in consort with the Democratic deficit hawks as political blackmail. Bentsen then laid out his menu of possible tax hikes. They could soak the rich. They could close loopholes and increase taxes on corporations. They could boost sin taxes on cigarettes and booze. Or they could raise the gasoline tax.

Then Gore surprised everyone by saying he favored an energy tax, based on the British thermal unit, or BTU. He explained that this tax would help fulfill pledges to the environmental movement, since it would fall most heavily on fossil fuels, particularly coal and oil. In the longer term, he argued, it would also encourage conservation and a shift to alternative fuels, meaning natural gas and nuclear power. Gore claimed that the Europeans and the Japanese were waiting for the United States to show leadership and would soon follow suit. Deficit reduction, combined with the energy tax, would be painful medicine, Gore continued, but it would be a bold stroke, comparable to the heady initiatives of FDR's New Deal. This prompted another sarcastic outburst from Clinton: "FDR was trying to help people. Here, we help the bond market and hurt the people who voted us in."

Lloyd Bentsen wasn't interested in reviving the New Deal, but he wagged his head in disbelief at Gore's BTU proposal. Unlike the vice president, he had studied the career of LBJ and knew how energy politics played on Capitol Hill. Any tax threatening coal and oil producers would instantly arouse the vigilant fury of two powerful senators: Robert Byrd of West Virginia and Bennett Johnston of Louisiana, the prime political guardians of the interests of the coal and oil companies, respectively.

Cunningly, Bentsen gave Gore enough rope to hang himself, sitting back as the White House lobbied furiously on the Hill for an economic package that included the BTU tax. It was uphill work and in the end it seemed it would even lose in the House, where the Democrats still had a big majority. It came down to some last-minute deal-making by Bentsen and Clinton's chief of staff, Mack McLarty, who'd previously been running Arkla, a big natural gas company. In negotiations that were shielded from Gore, they struck a deal with Oklahoma's Dave McCurdy, tribune of the Oklahoma oil patch. McCurdy would put the package over the top in the House, but at a price. When it came to the Senate version of the package, they would have to kill the BTU tax, slash more entitlements and kick out the economic progressives in the White House.

The package squeaked through the House but in the Senate the fix, as extorted by McCurdy, was in. Gore's cherished BTU tax was done in by Oklahoma's David Boren, a fellow eminence on the Democratic Leadership Council, and John Breaux, famous for saying "I don't sell my vote, but you can rent it." Gore sensed betrayal and rushed up to Breaux, angrily shouting, "Are you going to screw us?" Breaux laughed in his face and walked away. Bentsen went on the McNeil-Lehrer show and made it official: "It will not be a so-called BTU tax." Watching in the White House, Clinton played along with the charade, telling Gore he couldn't figure out what Bentsen was up to.

Desolate over the death of the BTU tax, Gore consoled himself with trying to implement McCurdy's other two demands—more cuts in entitlements and an onslaught on his enemies in the White House. There were better options for raising money, but in theory some kind of BTU tax wasn't a bad idea. Gore undercut the idea right from the start, though, agreeing to exempt industrial consumers of coal, thus annulling the biggest environmental benefit and passing the economic burden onto residential consumers. As always, they got it in the neck anyway with Bentsen's substitute, a 4 cent-a-gallon tax on gasoline. As Clinton himself said, the new budget was of "Eisenhower Republican" cast.

Peter Edelman, who was a top-level official at the Department of Health and Human Services before resigning in protest over the welfare bill in 1996, said of the new administration's obsession with deficit cutting: "It turned out that after all the noise and heat ... about balancing the budget, the only deep multi-year budget cuts actually enacted were those ... affecting low-income people."

Even by its own standard of timid promises, by the late spring of 1993 the Clinton Administration had failed to offer any opposing, progressive challenge to business-as-usual. Clinton's economic program outlined the terms of surrender and defeat. On top of that had come the catastrophic handling of the issue of gays in the military. In return for its energetic support in 1992, Clinton had promised the gay voting bloc that one of his first orders of business would be to end discrimination in the armed forces. Once in office he vacillated, with talk of hearings and working groups. While he displayed his inexperience, Senator Sam Nunn and the head of the Joint Chiefs of Staff, Gen. Colin Powell, seized the initiative. With lightning speed, the Pentagon had its majority in Congress, and the Christian right was trumpeting renewal and victory.

It remained to signal the coup de grace for Clinton's program of "putting people first", and here Gore was the facilitator. He lobbied hard for the recruitment of an old Reagan hand, Dave Gergen, to handle White House affairs. Clinton numbly agreed. Gore himself tapped out the press release at 6:15 AM on a Saturday morning in the office of Dee Dee Myers, then the White House press secretary. This meant sunset for George Stephanopoulos as a power in the White House. As he typed the release, Gore startled those not in the know by disclosing that Gergen would not be merely communications director but White House counselor. In terms of many of its campaign promises, it was the end of the Clinton Administration.

10 TRADE WARS

*The battle to pass NAFTA; Gore coopts big green
groups; a deal with Newt is struck; Gore debates
Ross Perot on Larry King Live; press cheers veep: "A
refreshingly dirty fighter." NAFTA passes and the
dire consequences predicted by its foes duly come to
pass; Gore wows big labor with pledges to affirm the
right to strike.*

At the level of symbolism, the arrival of Gergen
represented the defeat of those forces within the
administration who had carried the flame for the idea that the
Clinton-Gore victory in 1992 indicated a decisive break with
the corporatist politics of the Reagan era. In terms of policy,
though, his presence fit perfectly within the logic of the duo's
actual program.

Look no further than the North American Free Trade
Agreement, already touted by George Bush and the Republican
Party and at the top of Clinton-Gore priorities from the start.
In the fall of 1992 the Clinton campaign had remained
noncommittal for as long as it could on NAFTA. Why offend
labor prematurely? Finally, the week after Labor Day, the
campaign put out the word that if elected Clinton would push
for ratification of the treaty, while of course remaining granite-
like in his resistance to any threat it might pose to labor or the
environment.

There was no mystery as to where Gore stood on the
question, which was a fraught one in those months, as polls

showed the bulk of Americans opposed to any trade deal. As a senator, Gore had backed the Caribbean Basin Initiative of Reagan-time, which had encouraged the growth of the *maquiladoras* just south of the US-Mexican border. After the election, Gore helped put together the NAFTA sales force: Mickey Kantor as US trade rep; Bill Daley as the so-called NAFTA czar. Years later Gore slotted Daley in as secretary of commerce, where he maneuvered the China trade bill through the Congress before leaving to replace Tony Coelho as general chairman of Gore's 2000 campaign.

With NAFTA the sales problem was acute. Two of the core constituencies opposed it: organized labor and the greens. Another factor was Ross Perot, whose United We Stand party [precursor to the Reform Party] was using the NAFTA issue to build support toward the 1994 midterm elections. The Clinton-Gore strategy was to steamroll labor, divide the environmental movement and make Perot self-destruct.

Gore's first calls were to his friends in the environmental movement. Out of 800 groups, 795 were strongly opposed to the trade agreement, on the grounds that it would weaken US and Canadian environmental laws and exacerbate already wretched conditions inside Mexico. For reasons mostly to do with currying favor with the administration, five groups, on the neoliberal or conservative end of the green spectrum, offered their support. They were the Environmental Defense Fund, National Audubon Society, World Wildlife Fund, National Wildlife Federation and the Natural Resources Defense Council. This minuscule fraction of organized American greens was then used by Gore and the pro-NAFTA strategists for lobbying on the Hill and as conduits for pro-NAFTA propaganda in a national ad campaign.

Particularly shameless was Jay Hair, then head of

National Wildlife Federation and, at $250,000 a year, the highest-paid green CEO in the country. "There's going to be a near-term resolution of some incredibly difficult environmental degradation problems", Hair said, "and there's going to be a long-term benefit of NAFTA, by ripening the very investment process, that environmental impacts will be increasingly considered." The claim was that although manufacturing along the Mexican-US border in the *maquiladora* zone was an environmental disaster, NAFTA would prompt business to redeploy away from the border and spread the drift of pollution south instead of north. Hair's cohort, John Adams, head of NRDC, later bragged that he had helped "break the back of the environmental opposition to NAFTA".

For Gore it was an early field test of what came to be described as triangulation politics, meaning the courting of Republicans and pro-business Democrats in order to overwhelm the rest of his party. This put him once again into direct conflict with Richard Gephardt and also with David Bonior, one of the leaders of the Congressional Democrats' progressive wing. As the fall of 1993 approached, Gephardt and Bonior seemed to have the upper hand, with 228 votes, ten more than were needed to kill the trade pact.

Gore and his team approached Newt Gingrich, and elicited a promise that, as minority Republican whip, he would produce 132 votes. It was still necessary to peel away some of Bonior's votes. Gore began to raise the ante.

A week before the vote Gore went on *Face the Nation* and announced in grave tones that the fate of the Clinton presidency hung on the outcome of the NAFTA vote. "It is a foreign policy issue as well as an economic issue. The consequences of a defeat for NAFTA in the foreign policy arena would be really catastrophic. It would be a terrible thing to do to the president and the country." This was triangulation with a vengeance, since rhetoric of this voltage is normally reserved for the other party. Gore's press gallery seized upon the theme. *The Washington Post*'s David Broder, a man so pompous he makes Polonius sound like Charlie Chaplin, put on his gravest mien: "If NAFTA is voted down it will literally be a defeat of historic proportions. For a president with a shaky election mandate and a weak political base, it would reduce his international standing to a point unparalleled since Richard Nixon was careening towards resignation."

The next stratagem of the NAFTA forces was to eviscerate the man who helped them vanquish George Bush, Ross Perot. Gore challenged Perot to a debate in Perot's favorite venue, the Larry King show. This was no impromptu throwing down of the gauntlet. White House pollster Stan Greenberg had been keeping tabs on public opinion about Perot for months. Clinton was said to view Perot with contempt and yearned to see him humiliated. The game plan was to paint him as a hypocrite, an unstable autocrat. Gore prepped intensely for several days. One of his main trainers was Bill Bradley, a man so enthusiastic for NAFTA that earlier that summer he had confided to *The National Journal* that ratification of NAFTA would be a defining moment of the Clinton presidency, that it rivaled Thomas Jefferson's Louisiana Purchase in importance.

The White House built up a dossier on Perot's use of lobbyists, also his attempt to turn the area surrounding the Dallas-Fort Worth airport into a free-trade zone. Both before and during the debate the NAFTA proponents were sedulous in linking Perot at all times with two other opponents of the Treaty, Jesse Jackson and Pat Buchanan.

The face-off itself was the highest-rated show in the history of CNN to that date. Twelve million watched Gore rile up the thin-skinned Texas millionaire. To read the transcript seven years later is to find that the debate was about everything but the supposed topic, NAFTA. Early on, Perot tried to raise the entirely accurate point that the Mexican government had hired a legion of DC lobbyists, many of them former US government officials, to push the NAFTA case. Gore interrupted Perot, saying, "I served in the Congress and I don't know of anyone who lobbied the Congress more than you did, Ross, to get tax breaks for your companies." Perot was rattled; he told Gore, "You're lyin' now" and never fully recovered. In fact, Perot had hired a lobbyist to work for his company on tax breaks, but it was in 1975, two years before Gore was elected to Congress. As Perot said, Gore was lyin', but no one cared.

The White House had carefully field-tested the charge of doom-mongering and had discovered it struck a chord in test audiences. Gore duly taunted Perot with his opposition to the Gulf War and his prediction that 40,000 American soldiers would die. History, Gore said (cribbing from Bradley) was always an invitation to daring: "Sometimes we do the right thing: the creation of NATO, the Louisiana Purchase—Thomas Jefferson did the right thing there—the purchase of Alaska." In the end what counted were Gore's constant interruptions and King's incapacity to push the exchange toward substantive issues raised by Perot.

The media critics, used to reviewing TV shows, were merciless about King's performance. Tom Shales of *The Washington Post* also went after Gore, saying, "The veep has the unfortunate habit of sounding as though he's addressing kindergartners when he tries to make a point or describe a position." But the political correspondents, who were pro-NAFTA, anti-Perot or both, reported the encounter as an unqualified triumph for Gore. Perot, they said, had been "dismembered". Richard Cohen of *The Washington Post* was ecstatic at the discovery that Gore was "a refreshingly dirty fighter".

The conventional wisdom is that Gore's TV debate with Perot turned the tide in the House for NAFTA, which came to a vote shortly thereafter and succeeded by a margin of twenty votes. The White House had every interest in pushing the line that the Perot debate had been decisive, since this directed attention away from the fact that the vote was won the old-fashioned way, with pork barrel promises to swing votes. On one estimate the bribes totted up to $50 billion. Representative Bill Sarpalius of Texas was promised that Clinton would reverse course and retain $47 million worth of subsidies to a helium plant in his district. Sarpalius also won a promise for federal funding of a new plutonium lab at the Department of Energy's nuclear weapons factory in Amarillo. Representative Floyd Flake of New York was pledged a robust infusion of Small Business Association loans in his district. Representative J.J. Pickle of Texas was promised a trade center. And so it went, in a cornucopia of federal commitments for highways, obsolete military cargo planes, ships, building projects and other delights.

Some of these deals sabotaged the public commitments the administration was making to protect the environment. Trade rep Kantor, for example, won the support of twenty members of Congress from California and Florida by promising that the upcoming cutoff date for the use of the fumigant methyl bromide, targeted for elimination by the Montreal protocol on ozone depleting chemicals, would be pushed back from 2000 to 2100, with a loophole that might allow for agricultural exemptions even after that date. Another allurement for Texas and Florida reps was a pledge to shelter tomato growers from any sudden rise in tomato imports from Mexico. The pledge was empty. A report by the International Trade Commission found that between 1995 and 1999 tomato acreage in Florida and California declined precipitously. In Florida the number of tomato farms fell from 320 before NAFTA came into force to less than 100 in 1999. Meanwhile, Mexican imports into the US doubled over the same period.

After NAFTA went through, labor and the Democratic progressives were furious and vowed to exact retribution at the polls. In turn, Clinton and Gore said they would campaign for anyone, including Republicans, who voted for NAFTA. In 1994 the Democratic Party paid the price forecast by the labor leaders, losing control of both the House and the Senate. Ralph Nader and Jesse Jackson talked about building a third party movement. In the wake of the vote Nader said, "The word in the White House is that these Democrats who were against NAFTA have nowhere to go and must follow Clinton and Gore no matter how often they don the cloaks of crypto-Republicanism and corporatism. But they are pushing the fracturing of the Democratic Party toward its limits. Americans are going to be seeking a political realignment, a new political party." In fact they got two: the Reform Party and the Greens.

As for NAFTA, a 1997 study by Robert Scott and Jesse Rothstein on behalf of the Economic Policy Institute, a progressive think tank supported by the AFL-CIO, examined the economic effects of NAFTA's first three years. The results were stark. They estimated that there were 394,835 US jobs lost within those years. Especially hard hit were women, hispanics and blacks. Most of the jobs eliminated by NAFTA were high-paying manufacturing jobs. A later study, in 1999, showed that by January 1, 1999, this trend had persisted, with 600,000 jobs lost to Mexico.

It is frequently argued by free-trade zealots that deals like NAFTA help raise up the poor of the world, that opposition to such deals in this country reflects the selfish protectionism of American workers and the hypocrisy of young activists who speak of the immiseration of the Third World. Yet the average wage for Mexican workers sank by 29 percent over the first five years of NAFTA. By 1999 the average Mexican worker was making only 9.6 percent of what US workers make. In the same period 8 million Mexicans dropped from the middle class into poverty. Mexican subsistence agriculture has virtually collapsed in the face of cheap imports of corn and wheat from the north. Poverty had undermined public morals to the degree that the government was forced to disband some police forces in Mexico. The drug trade has flourished. NAFTA's passage prompted the Zapatistas to armed rebellion in Chiapas, demanding land and autonomy, and broadcasting the most eloquent and persuasive arguments against neoliberalism and a trade treaty that spelled death to them.

Gore had insisted that with improved economic conditions consequent upon NAFTA's passage, environmental standards would rise in Mexico. But by 1999 it was clear to everyone that in Mexico and along the US-Mexico border conditions were getting worse. Within the first five years of the NAFTA agreement, Mexico cut its environmental budget by 10 percent, as the crash of the peso reverberated through the economy. As manufacturing and assembly work headed south into Mexico, that country's toxic problems soared. In 1995, Oscar Canto Certina, chairman of the Mexican ecology commission, said, "Each year 7 million tons of toxic waste are without control, illegally dumped in drains and marine waters. Only 1 percent is under our surveillance." To take one example, a river in Baja was described by Dr. Lee Cottrell, a former public health officer for Imperial County, California, as "a ticking time bomb waiting to explode on both sides of the border," with a level of toxicity more than 1,000 times that considered fatal to humans. The river was a soup of PCBs, DDT, TCE, toluene and raw sewage.

In his 2000 campaign Gore chivvied George W. Bush by citing Texas's poor air quality. He was wielding a two-edged sword, because much of the air problem plaguing the Southwest can be traced to the *maquiladoras* and NAFTA. Ozone alerts in El Paso, spiked by burning rubbish piles and coal-fired brick factories along the border, have nearly doubled since NAFTA's passage. Farther west in the Nogales region, the atmosphere is a haze of carbon monoxide and sulfur dioxide. The high levels of pollution have been linked to clusters of lupus and multiple myeloma, a rare blood cancer.

Gore's promises that US environmental laws would not be undercut soon turned out to be empty as well. An Ohio company soon sought and won permission under NAFTA to import PCBs from Canada and Mexico. There was a shortage of raw material for the PCB recycling industry in the United States, but before the agreement passed, US laws forbade the import of any toxic waste. The Ethyl Corporation used NAFTA to bring a $251 million lawsuit against the Canadian government, which had banned the import of one of Ethyl's main products, the gasoline additive MMT. In 1999 a Canadian chemical company, Methenex Corp., filed a $1 billion lawsuit against California, using NAFTA to challenge an executive order by Governor Gray Davis directing that the gas additive and toxin MTBE be banned after the end of 2002.

The Methenex case convinced even NAFTA's most fanatical supporters in the environmental community that perhaps they'd made a tragic miscalculation. "The Methenex lawsuit is the latest attempt to use NAFTA as a tool for rewriting domestic environmental laws", said David Schorr, of the World Wildlife Fund. "Instead of protecting investors, NAFTA's rules are being used to attack legitimate environmental policies."

Baneful in and of itself, NAFTA merely opened the floodgates. Over the next six years Clinton and Gore pushed through more than 200 trade agreements and pursued kindred avenues toward unfettered license for corporations to roam the planet, to plunder without hindrance. There was the General Agreement on Trade and Tariffs, elevated into the World Trade Organization, a star chamber that can be used by corporations to undermine environmental, labor and human rights protections built up laboriously since the second world war. Such protections have been stigmatized as intolerable hindrances to the motions of corporate trade. Within a year of the passage of the enabling legislation for the WTO, the organization had been employed to assail US and European laws such as the Endangered Species Act, the Clean Air Act and the European Union's restrictions on the import of genetically engineered seeds. Citizen outrage finally exploded in 1999 in Seattle.

On the trade issue Clinton and Gore choreographed an intricate dance, alternately undercutting and courting labor, especially since Clinton's re-election and the simultaneous inauguration of Gore's quest for the nomination in 2000. In the early fall of 1997 the AFL-CIO met in Pittsburgh for its biennial convention, mustered against a backdrop of acrid Congressional debate over "fast track" authorization, which would allow the president to freelance international trade agreements without consulting Congress. Gore made haste to schedule an appearance during the pre-convention meetings, in which, with his usual measure of unctuousness, he recounted the travails of workers abused for trying to form unions, expressed shock that such a thing should happen in the United States of America and vowed to strain every muscle in the fight for workers' rights. Fast track, NAFTA—they were noted in passing but drowned in the wash of Gore's effusions on the right to organize, which coincided nicely with the theme of that year's convention. Meanwhile, President Clinton, instinctive triangulator, voyaged to Pittsburgh four days later to lecture the full convention on labor's narrow-mindedness toward free trade. Michael McCurry, Clinton's press secretary, later told *The New York Times* that Clinton wanted to reserve for himself the prime-time union-baiting function.

The two-sided approach backfired for Clinton but worked splendidly for Gore. Convention delegates booed the President and left Pittsburgh inflamed with zeal to stop fast track, which they duly did. Meanwhile, they lavished praise on Gore, persuading themselves that he was somehow not implicated in White House trade policy and setting the stage for the 1999 convention, when they would honor Gore with the earliest endorsement they had ever made of a presidential candidate. In 2000 the AFL-CIO would exhibit the same myopia after Congress approved normal trade relations with China, despite the biggest lobbying mobilization in big labor's history. President John Sweeney blasted Clinton and the Democrats who voted with him but spared Gore, saying, remarkably, that the pro-China vote would only make labor's job of electing Al Gore harder.

In 2000 Gore, battling his primary opponent, Bill Bradley, found himself in Iowa at a conference sponsored by the United Auto Workers. "You know why I'm here", Gore began. "We need to talk." The delegates began to throw questions at the vice president. "We're of the opinion that NAFTA does not work", said Dave Neil, the UAW's top man in Iowa. Another union man asked, "How come you don't twist arms on labor laws like you do on NAFTA?" Gore went on the defensive but, still playing to reporters, said: "If you want perfection, keep on looking. If you want someone who agrees with you 100 percent of the time, keep on looking."

Some union people took Gore up on his offer. By midsummer of 2000 James Hoffa, leader of the Teamsters, was being feted by the Republicans while simultaneously making friendly noises about Ralph Nader, the Green Party candidate. The UAW's Steve Yokich was also under such pressure from his membership that he felt it necessary to express disgust about Gore, and to make friendly remarks about Nader's candidacy.

11 REGO

Reinventing Government, aka Warcry of the Wonks: "Intervention at the Systems Level". Gore fights The Blob (or was it Dad?); feeding frenzy as public assets go on block. Gore's maddest claim: he turned Pentagon into "well-run business". So what about $2.3 trillions' worth of bookkeeping errors? He wanted to end affirmative action; Blacks in Government denounce REGO.

Gore wanted health care, but that went to Hillary. Then he lobbied hard to head a team that would dismantle the federal welfare system. Here too he was foiled. Some inside the White House, notably liberals like George Stephanopoulos, secretly hoped that welfare reform would fall off the agenda. Hillary and her people didn't want it competing for the spotlight with health care. And chief of staff Mack McLarty, Clinton's boyhood chum and a former natural gas company executive, didn't want Clinton to lose his direct identification with what was seen as a core issue of the New Democrat philosophy. Clinton had made "ending welfare as we know it" a constant refrain in his stump speeches, particularly across the South.

So Gore was assigned the task of heading a six-month review of federal agencies in an attempt to ferret out waste, a kind of Grace Commission (an earlier Republican-mounted attack on government) for the 1990s. The program became known as the National Performance Review, *a k a* Reinventing

Government, or simply REGO. Many White House staffers thought it was a political dead end and a good way to get Gore, who seemed omnipresent in the West Wing, always "peering over their shoulders like a nosy teacher", out of their hair for a while.

But Gore seized on the task with his usual plodding tenacity, huddling with management gurus, like Tom Peters, and DLC veterans, such as David Osborne, who had written a book called *Reinventing Government*. Osborne was a kindred spirit, who viewed the workings of the bureaucracy in the same terms Gore had used to describe attitudes toward the environment in *Earth in the Balance*. Osborne piously warned that the government was in meltdown, that the entire political system was "dysfunctional" and that it called out for dramatic "intervention at the systems level". The intervention he had in mind was a kind of disgorgement, a shedding of many of the government's activities to the private sector. It was the kind of activity Republicans loved to thunder in favor of on the campaign trail, then abandon in the face of Democratic opposition when it came to the level of practical reality.

Gore hired Elaine Kamarck, one of Osborne's converts, to run the operation. Kamarck was a policy wonk at the Public Policy Institute, the white-paper outpost of the DLC. In a later incarnation she supervised the drafting of Gore's platform for his 2000 presidential race. Kamarck marshaled strike forces of cost-cutters, scouring every agency in the federal government, seeking at least $100 billion in savings.

Early on, Gore addressed the REGO leaders, assembled by Kamarck into 200 reinvention labs. He cast their mission as "an historic event". He said it was their task to engineer "one of America's most important transitions—-the transition from yesterday's government to the government of the twenty-first century ... the government of our parents and grandparents to our children and grandchildren." As with much of Gore's political rhetoric, there is a distinctly Oedipal flavor to this. The very government he was seeking to overthrow embodied nothing less than the New Deal/Great Society programs that his own father had helped construct and defend. Indeed, Gore has often described the federal bureaucracy as "the blob that keeps coming back at you like a character in a horror movie". REGO, Gore said, was to be the silver bullet, a seek-and-destroy mission on the vestiges of FDR's programs, with the cost-cutters ever on the alert to "discard the remnants of yesterday's government".

With Hillary's health care proposal mired down and the rest of the administration stumbling from one embarrassment and misstep after another, Gore took REGO prime time. He appeared on *Late Night with David Letterman* wearing a pair of safety goggles and wielding a hammer to demonstrate the job of the federal ashtray safety inspector. He joked about the military specifications for making chocolate chip cookies and the twenty-three-step process for determining veterans' benefits.

The liberals in Clinton's inner circle thought it was "bullshit" but it turned out to be the Clinton administration's first big hit with the public. Stan Greenberg's polling showed REGO to be more popular than health care reform and the middle-class tax cut. This was a green light for Gore to take it even further. By 1994, REGO was engaged in a project that can best be described as an attempt to corporatize the federal government, privatizing parts of it and paring down the rest the way a corporate raider would after a hostile takeover.

Gore's notes from an August 2, 1994, meeting of the Clinton Cabinet show him urging department heads to go on a job-slashing rampage. "The cuts are aimed at headquarters, multiple layers of bureaucracy, auditors, and the offices that deal in the arcane rules of personnel, procurement and finance", Gore said. "With a few exceptions, the streamlining plans we've gotten aren't big enough, fast enough, or on target."

He demanded that agency headquarters cut their staff by at least 50 percent. "In the private sector, General Electric cut their headquarters' size in half while doubling their economic size", Gore said. "In retrospect, Frank Doyle told me that GE didn't move fast enough or boldly enough. Amoco just announced they are cutting from 4,200 to 400 in a year." Gore told the department heads: "I want you all to plan big, dramatic headquarters cuts like that." He warned them, if they didn't do it themselves he would "have to have my staff design it".

In a 1995 speech to REGO leaders, Gore instructed the teams to find ways to turn over government functions to "the vigor of the competitive private marketplace to produce better services, higher quality products, and greater efficiency than public or private monopolies." Through REGO, Gore also promoted a theme that would become a hallmark of the administration, allowing corporations to comply voluntarily with federal laws and regulations. "Reinventing government", Gore said, "is about giving businesses new opportunities to become trusted partners in enforcing laws." He then pointed to opportunities to lessen the burden on industry in areas such as "worker safety, environmental protection and the whole range of regulatory functions".

Gore's attacks on federal regulations displayed the same fervor as had Dan Quayle's Council on Competitiveness, which sought to emasculate environmental and labor rules during the Bush presidency. Like Quayle, Gore showed a particular animus toward the Code of Federal Regulations, the 150,000-

175

page encyclopedia of government rules and regulations. Gore poked fun at government rules for food inspectors on how to determine the freshness of fish through a smell test. "Of course, government must be involved in food safety", Gore declared. "But is there a way we could rely on market incentives and people's common sense instead of government interference? Can't we get the government's nose out of this business?"

So the teams went on their way, slashing with abandon. Gore told them "No idea is too outrageous." And apparently he meant it. Among the casualties: the Clean Coal Technology Program, an odd victim given his emphasis on reducing greenhouse emissions. The federal honey, wool and mohair programs also got the axe. REGO recommended an end to "unfunded mandates"—-regulations, such as clean air rules and OSHA requirements, that are imposed on states with no federal largesse to ease the pain of compliance.

The teams that came up with the most innovative ideas for slashing programs were given the Hammer Award, named after Gore's old patron Armand Hammer, one of the most accomplished thieves of the federal purse in the twentieth century. Since 1993, more than 1,700 of these awards have been handed out to cost-cutting grouplets with names including the Transgenic Arthropods Team, Alaska Volcano Lab, Automated Battlefield Development Team, Blue Crab Partnership, CIA Retirement and Investments Group, Dynamic Seat Certification Revised Method of Compliance Team, F-15 Ejection Natural Working Group, Plain English Team, KC-135 Aircraft Elevator Control Tab Corrosion Defect Team and, one of the most telling, the Government-Industry Partnership to Re-Engineer Federal Oversight Team.

In an especially miserly move, the Forest Service was directed to begin charging people to hike trails and go for picnics on National Forest lands. The Park Service was told to investigate the possibility of corporate sponsorship of the national parks.

Another scheme involved marketing reform at the Bonneville Power Administration, which oversees operations of the federal hydroelectric dams in the Columbia River basin and had kept electric rates in the Pacific Northwest the lowest in the nation. After the REGO reforms, the BPA raised costs on residential consumers and made sweetheart deals with big industrial power users, such as pulp mills and aluminum factories. The salmon fared even worse.

The National Labor Relations Board also fell victim to REGO's buzzsaws, seeing its staff slashed and its budget starved. Its general counsel, Fred Feinstein, was later given an award by Gore for how effectively he'd handled the downsizing, but the fact that the administration was squeezing an already overworked agency didn't sit well with many labor organizers.

"Because of the chronic backlog of NLRB cases—due in part to the acute shortage of staff—Fred Feinstein was forced to shift cases between offices to try to get the job done", said Chris Townsend, political action director of the United Electrical, Radio and Machine Workers of America. "Fred deserves an award for this heroic juggling effort. And Al Gore should be denounced for this latest 'reinvention' disgrace. Does the vice president support a real solution to this outrageous backlog of NLRB cases? Not at all. Does Gore support a doubling of NLRB staff so that union elections and unfair labor practice cases could be processed in a week or two? No."

On the block was the Elk Hills Oil Reserve in California which, as discussed here in chapter 13, was to become the single biggest sell-off of government assets in history. Bill Clinton himself praised the plan, saying: "The National

Petroleum Reserve in Elk Hills was created during World War I because America's new battleships needed oil. Well, World War I is over, and I know that the strategic need for the Navy to have its own oil fields has long since passed." What Clinton didn't mention was that the beneficiary of this sell-off would be Gore's favorite oil company, Occidental Petroleum. Nor did he bring up the touchy subject that the Elk Hills property contained important habitat for rare and endangered species and that the sale was fiercely opposed by biologists with the US Fish and Wildlife Service.

At a September 7, 1995, Rose Garden ceremony celebrating the second phase of Gore's REGO scheme, Clinton lavished praise on Interior Secretary Bruce Babbitt for undermining his own biologists and field staffers in the name of reducing the "burden of federal regulations", such as the Endangered Species Act. "The Secretary of the Interior is not here, but he's done his best now to try to resolve some of the thorniest conflicts between the federal government and various groups in the western part of our country by pushing these decisions down to local councils of people who can make them a long way from Washington", Clinton said. More often than not, those "people" turned out to be real estate tycoons or representatives from big timber, oil and mining companies.

Also slated for privatization: the US Enrichment Corporation (USEC), created in the 1950s to process uranium for use in nuclear weapons and submarines. The company went public in 1998, with an Initial Public Offering of 100 million shares of stock valued at $1.7 billion. The $1.7 billion went to the feds. The principals made a lot of money. So did the Wall Street traders. And the lobbyists. In all, the firms involved in the sell-off made more than $75 million. A 1999 report by the Center for Public Integrity chronicled the way several firms close to Gore cashed in on the multiyear process of privatizing the company, including Goldman Sachs, JP Morgan and the law firm headed by lobbyist extraordinaire Tommy Boggs. Gore's former chief domestic policy staffer, Greg Simon, was retained by JP Morgan for $10,000 a month in order to help pick a board of directors for the newly privatized company.

Once again, the nuclear power industry found itself the beneficiary of a Gore plan. Shortly after the privatization, USEC's chairman, William "Nick" Timbers, gave a speech at the Uranium Institute in London. "Another big winner coming out of USEC's privatization is the nuclear industry itself", Timbers gloated. "Yes, successfully selling 100 million shares of stock is a big voice of confidence in our company. But it is also a very visible demonstration of support for all of us in this business. Tens of thousands of investors voted with their checkbooks in favor of nuclear power and its potential."

But it wasn't a good deal for the workers. USEC almost immediately slashed 500 jobs. But even with lucrative government contracts, including a deal hatched by Gore to reprocess radioactive material from Russia, the firm had a difficult time making a profit. In the spring of 2000, it announced it was considering shutting down its Portsmouth, Ohio, plant, resulting in the loss of 2,000 jobs. Timbers requested a $200 million federal handout to keep the plant open.

All this prompted a Congressional hearing, at which several legislators lamented that USEC had ever been spun off to the private sector. "USEC came around in less than two years after they went public looking for us to bail them out", said Representative Tom Strickland, a Democrat from Ohio. "We cannot allow these plants to cease functioning. As a government we cannot allow this industry to fail, but we can let this corporation fail." Timbers blamed the problem on globalization. "The cold war is over and we are now fighting global competition", Timber said. He promised to look at other ways to cut costs. "Everything is on the table for reconsideration." Timbers was asked whether that included his own $1.2 million salary. The executive emphatically shook his head: "My salary has not been discussed in this context."

So where did all the new REGO money go? To health care? The environment? Investments in civilian infrastructure? No. As Leon Panetta, then head of the Office of Management and Budget, told an astonished White House press corps, most of the money, some $30 billion worth, was going to fund the Clinton-Gore 1995 crime package. "We would commit $10 billion for savings and the ability to reduce the deficit", Panetta said. "The amount above that would go to fund the crime bill.... We're not looking at entitlement spending on the crime side. But discretionary spending: money for cops, money for prisons, money for law enforcement generally."

REGO didn't stop there. It went on well into 2000, cutting jobs, contracting out work and privatizing federal assets. By the time Gore announced his presidential candidacy, he boasted that 377,000 federal jobs had been slashed (an odd claim for a Democrat), 1,500 federal regulations had been pared away, and the taxpayer had been saved $136 billion in federal spending. In all, Gore said his team had shrunk the government to its smallest size since the Eisenhower administration.

But the numbers didn't add up. In 1999 a General Accounting Office report determined that Gore and his team had grossly overestimated the savings from REGO, perhaps by as much as $21.8 billion. It accused the REGO accountants of double-counting, tallying savings for two years that hadn't yet occurred, taking credit for savings that were the result of other factors and not fully assessing the costs of restructuring.

Gore was proudest of REGO's transformation of government procurement, particularly at the Pentagon, which he said had begun to operate "using quality management the same way a well-run business uses it". But, as usual, it turned out to be the businesses that were making a killing at the Pentagon, an even better one than they had before the REGO reforms went into effect. An investigation by the Defense Department's inspector general discovered that the REGO reforms dovetailed nicely with the interests of military contractors, such as Boeing and Lockheed Martin.

By adopting so-called commercial practices, the Pentagon ditched important protections against contractor fraud and billing abuse, including a provision that exempted thousands of purchases from oversight by auditors. Soon there were reports of Pentagon spending sprees rivaling the spare parts stories of the 1980s. The Allied Signal Corporation, for example, was found to have overcharged the Pentagon on some spare parts by as much as 618 percent.

The inspector general's report noted that the REGO procurement reform "qualifies most items that the DoD procures as commercial items", which are exempt from oversight. This led to a situation in which the Pentagon was almost blindly accepting the costs and prices claimed by the contractors. The report noted that the rapid pace of mergers of defense companies during the Clinton-Gore years only exacerbated the problem. "If anything, the risks may be greater today because there is such market dominance by a few very large suppliers", the inspector general wrote. "In this environment, getting cost information and maintaining audit rights is a prudent business practice. Failure to do so will be very costly for the Department and ultimately the taxpayer."

Consider the case of Mark Krenik, an Air Force employee who did well for a while out of the reinvention of his government job. He worked in an office called Single Agency Manager, or SAM. That office purchases computer audio-visual equipment, supplies and services for many DOD organizations. Krenik pled guilty to false claims totaling more than $500,000. Senator Charles Grassley described the case in a hearing into the huge mess of Pentagon accounting. "In his office, there was no separation of duties. Therefore, Krenik himself was able to cover the waterfront. He developed requirements for goods and services; he wrote purchase orders; he steered contracts to favored vendors; he received and accepted deliveries; he signed receiving reports; and he submitted invoices for payment. It was a piece of cake for Krenik to fabricate phony invoices and receipts, and then get paid. With separation of duties, it would have been very difficult—if not impossible—for him to do what he did. But there was no separation of duties. How did Krenik get caught? Not by effective internal controls. An alert bank teller in Maryland got suspicious. Mr. Krenik sent the payments to his own bank account. The teller noticed the large deposits in his account were abnormal. She called the Secret Service. Mr. Krenik was caught, and is presently serving a two-year probation."

In fiscal year 1997 alone, the Justice Department reviewed 802 similar cases involving financial crimes at the Defense Department. As one very seasoned Pentagon watchdog put it, "The reinventors took practices that were already scandalous and turned them into virtues. Take 'pay and chase', a streamlining measure extolled by the reinventors, which made the paying of bills without paperwork a virtue. We do not require double-entry bookkeeping, just an "Accounts Payable" obligation. We just have money flowing in and flowing out, with impunity. With streamlining you don't have to check to see if someone had actually ordered something, and had got what he ordered. You get a bill, you pay it."

Robbie Miller was a staff sergeant in the Air Force at Dayton, Ohio, which is the location of the Defense Finance and Accounting Service. He stole about a million dollars, sending fake invoices to his mother, girlfriend and himself, at phony addresses. His only mistake was to change girlfriends in the middle of these streamlined financial maneuvers. Miller drew a twelve-year sentence. The Defense Finance and Accounting Service at first set out to do defend the Air Force but, in the words of one investigator, "when they got into it, there was not enough sand in a cat box to cover it."

A 1999 report by the Project on Government Oversight, which exposed many Pentagon scandals of the 1980s, showed that the REGO reforms had cut deeply into the budget and staff of the Defense Contract Audit Agency, the outfit charged with keeping an eye out for waste and fraud at the Pentagon. From 1993 to 1997, its staff and budget had been cut by 19 percent, despite evidence that the auditors had saved the government nearly $10 for each dollar spent in its budget. By 2002 the agency is projected to have lost more than 3,000 staffers, a 44 percent cut from the levels of the Bush administration.

As a measure of how short REGO fell in curbing or even confronting the staggering fraud and waste that is endemic to the Defense Department, consider that in 1998 the General Accounting Office and the Defense Department's inspector general found that the Pentagon had made more than $2.3 trillions worth of bookkeeping errors, a sum that is larger than the entire federal budget. They also pointed out that the

Pentagon had no idea where nearly $120 billion worth of equipment was located, including trucks, tanks and ships.

Amid these dismaying discoveries the Pentagon was given a green light by the Clinton-Gore Administration to pursue its own privatization schemes in two ways: through increased outsourcing of contracts, and through sales of surplus parts. Both programs were saturated with fraud. A 1999 GAO report found that the Pentagon was selling off "potentially dangerous aircraft parts". Indeed, the US Army alone sold more than 4,500 faulty parts to civilian aircraft firms.

Among the more sinister REGO proposals offered up by Gore is one recounted in George Stephanopoulos's memoir of his time in the Clinton White House, *All Too Human*. Stephanopoulos, then a top aide to Clinton, describes fielding frantic calls from fellow liberals in the White House who had learned that Gore's REGO team was proposing to abolish affirmative action hiring and contracting guidelines at the federal level. He said that he was handed a letter from the US Civil Rights Commission opposing the plan, but was told that the fix was in. Stephanopoulos says he charged over to Gore's office to denounce the plan, calling it "a cluster bomb into the middle of our base".

Gore bristled, telling Stephanopoulos to back off. "Now, wait a second", Gore said. "Let's start off on the premise that the president has already made this decision." But Gore apparently was bending the truth. Stephanopoulos says he immediately sought out Clinton and asked him if he had okayed Gore's affirmative action plan. Clinton shook his head: "No, no, no. I mean, Davis-Bacon, I knew about, but never affirmative action." Davis-Bacon is the federal law requiring government contractors to pay their workers a prevailing wage;

an effort to kill it (something the Reaganites tried) should have made headlines in its own right. Stephanopoulos says that Gore's scheme — both the affirmative action and the Davis-Bacon "reinvention" plans — then died "a bureaucratic death".

Astoundingly little press attention was ever given to government reinvention by Gore's people. But in July of 1999 the national legislative review committee of Blacks in Government published "National Partnership for Reinventing Government: The New Spoils System". It is a savage assessment of what Reinventing Government has done to the civil service. "Reinventing", the report concludes, "has been generally silent about fairness and equality issues" and "has had a devastating impact on federal workers, particularly racial minorities."

In one caustic paragraph after another "The New Spoils System" describes how the "private-sector does it better" philosophy has proven to be a breeding ground for cronyism, corruption and burgeoning racism within government agencies. In their zeal to cut red tape by slashing regulations, easing restrictions and procedural controls, and giving increased power to line managers, the reinventors sabotaged the merit principle and engineered "the government-wide downsizing of racial minorities".

Under the bleak headline "A Catalyst for Economic Genocide" the report lays out in bitter detail how rules designed to protect federal employees from unfair treatment have been discarded. Agencies—like the USDA and Interior Department– already notorious for the poor treatment given minorities were now being given a license by the reinventors to perpetuate unfair treatment and inequality. "Discriminatory managers will be allowed to use 'human resources management' initiatives to 'ethnically cleanse' the Federal sector work force."

The report from Blacks in Government is particularly vitriolic about one administrative change imposed by Gore's reinventors, known as "broadbanding". This plan aimed at reforming the job classification and basic pay systems of government workers by eliminating the General Schedule (GS) system, which had standardized personnel classifications and pay rates since it was introduced, in 1949.

Nothing infuriates and demoralizes a civil servant—particularly one who is black or hispanic—more than the sight of colleagues with less experience or fewer credentials undeservedly getting higher pay or preferment. Adequate merit protections and the control of favoritism and corruption have been the concerns of every civil service since the dawn of civilization. Yet Gore's cocksure reinventors, with "re-engineering" blueprints from the corporate sector in their briefcases, staked all on "flexible" management tools, meaning that managers could now, without accountability within the larger civil service framework, establish their own buddy systems.

Under broadbanding or paybanding, an employee's maximum pay varies, depending on how he or she is classified, with this same classification now being the purview not of personnel officials but of managers able to manipulate the system to award different rates of pay to employees doing the same job. For example, a manager can classify one worker as an economist (maximum salary in fiscal year 1995, $47,167) or as an accountant (maximum salary, $43,991), with no difference in the worker's actual duties. In 1995 the same "broadband" offered someone classed as a statistical clerk a maximum salary of $34,094, but a budget clerk only $23,491.

Furthermore, with this re-engineering tool, managers can

discriminate against women and minorities, because there's little or no objective documentation required to support the manager's allocations. As the report puts it, the biased manager could set a newly hired male accountant at the top of his band range, at $41,468, and a newly hired female accountant with the same experience at the bottom of the same band, at $23,678.

It's fortunate for Gore that on the journalistic radar screens of newspaper editors and TV producers the concerns of civil service employees in the US government have zero visibility. Otherwise the vice president might have been more troubled politically by the fact that many black Americans in government—a substantial group—regard him as a relentless foe of affirmative action, a man who actively sought to reduce their opportunities and degrade their conditions in government service.

Give Elaine Kamarck, Gore's own lieutenant in implementing this project, the last word on reinventing government: "There was a lot about reinventing government that was 'Nixon goes to China'. The unions would sabotage Ronald Reagan [for this], but not Bill Clinton and Al Gore."

12 WAR ON THE POOR

Enter Dick Morris, sees Gore as soulbrother. The
pact with Republicans: When all else fails, go after
the destitute. The "values agenda". Gore the man
who pushed Clinton to sign welfare bill; Moynihan
says "It's not welfare reform, it's welfare repeal".
Clinton, Gore and the Jackboot State. Anatomy of
Clintonomics.

In November of 1994 two years of ramshackle
government, breached pledges and the Clinton
Administration's frequently manifested contempt for its
traditional base, exacted their price. In the midterm elections
Republicans won both the House and the Senate for the first
time since the Eisenhower period. The rout extended to
governors' mansions across the country, where the Republicans
captured the majority of governorships for the first time in a
quarter-century. Newt Gingrich, the new speaker of the House,
became the nation's political *Wunderkind*.

Yet for Clinton and Gore the Democratic defeat held its
paradoxical allure. The old-line Democratic Congressional
leadership no longer held sway on the Hill. Tom Foley and Dan
Rostenkowski had gone altogether—one back to the Inland
Empire of the Pacific Northwest and the other to a
penitentiary. The White House no longer had to dicker with
hostility to its agenda from New Deal-oriented Democrats.
Without the threat of a presidential veto to lend clout to their

resistance, the liberal Democrats on the Hill were impotent against the Republicans flourishing their Contract With America. Thus unencumbered, the administration could cut deals with the Republican leadership.

All this strategy needed was a name, and soon after the election Bill Clinton summoned in the man who would introduce "triangulation" into the lexicon of the late 1990s.

Dick Morris, a man of elastic political scruple, had enjoyed a fluctuating relationship with Clinton. He'd bailed out the young governor of Arkansas after the latter's first comeuppance at the hands of the voters, in 1980. Since then Morris had served many masters, ranging from the millionaire socialist from Ohio, Howard Metzenbaum, to Bella Abzug of New York, to Trent Lott of Mississippi ("I love his feisty, shit-on-the-shoes style") and Jesse Helms of North Carolina. Morris worked as a consultant for Helms in 1990, in a particularly foul campaign against the black Democratic challenger, Harvey Gantt.

Morris came to the White House with the purpose of providing new ideas and a new strategy. He says Clinton told him, "I've lost confidence in my current team." Morris commenced his mission of refreshment under conditions of secrecy, code-named Charlie, his function at first known only to the Clintons. His advice: steal the Republicans' thunder, draw down the deficit, reform welfare, cut back government regulation and "use Gore's reinventing government program to cut the public sector's size". Clinton should demonstrate toughness, Morris counseled, with decisive action overseas.

As the new Republican leadership took over in January of 1995, Clinton summoned Gore, disclosed the hiring of Morris and instructed the vice president to work with him. "Charlie" then laid out the new agenda for Gore. Morris later wrote, "He grasped what I was saying at once and offered his full support.... Gore told me that he had been increasingly troubled by the drift of the White House.... He said he had tried, in vain, to move the administration toward the center, but the White House staff had shut him out. He said that he had only recently heard of my involvement and did not know me at all. But, he said, 'we need a change around here, a big change, and I'm hoping and praying that you're the man to bring it.' We shook hands on our alliance."

Soon they came to two fateful decisions, one of them with some adverse consequences for Al Gore. As part of the strategy of stealing the Republicans' thunder, Morris urged an intensive fundraising drive, aimed at amassing "soft money" for TV spots designed to boost the new Clinton agenda, trump the Republicans and detour the old-line concerns of the Democrats at the other end of Pennsylvania Avenue. Soft money earns that much-abused name because it can be raised in amounts not limited by campaign spending laws; it can be procured directly from corporations, labor unions or other institutions so long as the money is used to promote "issues" rather than specific candidates. That at least is how the law supposed soft money would work. Morris knew very well that the issue ads would be identified directly with Clinton, because they would sound the themes Morris himself had prescribed. To execute these ads Morris and Gore turned to the latter's longtime media consultant, Bob Squier. Down the road lay many a funding scandal, not least the Buddhist temple imbroglio that found Al Gore on the receiving end of thousands of dollars in contributions from monks and nuns supposedly ennobled by the spiritual distinction of poverty. But such things were more than a year away.

The time had come to go public with the new line. Morris

drafted a speech for Clinton in which the president would announce that he was ready to work with the Republicans. It laid out the grounds on which the President was prepared to meet Newt Gingrich. Within the White House there was a storm of protest, led by Leon Panetta, Clinton's chief of staff and onetime California congressman, who was aghast at what he correctly perceived to be the betrayal of his former Democratic colleagues on the Hill.

As Panetta laid out his case, Clinton began to tilt toward his position. Morris saw crisis at hand. At the crucial moment, so he relates, Gore, who had been silently following the debate, made a decisive intervention. "I agree with Dick's point, that we need now to emerge from the shadows and place ourselves at the center of the debate with the Republicans by articulating what we will accept and what we will not in a clear and independent way." It was music to Morris's ears, and he cried "Bravo!" In his memoir, he added, "I began to understand how important the vice president was to the president. Gore is the single person in the world whose advice the president most values. He sees Gore as a junior president—not at the top yet, but good enough to serve when the time comes." We should note that the ever-opportunistic Morris wrote those words in 1997, knowing that it was quite possible that Gore might one day need his services. So he may be overemphasizing Gore's role. But accounts by Morris's rival, George Stephanopoulos, the man Gore had already cut down, confirm the collegial relationship between Morris and Gore, and the success of their alliance.

For Morris, as for his employer, polls were everything. He developed what he called a "neuro-psychological profile" of the American voter, and established an iron rule that no initiative could be undertaken by the White House unless polling showed that it enjoyed an approval rating of 60 percent. By constant polling he developed what he called "a values agenda". At the top of the list was affirmative action. "Mend it, don't end it" was the mantra, which meant, in practice, destroy affirmative action from the inside while professing support for the general principle. Second came tobacco. Attack the companies. Focus on the effects on children but expand exports (which of course are targeted at Asian teenagers). Third was TV violence. Intimidate the networks into adopting a "voluntary" system of ratings for TV shows and movies. Soon media executives were summoned to the White House for a session with Clinton and Gore. Simultaneously the administration pushed for installation of the so-called V chip in all new sets, which would allow parents to block offensive material. Fourth came teen pregnancy, an issue pounded on by the White House even though the rate had been falling. Education: go after tenured teachers, an attack increasingly popular in Morris's focus groups, and demand that at least they be tested. Youth: advocate school uniforms and curfews for teenagers. Gay marriage: on Morris's advice Clinton and Gore embraced the Defense of Marriage Act, a purely grandstanding piece of legislation which preemptively bars gay marriages, should any state actually sanction them (Vermont has since passed a civil union law), from recognition under federal law for any purpose. Immigration: the poll figures were off the chart, and the White House duly set a goal to double the number of turn-backs by the Immigration and Naturalization Service—among other things, enlisting the Labor Department to help speed the pace and breadth of workplace raids. Taxes: Morris thought that Main Street America was now playing the market, so that a 20 percent reduction in the capital gains tax would be hugely popular.

But there were two items that towered above the rest in Morris's assaying of public opinion: welfare and crime. In the 1992 campaign Clinton and Gore had pledged to "end welfare as we know it". They had also blustered on the issue of crime. In 1993 Gore had urged a war on welfare as part of the first 100 days and had implored Clinton to let him lead the charge. After all, Gore argued, he was one of the few Democratic senators to have supported a welfare-to-work law narrowly approved in 1988, forcing states to require parents getting welfare cheques to work at least 16 hours a week in unpaid jobs. But Hillary thought an attack on welfare would divert energy from her health package, and Gore lost the battle.

By 1995 the welfare rolls were shrinking, from a peak of 18 million in the recession of 1991 to about 12.8 million. Defenders of the system in Clinton's Cabinet, Labor Secretary Robert Reich and Donna Shalala of Health and Human Services, argued that the total budget for Aid to Families with Dependent Children was a tiny fraction of the federal budget; indeed, it was only 14 percent of the amount devoted to Medicare, a middle-class entitlement. The real problem, they argued, was lack of training for the chronically underemployed and unemployed.

Reflexively hostile to welfare and fortified by Morris's polls, Clinton, further fortified by Gore, pressed ahead. The administration began granting waivers to states to implement their own onslaughts on welfare, featuring "workfare" requirements, time limits and "family caps", a punishment to women who dared to have more than the approved number of children the government would help support. Through 1995 and early in 1996 the Republicans had passed and sent to Clinton two welfare bills. He vetoed both, stressing that he agreed with much of their content in principle. Peter Edelman, a high-level official at HHS, described this as "the squeeze play", whereby Clinton would reap approval from Democratic New Dealers for standing up for poor kids while at the same time signaling that in the long run he'd throw the mothers of those kids off the rolls altogether.

As they approached the Democratic convention in the summer of 1996, Clinton was floating on Morris's magic carpet. Assisted by staggering blunders by Gingrich and a lackluster candidate in the form of Bob Dole, Clinton was ahead by no less than 27 percent in the polls. The Republicans were eager to wrap up their legislative work before the conventions in July and August. They pushed through a welfare bill arguably worse than the ones Clinton had vetoed. Many Democrats on the Hill thought Clinton would veto this bill too. But Senator Daniel Patrick Moynihan of New York had more sensitive political antennae. He warned, "I've heard that the leaders of the Cabinet recommended a veto but that the president remains under the sway of his pollsters."

On July 30, 1996, Clinton mustered his Cabinet to hear arguments on whether or not he should sign the Republicans' bill. One by one his advisers said he should not. No's from people like Shalala and Reich came as no surprise. But similarly disapproving were not only Laura Tyson, his chief economic adviser, but Leon Panetta, Henry Cisneros of HUD and even Treasury Secretary Robert Rubin, who said that too many people would be harmed by the bill and that it would be an act of political courage to veto it.

Not trusting Shalala's department to produce objective assessments of the consequences of the bill, the White House staff had commissioned a survey from the Urban Institute, a DC think tank. The numbers were dire. The bill would push 2.6 million people further into poverty, 1.1 million of them children. In all, the institute predicted that 11 million families would lose income. That was the best-case scenario. In the event of a recession the numbers would be far worse. In that fateful Cabinet meeting Rubin invoked this study, and the numbers seemed to find their mark with the president, while Gore remained mute.

The meeting came to an end and Clinton, Panetta and Gore headed for the Oval Office. All accounts agree that, first, Panetta again made the case for a veto, laying particular emphasis on an appalling provision in the bill that would deny legal immigrants federal assistance such as food stamps. Finally Gore broke his silence and urged the president to sign.

Clinton, Morris and Gore prepared a press statement, delivered by the president that same day. Clinton admitted that the bill had "serious flaws" but went on to say, "This is the best chance we will have in a long time to complete the work of ending welfare as we know it." No one at the press conference quizzed Clinton on this curious claim. After all, the election was only about three months away. The Democrats had a chance of regaining the House. Would not that recapture afford a better chance of crafting a welfare bill not composed by Gingrich and the others?

To this day many Democrats in Congress become incensed on the topic of what Clinton and Gore did. On the eve of a Democratic convention, with Gingrich already ensconced in the national imagination as the Bad Guy, Clinton had just made common cause with him, thus undercutting all plans to campaign against the Gingrich Congress. As for Al Gore, the consensus was that he was looking ahead to a possible challenge in 2000 from his old rival Dick Gephardt. With Morris's polls showing an attack on welfare to be well over the 60 percent bar, Gore would have the advantage over Gephardt, with the latter lamely defending public entitlements.

Suspicions about Gore deepened as the fall campaign proceeded. The president and vice president argued that it was crucial that they be re-elected so that they could fix the problems with the welfare bill they had just signed. The problems here concerned not the welfare bill but the denial of federal services to legal immigrants and a slash in the food stamp program. In October, with the presidential election no longer in doubt, Democratic candidates came to the Democratic National Committee urgently seeking infusions of cash to help them in the final weeks. Finally Senator Chris Dodd of Connecticut, then the general chairman of the DNC, organized a meeting with Clinton and Gore. Dodd explained that the two were home safe and there was a chance to recapture the House. Clinton seemed amenable to a release of funds. Gore adamantly disagreed. On one account, he was the only person in the White House to oppose this transfer of funds from the presidential campaign to Congressional races. It's a measure of how a number of Democrats view Al Gore that some participants in that meeting felt the only explanation for his conduct was that he did not want the Democrats to recapture the House because victory would elevate Gephardt to the prominence of Speaker of the House.

The cynicism may not have stopped there. Why did Clinton and Gore decide to sign on to that third Republican bill? The only major difference from the previous ones came in the form of the denial of federal services to legal immigrants and a $25 billion cut in the food stamp program. It's likely that these two Republican add-ons were what allured the White House, because (as noted above) Clinton could then turn to the liberals saying they needed him to be re-elected so he could repair part of the damage wrought by the very bill he had signed. In fact the White House probably could have insisted the riders be dropped, because Dole wanted a legislative victory under the Republicans' belt.

The welfare bill that Gore steeled Clinton to sign ended the federal entitlement that had been a cornerstone of the New Deal. It caps the federal contribution to welfare programs at $14.6 billion a year and hands the money over in block grants to the states to distribute as they see fit. The main requirement is that the states agree that welfare recipients can spend no more than a total of five years in their lifetime on welfare. It allows states to adopt even harsher standards. Finally, under the old system, welfare money came to the recipient as cash. Under the new system, the money can be given to intermediaries, for possible conversion to other services such as housing or food. Al Gore particularly liked that provision. In Atlanta in May of 1999 he told an audience why: "It allows faith-based organizations to provide basic welfare services. They can do so with public funds—without having to alter the religious character that is so often the key to their effectiveness. We should extend this approach to drug treatment, homelessness and youth violence prevention. People who work in faith- and values-based organizations are driven by their spiritual commitment. They have done what government can never do: provide compassionate care. Their client is not a number but a child of God." In other words, treat welfare payments like school vouchers. How about a block grant to Jimmy Swaggart, or to Al ("Tired of Being Alone") Green's church in Memphis, where the Rev Al regularly denounces gays: "It was Adam and Eve, not Adam and Steve!"

Not long after Clinton signed the bill, judgment came from Senator Moynihan, who had begun his service to the state back in the sixties with sermons about the "pathology" of the black family and now, bizarrely, was defending the system he'd denounced for years. Even this man of all seasons and all masters was shocked: "It is a social risk no sane person would take, and I mean that. If you think things can't get worse, just wait until there are a third of a million people on the streets.... It's not welfare reform, it's welfare repeal."

Hugh Price, president of the National Urban League, called the bill "an abomination for America's most vulnerable mothers and children" and accused Clinton, Gore and the Congress of defecting from a war on poverty and "waging a war against poor people instead."

Within weeks three high-ranking officials in the Department of Health and Human Services had resigned: Mary Jo Bane, Walter Primus and Peter Edelman. That was it. Across the length and breadth of the Clinton administration, only these resignations were tendered in principle against this abandonment of the New Deal and the shafting of America's poor. Since that time Edelman has missed no opportunity to denounce the bill as a punitive strike against defenseless people. "The bill closes its eyes to all the facts and complexities of the real world and essentially says to recipients: find a job."

The edict "find a job" was central to the bill and to the mythology nourished by opponents of welfare, that freeloaders with jobs available to them were abusing the system. Of course there is always some abuse, but study after study had shown that most welfare recipients had looked for jobs and couldn't find a suitable one or had been on welfare for a limited period, then found a job and got off the rolls. In 1999 a University of Michigan study making an assessment three years after the welfare bill found that the welfare population faces "unusually high barriers to work: such as physical and mental health problems, domestic violence and lack of transportation". More than 30 percent of the families that are on welfare are constrained by disability, a sick child, no child care or an infirm relative, and those that want to find work are faced with narrow options even in an economy hyped as in mid-boom. In 1996 the Congressional Budget Office offered some bleak realities about the reserve army of the unemployed. With an official unemployment rate of 4 percent (the unofficial rate is roughly twice that, since government figures don't count frustrated people who have given up looking for work), there are still three to five people needing work for each available job. In times of recession this ratio rises to more than ten to one.

In urban areas the job market is even more constrained. A 1998 study in Harlem showed just how brutally competitive the low-wage job market is. Over a five-month period, an average of fourteen people applied for each job opening at a local McDonalds. A year later researchers from the University of Chicago found that 73 percent of those same job searchers still hadn't found work.

In many states, there's the last resort of workfare, which compels welfare recipients to accept public jobs, such as highway clean-up or garbage picking with the Parks Department, in return for benefits. Some states and localities call this job training. Nationally the average benefit for workfare jobs is $381 a month, which works out to $4.40 an hour, or 80 percent of the minimum wage. But in some places it's much worse. Mississippi, for example, requires single parents to work twenty hours a week at $1.38 an hour, and a two-parent household to work fifty-five hours at 50 cents an hour.

On top of this the people in the workfare labor force are denied such basic rights as collective bargaining, unemployment insurance, the earned income tax credit and Social Security credit. States are finding it to their budgetary advantage to fill job vacancies with these "slavefare" workers. A Senate study in 1996 estimated that this consequence of welfare reform would depress the wages of the working poor by 12 percent.

Allowing the states to freelance their welfare programs has resulted in some particularly cruel policies and inequities. Minnesota spends $50 million a year on child care for single mothers receiving welfare benefits who are working or looking for work. New York spends $54 million, to serve a population six times as large. Gore has repeatedly touted Indiana because its welfare program was initiated and implemented by a Democratic governor, Evan Bayh, and his successor in the governor's mansion, Frank O'Bannon. The pair has presided over the shrinking of Indiana's welfare rolls by 30 percent. There's no way to know if those people actually found work. It's possible that the conditions of supervision of welfare recipients simply became unbearable and they left the program and perhaps the state. Under Indiana's scheme, one missed job-training course means the loss of a welfare check for two months. A second infraction means the loss of benefits for a year. A third strike and you're out.

The welfare reform bill includes a provision that allows states to begin drug-testing welfare recipients. In theory the provision was aimed at people suspected of having drug problems. Oregon initiated a testing policy but soon reversed course when recipients began dropping out of the welfare program in order to avoid testing. The state found it was better to stop drug testing, keep people in the program and steer addicts into treatment. Michigan took a different approach. In 1999 the state adopted a mandatory drug-testing policy for all welfare recipients, which prompted a lawsuit brought by the ACLU. A federal judge ruled in 1999 that the policy was unconstitutional. He noted that in the five weeks of the program's operation there were positive drug tests in only 8 percent of the cases, and all but three of those were for marijuana.

In the first half of 2000, Gore campaigned with a call for Welfare Reform II, saying that more remained to be done to weed out cheats and freeloaders. He was particularly vehement in attacking dads behind on child support, saying that he will make it easier for credit card companies to deny credit to such fathers. This would come on top of a program, initiated by Janet Reno in her Florida years, whereby fathers behind on their payments get their drivers' license lifted, meaning that they can't go to work. In 1995, Clinton, Gore and Morris put into operation a program that saw these fathers' mug shots up in post offices, their federal benefits garnished and the IRS on their tail. This pattern of inflicting administrative conviction outside the court system and due process is integral to Gore's philosophy on crime.

The crime bill of 1994 introduced mandatory life imprisonment for persons convicted of a third felony in certain categories. It maintained the 100-to-1 disproportion in sentencing for crimes involving powder and crack cocaine, even though the US Sentencing Commission had concluded that this disparity—i.e., someone caught with crack getting a penalty far, far harsher as that of someone caught with powder(—is racist. It expanded to fifty the number of crimes that could draw the death penalty in a federal court, reaching to crimes not including murder—the broadest expansion of the federal death penalty in history. Pell grants giving prisoners an avenue to higher education were cut off. Federal judges were stripped of their powers to enforce the constitutional rights of prisoners, and the power of states to set sentencing standards for drug crimes was diminished.

This curtailment of states' rights went further. Grants for new prisons contained the provision that receipt of the money was dependent on the states ensuring that prisoners served at least 85 percent of their sentences. These inmates, remember, had been convicted in state, not federal courts, so this was simply federal blackmail to curtail parole at the state level. The Clinton Administration also pressed the states to try juvenile offenders as adults. Gore articulated the administration's position: "When young people cross the line, they must be punished. When young people commit serious, violent crimes, they should be prosecuted like adults." Nonviolent offenders were to be sent to boot camps. Not, it should be noted, his own kids, who evaded punishment for nonviolent infractions such as smoking marijuana and having an open alcohol container in the car.

Gore was particularly assiduous in his assaults on the Fourth Amendment, protecting citizens against unreasonable searches and seizures. In 1994 he successfully pressed for a bill requiring all communications providers to make existing and future communication systems wire-tap ready. He also pushed hard for the so-called clipper chip, an encryption device that makes it easy for law enforcement and intelligence agencies to snoop on private messages.

The high-water mark in the Clinton Administration's attack on the Bill of Rights came in 1996, with the Counter-Terrorism and Effective Death Penalty Act, which among other horrors allowed the INS to deport immigrants without due process, and denied prisoners appeals to the federal bench based on *habeas corpus* petitions. "When historians write the story of civil liberties in the twentieth century", said Ira Glasser, head of the ACLU, "they will say that the Clinton Administration adopted an agenda that has everything to do with weakening civil rights and nothing to do with combating terrorism."

In May of 2000, Gore outlined his campaign posture on crime and drugs in another speech in Atlanta. The erstwhile dope smoker from Tennessee evidently feared that the man who refused to discuss cocaine use in his early years, George W. Bush, had the edge on the crime issue. Gore proclaimed he wanted to swaddle communities "in a blanket of blue". He swore that the minute he settled into the Oval Office, President Gore would call for 50,000 more cops (i.e., more half-trained recruits like the ones who shot Amadou Diallo forty-one times in the Bronx) and would allow off-duty cops to carry concealed weapons (which they almost all do anyway).

Gore promised prisoners "a simple deal: before you get out of jail you have to get clean. If you want to stay out, then you better stay clean. We have to stop that revolving door once and for all. First we have to test prisoners for drugs while they're in jail." Gore was so blithe in his disregard for elementary rights that he was unable to see a distinction between a prison sentence fully served and a further punitive add-on: "We have to insist on more prison time for those who don't break the habit." Even after prisoners are released the eye of the state would still follow them: "We should impose strict supervision on those who have just been released—and insist they obey the law and stay off drugs."

Another feature of Al Gore's prospective war on crime was the especially vigorous targeting of minority youth: "I will fight for a federal law that helps communities establish gang-free zones with curfews on specific gang members, a ban on gang-related clothing and the specific legal authority to break violent teen gangs once and for all."

By 2000 the US prison population had reached 2 million, with no sign of slowing. Yet public opinion has been shifting both on the death penalty and on the War on Drugs. A sizable chunk of the population believes there are some serious flaws in the justice system. In January, 2000, the Republican governor of Illinois, a supporter of capital punishment, suspended the death penalty in his state because he no longer thought it could be fairly administered. In the late 1990s New York and Los Angeles were in uproar over racist, trigger-happy and corrupt cops.

The federal agents' armed snatch of Elian Gonzalez from his relatives' home in Miami's Little Havana prompted cries of outrage from lawmakers who had glibly signed on to the repressive Clinton-Gore anti-crime measures. They now were denouncing the Jackboot State, alerting mainstream America to the fact that the Bill of Rights has disappeared, restrictions on the role of the military in domestic affairs have been thrown overboard, and all the appurtenances of a police state have been put in place. Upon the removal of Elian, House Speaker Dennis Hastert proclaimed sternly, "Our government has invaded the home of American citizens who deserve the protection of our laws and a certain respect for their rights." (In a foolish spasm of opportunism, Gore sided with the Miami relatives in the Elian case, then doubled back after the raid, as he saw poll numbers climb in favor of Elian's return to his father.)

For blacks and hispanics the reactions of some pundits and politicians (Chris Matthews expended his usual lung-power on the topic) to that famous photograph of Elian face-to-face with the gun of a federal agent was comic in a macabre sort of way. They had been putting up with these no-knock forcible entries by heavily armed cops or INS agents for decades. On the far right, fears about the onrush of tyranny had hardened into certainty back at the time of Waco.

The week before the Elian raid, the left saw the state in action against their demonstrations in Washington DC against the World Bank and the International Monetary Fund. Here's how Sam Smith, longtime Washington reporter and editor of *The Progressive Review*, evoked the events unfolding in the capital in April: "Illegal sweep arrests. Print shops intimidated into closing by police. Universities canceling public forums under pressure from officials. Homes of opposition leaders broken into and ransacked. Headquarters of the opposition raided and closed by police. These were the sort of things by which we defined the evil of the old Soviet Union. And now they have become characteristics of the federal government's handling of the current protests."

In Washington, as in Seattle during the protests against the World Trade Organization, the treatment of arrested people made for hair-raising reading, with random beatings, denials of food and water for twenty-four hours, racial abuse, threats of rape, refusals to allow consultations with attorneys. As in the 1960s white middle-class demonstrators (and their parents) are learning what happens to poor people all the time. Mainstream politicians were not a whit perturbed by police conduct in Seattle or Washington DC.

Both parties have eagerly conjoined in militarizing the police, extending police powers and carving away basic rights. Often the Democrats have been worse. It was Republican Representative Henry Hyde of Illinois who led the partially successful charge in 1999 against the seizure of assets in drug cases. It was Democratic Senator Charles Schumer of New York who was the factotum of the Justice Department in trying to head off Hyde and his coalition.

The rise of the Jackboot State has marched in lockstep with the insane and ineffective War on Drugs, and this has been a bipartisan affair. Its consequences are etched into the fabric of our lives. Just think of drug testing, now a virtually mandatory condition of employment, even though it's an outrageous violation of personal sovereignty, as well as being thoroughly unreliable. In an era in which America has been led by two self-confessed pot smokers—Clinton and Gore—the number of people held for drug crimes in federal prisons has increased by 64 percent.

No-knock raids are becoming more common as federal, state and local politicians and law enforcement agencies decide that the war on drugs justified dumping the Fourth Amendment. Even in states where search warrants require a knock on the door before entry, police routinely flout the requirement.

The Posse Comitatus Act forbidding military involvement in domestic law enforcement is rapidly becoming as dead as the Fourth Amendment. Because of drug war exceptions created in that act, every region of the United States now has a Joint Task Force staff in charge of coordinating military involvement in domestic law enforcement.

In many cases, street deployment of paramilitary units is funded by "community policing" grants from the federal government. The majority of police departments use their paramilitary units to serve "dynamic entry" search warrants. The SWAT Team in Chapel Hill, North Carolina, conducted a large-scale crack raid of an entire block in a predominantly African-American neighborhood. The raid, termed Operation

Redi-Rock, resulted in the detention and search of up to 100 people, all of whom were black. (Whites were allowed to leave the area.) No one was ever prosecuted for a crime. In Albany, New York, not long before the change-of-venue trial there of the four white cops who had killed Amadou Diallo in the Bronx, police in camouflage uniforms went on a ransacking spree in the black neighborhood of Arbor Hill, beating down doors house to house in search of a black suspect.

Right now the swelling Jackboot State is an expression of the War on Drugs. No politician who does not call for a ceasefire and a rollback in that cruel, futile war—our domestic Vietnam—has any standing to bewail the loss of our freedoms. There are signs of popular mutiny. In 2000 the ACLU and the National Rifle Association jointly called for President Clinton to appoint a commission to investigate lawlessness in law enforcement. States with democratic processes such as ballot initiatives have seen brave efforts to curb the drug war. Meanwhile, Al Gore has consistently called for a widening of police powers, an intensification of that war, a whittling away of the Bill of Rights.

Where there is no social program, there's always a violence program. For the Clinton-Gore Administration welfare reform and expansion of the police state were not only means to trump the Republicans; they were also essential to economic policy. Intense competition for jobs at the lowest rungs would depress wages, pit poor and working-class people against each other, and, where workfare recipients displace municipal workers, weaken unions. The spectre and reality of incarceration would have the traditional effect of suppressing the dangerous classes, at a time when the gap between rich and poor grew wider than at any time in recent history. A side benefit would be that all those prisoners would brighten the statistical profile of Clintonomics, since they aren't figured into unemployment rates.

Gore's Campaign 2000 continued to prescribe the medicine of Clinton time, while advancing its candidate as co-author of the policies that had supposedly worked wonders of prosperity for the majority over the past eight years. In *New Left Review* for May/June 2000, Robert Pollin, an economist at the University of Massachusetts, Amherst, published an "Anatomy of Clintonomics", and it did not offer much comfort to those trying to run the "lesser of two evils" flag up the pole one more time.

Pollin concluded his survey thus: "The core of Clinton's economic program has been global economic integration, with minimum interventions to promote equity in labor markets or stability in financial markets. Gestures to the least well-off have been slight and back-handed, while wages for the majority have either stagnated or declined. Wealth at the top, meanwhile, has exploded. But a stratospheric rise in stock prices and a debt-financed consumption spree make for a mortgaged legacy. Clinton will hand over to his successor the most precarious financial pyramid of the post-war epoch."

Pollin detailed the record. "Clinton has done virtually nothing to advance the interests of working people or organized labor." What about the two-step rise in the minimum wage? Answer: the overall rise from $4.25 to the current $5.15, set in September 1997, has done little to offset the plunge in the real value of the minimum wage. By Pollin's calculations, that $5.15 is 30 percent below its real value in 1968, even though the economy has become 50 percent more productive across that thirty years.

How about antipovery programs? Pollin looked at all the claims made by the administration for the glories of the earned income tax credit, offset those against the destruction of Aid to Families with Dependent Children, (now known as Temporary Assistance for Needy Families), factored in the decline in the number of people getting food stamps (five times greater than the decline in the number of people in poverty) and spelled out the conclusion: the combination of a low minimum wage and a widening of the earned income tax credit "have allowed business to offer rock-bottom wages, while shifting onto tax payers the cost of alleviating the poverty of even those holding full-time jobs".

Nor could it be said that, under Clinton-Gore, organized labor enjoyed much of a renaissance. In 1988, Reagan's last year, the percentage of the total workforce in unions stood at 16.8. In 1998 it had fallen to 13.9. It has since risen but not to anywhere near its rate during the union-busting days under Reagan. Despite Gore's avowed concern for labor rights, workers have not had an easier time forming unions, winning certification elections, negotiating first contracts or striking under Clinton-Gore; nor have employers had a harder time decertifying unions.

In terms of compensation, both the average wages of non-supervisory workers and the earnings of those in the lowest tenth on the wage distribution scale remain, according to Pollin, well below those of the Nixon-Ford and Carter administrations and are also lower than those of the Reagan-Bush years. Wage inequalities have also shot up. "If low rates of unemployment have been a positive feature of the 1990s", Pollin wrote, "it is still quite possible that the overall condition of the poor will prove to have worsened in Clinton's final years of office."

13 "THE PRICE IS WORTH IT"

Gore sets Iraq policy, kills Iraq's leading artist. The deadly consequences of sanctions assessed. Gore as exponent of liberal interventionism. The laptop bombardiers. He pushes for military intervention in the Balkans. "We see through your veil of evil and will stop it." Human rights organizations charge war crimes. Gore and Chernomyrdin objectively compared. Gore promises all to Pentagon.

In the 1992 presidential campaign Gore had been told to tone down environmental issues and earn his keep with constant pummeling of Bush for having been soft on Saddam. Gore duly criss-crossed the country yoking Saddam and Bush in fervid denunciation, his press aides passing out speeches flatteringly footnoted with references to the work of the journalists covering his campaign. Gore charged that Bush had given Saddam "one of those milquetoast routines George Bush is so famous for". "The cover-up of Bush's arming of Saddam was", he shouted, "bigger than Watergate ever was." Right before the election he called for expansion of the no-fly zones in Iraq and said that any Iraqi plane venturing into such zones should be shot down.

Victory for the Democratic ticket brought Gore to the heart of US foreign policy making. Clinton had never served his apprenticeship in the US national security establishment, and he had spent the campaign on the defensive, trying to dance around the draft issue. Clinton had not even been inaugurated before Gore was able to grab an opportunity to cement his position. Thomas Friedman, a self-important columnist employed by *The New York Times*, interviewed Clinton in early January and, on the topic of Saddam, elicited this relaxed sentiment from the president-elect: "I always tell everybody, 'I'm a Baptist. I believe in deathbed conversions.' If he wants a different relationship with the US and the UN, all he has to do is change his behavior."

There was an immediate hubbub in the national security establishment, and Gore made haste to reformulate the position of the incoming administration. The "deathbed conversion" was tossed in the trash, as Gore announced that there could never be normal relations with Iraq so long as Saddam remained in power. He reiterated the call for a coup, if not by the Iraqi military then by the CIA (which in point of fact had a "presidential finding" from Bush, three months after the guns of the Gulf War fell silent, authorizing it "to create the conditions for the removal of Saddam Hussein from power").

From that moment on, the vice president was given authority within the Clinton administration on Iraq policy. "The Iraq issue is a natural one for Gore to do," said Roy Neel, Gore's former chief of staff. "He knows it. He had credibility on it because of his background and expertise and because he voted with Bush on the Gulf war. Clinton is perfectly comfortable to let Gore exploit this issue on his own."

Gore was eager for a chance to flex muscle against Saddam and his devastated country. Opportunity soon came. On April 14, 1993, George Bush embarked on a private trip to Kuwait City. In the course of this excursion Kuwaiti officials arrested seventeen people and charged them with plotting to kill Bush with a bomb that had been placed inside a Toyota Landcruiser. Despite ongoing probes by the CIA and FBI, Gore

211

made haste to assign Leon Fuerth to make his own inquiries
into whether the bomb could be linked to Saddam Hussein.

In early June there was said to be unanimity among the
investigators that Saddam Hussein should be held accountable.
Later it emerged that the FBI's Fred Whitehurst had deemed
the evidence inconclusive, but his reservations were concealed
by his superiors, who were excited to subscribe to the plan,
hotly advocated by Gore, to bombard Baghdad. The two
individuals most reluctant to endorse this plan were Bill
Clinton and George Bush. "Do we have to take this action?"
Clinton muttered to his national security team, as the cruise
missiles on two carriers in the Persian Gulf were being
programmed. His reservations were amply justified. Eight of
the twenty-three missiles homed in with deadly imprecision on
a residential suburb in Baghdad, one of them killing Iraq's
leading artist, Leila al-Attar. Feasting on shrimp, cocktail
canapés and diet Coke, the White House group watched CNN's
Wolf Blitzer announce the strike; the misfortune of the errant
missiles and al-Attar's death were never mentioned. First blood
for the Gore policy.

Clinton's pollster Stan Greenberg, who did daily surveys
on the popular sentiment, reported to the gratified
Commander-in-Chief that bombardment of Iraq caused an
uptick of eleven points. Since the Clinton Administration was
at that time in the process of its first meltdown, this was a
welcome ray, and one not forgotten. Four years later cruise
missiles once again, but far more profusely, descended on
Baghdad and other major cities, where the targets were
supposedly Saddam Hussein's palaces. And once again Gore
had been an instigator of the strikes, deemed essential to
avenge the US for the slight of having UN inspectors denied
access to those palaces. Initially, Clinton had been reluctant to

order the strikes, and in November of 1998 his reservations prevailed. But by December, Gore was even more insistent, and Clinton had ample reason not to press his objections, since the raids shortly preceded the vote on his impeachment by the House of Representatives.

But these cruise attacks were pinpricks compared with the frightful human toll of the sanctions. Back in 1996, when the number of Iraqi children killed off by sanctions stood at around half a million, Secretary of State Madeleine Albright made her infamous declaration to Lesley Stahl on CBS: "We think the price is worth it."

The White House viewed the truth about the sanctions policy with the same insouciance as Albright regarded the lives of Iraqi children. UN officials working in Baghdad agreed that the root cause of child mortality and other health problems was no longer simply lack of food and medicine but the lack of clean water (freely available in all parts of the country prior to the Gulf War) and of electrical power, now running at 30 percent of its pre-bombing level, with consequences for hospitals and water-pumping systems that can be all too readily imagined. Of the 21.9 percent of contracts vetoed as of mid-1999 by the UN's US-dominated sanctions committee, a high proportion were integral to the efforts to repair the water and sewage systems. The Iraqis submitted contracts worth $236 million in this area, of which $54 million worth—roughly one-quarter of the total value—have been disapproved. "Basically, anything with chemicals or even pumps is liable to get thrown out", one UN official revealed. The same trend was apparent in the power supply sector, where around 25 percent of the contracts were on hold—$138 million worth, out of $589 million submitted. The proportion of approved/disapproved contracts does not tell the full story. UN officials refer to the "complementarity issue",

213

meaning that items approved for purchase may be useless without other items that have been disapproved. For example, the Iraqi Ministry of Health has ordered $25 million worth of dentist chairs, said order being approved by the sanctions committee—except for the compressors, without which the chairs are useless and consequently gathering dust in a Baghdad warehouse.

In February of 2000 the US moved to prevent Iraq from importing fifteen bulls from France. The excuse was that the animals, ordered with the blessing of the UN's humanitarian office in Baghdad to try to restock the Iraqi beef industry, would require certain vaccines which, who knows, might be diverted into a program to make biological weapons of mass destruction. For sheer bloody-mindedness, however, the interdiction of the bulls pales beside an initiative of the British government, which banned the export of vaccines for tetanus, diphtheria and yellow fever on the grounds that they too might find their way into the hands of Saddam's biological weaponeers. It has been the self-exculpatory mantra of US and British officials that "food and medicine are exempt from sanctions". This, like so many other Western policy pronouncements on Iraq, turns out to be a lie.

The sanctions policy has always been marked by acts of captious cruelty. A partial review, courtesy of the Mariam Appeal in London:

- December 12, 1991. US vetoes a request by Bulgaria to ship baby food to Iraq, on the grounds that it might be consumed by adults.
- February 6, 1992. Ping pong balls from Vietnam are vetoed by US, UK, France and Japan.
- March 1992. UN sanctions committee blocks a Dutch request to supply children's hospitals with NCR

computers, essential equipment for specific hematology and hepatitis studies.

- April 26, 1992. Water purification chemicals are vetoed by US and UK.
- June 1992. Committee's US representative blocks a Danish request to ship heaters to children's hospitals, on the grounds that they might be used elsewhere.
- June 1992. UK vetoes an application by the United Nations Food and Agriculture Organization (FAO) to supply 300 tons of insecticide to Iraq, on the grounds that they might be used for other purposes.
- June 1992. Spanish consortium's application to help rebuild a medical syringe factory (bombed in the war) is vetoed by UK and France.
- August 4, 1992. Children's bicycles are vetoed by US and UK.
- October 29, 1992. Boxes of nail polish and lipsticks are vetoed by UK.
- April 3, 1993. Tennis balls, children's clothes, adult clothes, pencil sharpeners, erasers and school notebooks from Pakistan are vetoed by US, UK, France and Japan.
- July 24, 1993. Cotton for medical use (swabs, gauze, etc.) is vetoed by UK.
- August 14, 1993. Japan's application to supply communication equipment for hospital links (i.e., pagers, hospital-ambulance radios) is vetoed by US and UK.
- September 17, 1993. Shroud material is vetoed by US and UK. UK later relents but with stipulations. Export license is revoked under new UK regulations. Application process has to begin all over again.

Al Gore has always worked by simple recipes. In June of Campaign 2000, he publicly distanced himself from the president on Iraq policy, reiterating that Saddam has to fall, and pledging support to an exile group called the Iraqi National Congress (INC), led by Ahmad Chalabi. In the late 1990s Chalabi's cause was pressed by Republicans in Congress, most notably Jesse Helms and Trent Lott, and by that baleful schemer and hero of Israel's ultra-rejectionists, Richard Perle. A bizarre alliance, stretching from Helms to Perle and *The New Republic* to *Vanity Fair*'s Christopher Hitchens, pressed Chalabi's call for the US to guarantee "military exclusion zones" in northern Iraq and in the south near Basra and the oil fields, to be administered by the Iraqi National Congress. In 1998, Clinton reluctantly authorized an appropriation of $97 million from the Pentagon budget to go to Chalabi's group. But as a consequence of a fierce CIA attack on Chalabi's credentials and prowess, only $84,000 was actually released, and that merely to pay for offices and some training in public relations.

So Gore's stance on the INC in early summer 2000 was clearly preemptive groundwork for a fall campaign indicting the Bush family for being soft on Saddam and ratcheting up the possibility of another military strike against Iraq. He announced that he had differed with Clinton's refusal to release $97 million in military aid to the Iraqi opposition. These posturings remain precisely that, for the simple reason that any serious plan for full-scale war to topple Saddam would involve (a) the cooperation of Saudi Arabia, and (b) a warm-up of relations with Iran, neither of which contingencies are in the least likely.

The most gallant group denouncing the horrible consequences of sanctions against Iraq has been Voices in the Wilderness, based in Chicago. On June 29, 2000 news came to them that Al Gore was visiting Chicago to talk about "energy policy incentives for cities." Let Danny Muller take up the story:

"Kathy [Kelly] and I decided that we could not pass up this oppportunity, to at least be a presence near his speech, so I ditched her with all the mundane office tasks and last minute details and headed to Navy Pier. I entered Navy Pier, went to the Rooftop Terrace and showed my ID, which was all they asked for. I later found out it was by invitation only, supposedly, but they were letting anyone walk in who showed an ID. I passed through metal detection and made my way to the roof amidst a sea of ardent Gorettes and carefully placed Secret Service. The rooftop was filled with approximately 150 Gore supporters, Chicago's Mayor Daley, and every major media outlet.

"As Gore stepped out to a standing ovation, with a stammering introduction from the Mayor, 'These Are Days', blasted throughout the sound system. I had come not to hear the issues Gore was saying were important, but to ask him a question relating to an issue that is in the hearts and minds of 24 million people taken siege by sanctions. This question also weighs heavily on my heart and mind, since I recently returned from Iraq and witnessed the carnage so cavalierly bestowed upon the Iraqis by the US government.

"As Mr. Gore began to speak about how much 'me and Tipper love the Windy City,' I raised my voice and asked 'Mr. Gore, why should anyone vote for an administration that kills five thousand innocent children a month through sanctions in Iraq?' He stopped. And he laughed. He actually laughed. He said he would discuss this later in the day. I responded by saying that every ten minutes a child dies in Iraq due to sanctions and we do not have the time to wait. I told him that we need to stop giving military aid to the Middle East, which works to divide and destabilize, and that the billions wasted on bombing missions and sanctions could benefit the American people. I was also able to spout off the names of Denis Halliday, Hans Von Sponeck, and Jutta Burghardt as UN officials who protested the sanctions before I was removed.

"Mr. Gore did not answer my question directly, but many people expressed support, even the sticker-wearing Gore fans. I think of the song blaring while Gore walked to the podium as I think of what occurred this afternoon. I am more certain that at least one message from the afternoon is crystal clear. That 'These Are Days.' These are days to stand up and demand an end to bombing and to sanctions. These are days you'll remember. These days are ours if we take them in the spirit of nonviolence and love that conquers even the strongest hate."

For a vice president, Gore had virtually unprecedented influence in the formation of foreign policy, and not only with respect to Iraq. He exercised that influence both in his assiduous promotion of his own team and in his one-on-one lobbying of the president. As regards his own people, Gore made sure that Leon Fuerth was inside every loop. Fuerth was, as noted, on the so-called Principals' Committee of top foreign policy advisers to the White House. Anthony Lake, Clinton's first national security adviser, once described Fuerth's demeanor on this committee, saying Fuerth would articulate his "contrarian point of view" at great length, which would evoke the "spasmodic displeasure of the other principals", this point of view being almost invariably a hawkish one. Aside from Fuerth there was Woolsey, successfully touted by Gore as CIA director, replaced in turn by another Gore man, John Deutch of MIT. Back in the early 1980s Deutch had conducted a study on Midgetman. Gore's favorite for secretary of defense, Les Aspin, had made the cut, and when Aspin was later evicted from that position, yet another Gore ally, William Perry, took over.

These men shared a propensity for what became the keynote of foreign policy throughout two terms of the Clinton Administration: liberal interventionism. It was on display in Bosnia, in Somalia, in Haiti, against Iraq and against Serbia. And the commander in chief of these laptop bombardiers was Al Gore.

This is not to exculpate Bill Clinton from responsibility for the foreign policy adventures conducted in his terms. But with Clinton the essential calculus was of political expediency, expressed in terms of encouraging polls and an outmaneuvering of the Republicans in Congress — as witness his most cynically murderous actions, the bombings of Sudan and Afghanistan, and, once again, on the very cusp of the Senate's impeachment vote, Iraq. In essential outlook, however, Clinton lacked that edge of evangelical savagery that has characterized Gore and advisers such as Peretz and Fuerth in assessing the projection of American power and moral self-righteousness overseas.

Gore was still fresh from the cheers of the Democratic Party convention in New York in 1992 when he first began pressing the presidential nominee into calling for military intervention in the Balkans. He cornered Clinton on the campaign trail in St. Louis and lectured him on the evils of Slobodan Milosevic. He urged Clinton to pledge that the next Democratic administration would be far tougher on the Serbs. He also argued for lifting the arms embargo in the region.

Gore kept up this bellicose barrage after the election, but ran into the reservations of the head of the Joint Chiefs of Staff,

Gen. Colin Powell, whose basic position was the reasonable one: why get involved in a messy European affair? All the interminable rantings in *The New Republic* against the UN (loathed by Peretz for its resolutions on Israel, the Palestinians and also the illegal occupation of Lebanon) found their echo in Gore's fulminations about the spinelessness of the UN presence in the Balkans, "the self-delusional" nature of the Europeans and the need to make NATO the supervising force in the region.

By 1995, Clinton was beginning to wear thin from the sermons by Gore and the public clamor of liberal columnists, the laptop bombardiers, led by an entirely hysterical Anthony Lewis of *The New York Times*. Stephanopoulos reports Clinton fuming to him, "Lewis has to accept the fact that he's been against every American intervention for thirty years, and now he's the biggest hawk in the world. What would they have me do? What the fuck would they have me do?" Just as Clinton was ingesting Lewis's latest broadside, Gore would belabor him with news of how his daughter Karenna had read a news story about atrocities at Srebrenica and asked why the US wasn't doing something.

Now, the Serb atrocities at Srebrenica were later mirrored on a much larger scale by the Croatian atrocities against Serbs in the Krajina. There the US position was scarcely one of moral alertness but the consummately cynical one of sponsoring what was demurely described as "population exchange" or, as Secretary of State Warren Christopher put it, "simplifying matters". As it turns out, it was the single biggest ethnic clearance of the war, as hundreds of thousands of Serbs were evicted from their ancestral homes. As Croatia's fascist leader Franjo Tudjman roared hoarsely for his cleansers in the Croatian forces to drive out the Serbs, these same forces were being advised by US military and intelligence officers, with US ambassador to Zagreb, James Galbraith, supervising operations.

Gore's outrage at what he termed "genocide" in Bosnia was entirely selective. Himself an ardent laptop bombardier, *The Washington Post*'s Bob Woodward described the following scene on July 18, 1995. Woodward is reconstructing Gore's words to Clinton: "The worst solution would be to acquiesce to genocide and allow the rape of another city and more refugees. At the same time we can't be driven by images because there's plenty of other places that aren't being photographed where terrible things are going on. But we can't ignore images either."

Gore then flourished a photograph of a young Bosnian woman who had hanged herself. "My 21-year-old daughter asked about that picture. What am I supposed to tell her? Why is this happening and we're not doing anything? My daughter is surprised the world is allowing this to happen. I am too.... The cost of this is going to cascade over several decades. It goes to what kind of people we are. Acquiescence is the worst alternative.... We have to come up with something practical to make military sense. Acquiescence is not an option."

Thus admonished by his vice president, Clinton cast the die. Again according to Woodward, he said, "The situation underscores the need for robust air power being authorized. The United States can't be a punching bag in the world anymore." It was a classic instance of Gore's modus operandi. As Bill Richardson—one of Gore's intimates, US ambassador to the UN after Madeleine Albright, and secretary of energy in Clinton's second term—put it for *Time* magazine in 2000: "Gore comes in at the end, summarizes, moves the president his way."

Gore similarly advanced the cause of NATO's 1999 war against Serbia, and there the terrible consequences of liberal interventionism are even more glaring. Since the completion of that mission to end ethnic discrimination by Serbs against Albanians, we have seen wholesale slaughter and eviction of Serbs; we have seen a replay of Iraq in the destruction of Serbia's economic infrastructure. Power plants, factories, oil refineries, bridges, hospitals, schools, churches, national shrines and monuments were all blown to smithereens, with little impact on the Serbian military, which lost a few vintage tanks and emerged from the supposedly lethal barrage in very good shape.

The war on Serbia was just the sort of conflict Al Gore espouses. Plenty of high-sounding proclamations of moral intent; delirious invocations of techno-whizardry and credulity in the technical capacity of missiles and weapons; callous indifference to civilian suffering.

Assiduous polling by Dick Morris in 1996 had told the White House that the American people remained adamantly opposed to foreign interventions. But Morris also reported that when the words "humanitarian" and "moral imperative" were introduced as verbal adornments for adventures overseas, the numbers changed markedly. Yet even when aglow with the thought of merciful missions to beleaguered peoples, Americans still didn't like the idea of their boys and girls being committed in a ground mission. To soften public oppostion, it was also essential to demonize the foe. From this formula was engendered nineties-style humanitarian intervention, with human rights organizations dutifully playing their role, and Slobodan Milosevic joining the imperial bestiary, wherein, in our time, have been lodged Fidel Castro, Muammar Qaddafi, Saddam Hussein and Kim Il Sung.

In the early days of the US intervention in the Balkans, Richard Holbrooke was strongly touted by Gore as the appropriate US emissary on the ground. Holbrooke, ambitious and obsessed with publicity, headed off to the region and soon relayed the message that "we've got to bomb the Bosnian Serbs". Bomb they did, and the long-term consequence was the speedy recourse to bombing in the Kosovo conflict four years later. There the essential features of humanitarian intervention were brought to deadly refinement, with NATO bombardiers flying safely at 30,000 feet, dropping high explosives on "strategic infrastructure".

Historians of wars and propaganda will probably consider at length the Serbian-Kosovo conflict as a textbook example of the manipulation of public opinion by an administration and willing accomplices in the press. Even at the time, most of the claims were transparently specious, and retrospective research has confirmed such suspicions a thousandfold. Was there really a genocide of Albanian Kosovars by the Serbs? Clinton talked of 600,000 missing, presumed slaughtered. Other, slightly more restrained estimates, offered figures between 10,000 and 25,000 before NATO began its bombing, on March 24, 1998. By mid-2000 the estimate, secured after months of investigation and interviewing by the International Red Cross and by teams of investigators from the FBI and other groups, was that there were a total of 3,300 people from Kosovo unaccounted for since the beginning of 1998, including Albanians and Serbs combined. Of those, 2,200 were Albanians put into Serbian prisons during the period commencing in 1998, when Serbia was trying to suppress the Albanian independence movement headed by the KLA.; 370 Serbs were kidnapped and presumed murdered by the KLA, leaving 930 whose fate has not been determined. As a consequence of NATO's bombing, somewhere between 1000 and 1,500 Serb civilians died directly, and thousands more—many of them children—have suffered premature deaths from disease and lowered immunity from wretched conditions in Serbia after the bombing.

Amnesty International, which had been a vocal proponent of intervention in Kosovo, concluded that NATO's bombing raids violated the Geneva Conventions by targeting civilians. An Amnesty report cited a NATO attack on a bridge at Varvarin on May 30, where eleven civilians were killed. According to Amnesty, "NATO forces failed to suspend their attack after it was evident that they had struck civilians." The report also cited the destruction of a hospital and the April 23 bombing of a Serb TV HQ: "General Wesley Clark has stated, 'we knew when we struck that there would be alternate means of getting Serb television. There's no single switch to turn off everything but we thought it was a good move to strike it, and the political leadership agreed with us.' In other words, NATO deliberately attacked a civilian object, killing sixteen citizens, for the purpose of disrupting Serb television broadcasts in the middle of the night for approximately three hours. It is hard to see how this can be consistent with the rule of proportionality."

By the third week in April the White House was becoming increasingly distraught about the progress of the war. Opinion polls were below what Morris regarded as the sine qua non—60 percent support. The Serbs remained defiant, and even *The New York Times* and *Los Angeles Times* were beginning to run detailed articles about the civilian toll. Stories of divisions in NATO were also beginning to surface. At this juncture, on April 21, Gore went to Ellis Island to deliver a speech on the fiftieth anniversary of NATO.

There had been some speculation in the press that the war might not necessarily benefit his chances of succeeding Clinton, and that it would be wise for the vice president to yield the rostrum to Secretary of State Albright or Gen. Wesley

Clark, the demented supremo of NATO's forces. But it tells us something about Gore's disposition that he used the opportunity to make what remains the most belligerent, hyperbolic speech defending NATO's war.

"Some will say", Gore cried, "that because we cannot help people everywhere, we should help people nowhere. I believe that is wrong. We should work toward the day when there will be both the moral alertness and the political will on every continent to respond to human suffering. But this much is clear: in Europe today we see the need to act. Thanks to NATO we have the means to do it. Slobodan Milosevic is one person standing in the way. Ethnic cleansing is a phrase intended to mask the stench of its true meaning: the combination of mass murder and mass-expulsion. Ethnic cleansing means that a dictator can simply throw away the people he does not need like so much dirt and disease. It dehumanizes along ethnic lines so that murder and displacement become scientific, antiseptic, something other than atrocity. So I say to Milosevic: we are not fooled by your hateful rhetoric. We see though your veil of evil and we will stop it."

Just as Gore offered the administration's fiercest rhetoric, he also presided over the diplomatic framework of Serbia's defeat. Milosevic had always assumed that the former Soviet Union would in the end broker an acceptable settlement, but like many others he had underestimated the full extent of Russia's weakness and its leadership's venality. (On this latter point there is some interesting evidence that among the suasions exercised upon the Russian leadership to foster an accommodating attitude was a prodigious bribe to Yeltsin personally.) Early in the administration, Gore had formed a rapport with Viktor Chernomyrdin, the former prime minister, resurrected by Yeltsin as Russia's special envoy to Yugoslavia.

As the missiles pounded Belgrade Gore stayed in almost daily contact with Chernomyrdin, and finally summoned him to Washington in early May, where the two conferred with Secretary of State Madeleine Albright at the vice president's official residence at the Naval Observatory. For his subsequent mission to Belgrade, Chernomyrdin was equipped with a NATO escort in the form of Finland's president, Martti Ahtissaari. Off they went to Belgrade to intimate to the Serbs that they could expect no support from Russia and had best come to terms, which the Serbs duly did.

For those who had thought that the former Soviet Union might, even in its weakness, bestir itself on behalf of its ally in Belgrade, this Russian surrender, supervised by Gore, was the final proof that the country now has an international clout roughly equivalent to that of Brazil. As in the latter's case, Russia's urgent need for fresh loans from the US outweighs all other considerations. Having imposed "shock therapy", leaching the country's economy dry, the US got Russia's complaisance in the Balkans, and in return turned a blind eye to the Russians' atrocious bombardment of Chechnya.

Gore himself has said repeatedly that he thinks his greatest accomplishment as vice president was overseeing the administration's relations with Russia through a joint commission that he chaired with former Prime Minister Chernomyrdin. He told *The Washington Post*, "We have worked to help Russia make a transition to a market-based economy." He also boasted about getting the Russians to agree to NATO expansion into Eastern Europe, and touted agreements on nuclear materials, giving the impression that he had made significant contributions to the safety and cleanliness of the planet.

The realities are somewhat less exalted. Gore tended to

lecture his Russian counterparts about the "leakage" of Russian nuclear technology to countries such as Iran, but was indifferent to Russian concerns about Israel's nuclear weapons program. (Gore himself has supported Israel's refusal to sign the nuclear nonproliferation treaty.) Andrei Kokoshin, at the time head of Russia's Defense Council, later recalled, "We had too much talk from the American side just on alleged Russian violations rather than on a broader discussion of the nature of nonproliferation and efforts by both sides to prevent the spread of weapons of mass destruction. There were mostly specific cases raised by Gore and practically no discussion of what kind of world we want to see together."

On the environmental side of the nuclear question the author of *Earth in the Balance* had little to be proud of, setting a framework that would make Russia's outback the dumping ground for radioactive waste from the world's nuclear power plants. This scheme was brokered by a nebulous, US-dominated consultancy called the Non-Proliferation Trust, run by former military and CIA personnel plus Gore's favorite enviro group, the Natural Resources Defense Council, and Minatom, the notably corrupt Russian nuclear agency. Once again this plan capitalized on Russia's economic crisis, offering $10 billion to Minatom in return for the right to dump an estimated 200 tons a year of high-level radioactive material in Russian waste sites in the Urals.

Early in the 2000 presidential campaign Gore was rattled by allegations that he had ignored corruption in Russia despite frequent contact with its leaders. The vice president was vulnerable because between 1993 and 1998 he had taken a leading role in formulating US policy toward Russia through the Gore-Chernomyrdin commission. Gore had boosted the commission as evidence that he was a serious international statesman. The claim blew up in his face in 1999, when critics asked why, if he knew so much about Russia, he only learned from the newspapers about the scandal over the laundering of $10 billion in Russian money through the Bank of New York.

But Gore was telling the truth when he said he knew something about Russia. He could not publicly explain, however, that this knowledge stemmed from the relationship between his father and Armand Hammer, a man who had once served, according to secret Soviet documents since released, as the conduit for laundering money to Soviet intelligence operations and Communist parties abroad. Not surprisingly, Soviet and later Russian leaders—often the same people—favor Al Gore for the presidency as an associate of their favorite capitalist. Andrei Kortunov, president of the Moscow Science Foundation, and an expert on relations with the US, says: "The traditional establishment likes the Gore family." On meeting Al Jr. in Washington as early as 1985, he recalls being struck by the senator's knowledge of the Soviet Union.

Gore doesn't ever mention what seems to be his dominant concern in the meetings with Chernomyrdin—the opening up of Russia's oil fields to exploitation by US companies. Gore and Chernomyrdin both favored privatization of the Russian oil and gas industry, and Chernomyrdin was also complaisant to Gore's demand that US oil companies be given a big slice of the action. Gore said that the climate for investment would be much improved by locking in tax rates for more than twenty years, and once again Chernomyrdin wagged his head in agreement. The reason for the Russian's agreeable disposition in these matters can be at least partly explained by the fact that he was uniquely positioned to benefit from the privatization of Russian public property, since he set the terms of the sale and could then be first in line to buy the assets at knockdown prices. Chernomyrdin's personal fortune has been estimated at $5 billion.

Gore's and Chernomyrdin's empathy was not discommoded by a CIA report sent to the vice president and detailing the corrupt activities of the Russian prime minister. Gore sent the report back to the CIA, with "Bullshit" loyally scrawled across its cover. Among other the allegations, the CIA reported that Chernomyrdin had charged a German business executive a million dollars for a meeting.

But those who would see a contrast between the corruption of a former Soviet bureaucrat and the neotenic emissary of Western market-oriented liberalism should ponder some remarkable similarities. At the very moment that the CIA was proffering its report on Chernomyrdin, in 1995, Gore was known in the White House as the "solicitor in chief" on account of his pertinacity in extracting campaign funds from corporate chieftains. Some of the biggest cash infusions came from Arco, the Los Angeles-based oil company looking for cheap oil on federal lands in Alaska, an objective the company duly achieved when the National Petroleum Reserve was opened for oil drilling by the White House. The US Navy had jealously guarded the reserve for eighty years, and it could not have hurt Arco's prospects that from 1992 to 2000 the company had refreshed the Democratic National Committee by $405,000. In 1994, Arco's CEO, Lowdrick Cook, was invited to the White House, where President Clinton presented him with a sumptuous birthday cake.

As for maneuvering the private plunder of public assets, Al Gore succeeded where the administration of Warren G. Harding had failed, in privatizing Elk Hills, the huge oil field outside Bakersfield, California, set aside long ago as a strategic reserve for the US Navy. Back in the Harding days, interior secretary Albert Fall went to jail for taking a $300,000 bribe to approve the sale. For sixty years, lingering recollections of Teapot Dome remained strong enough to stymie attempted raids on the military's largest strategic fuel reserve. Nixon tried to sell it, so did Reagan, but each time Congress turned them down.

But Al Gore was pledged to "re-invent government", and in 1996, an item in the Defense Authorization Act under Gore's auspices finally approved the sale of Elk Hills to private interests. Various oil companies savored the prospect of acquiring this immense prize. In 1998, Occidental Petroleum emerged as the lucky winner, buying 78 percent of Elk Hills for $3.65 billion—the largest privatization in US history. Normally, the Department of Energy would have been responsible for examining whether the sale of this important national asset was in the best interests of the country. But the DOE was absolved from this task. Instead, Gore arranged for the consulting firm ICF/Kaiser International to assess the sale. On the board of ICF/Kaiser was none other than Tony Coelho, friend of Al and for a time overseer of the Gore presidential campaign. ICF/Kaiser delivered a whole-hearted and unqualified certification of the deal.

Acquisition of Elk Hills was vital for Occidental and its chairman, Ray Irani. Low in oil reserves, Occidental had previously been viewed as heading for ruin, but the Elk Hills deal tripled its holdings at a stroke, leading to a gratifying reversal in the company's fortunes. Although the bidding on the government asset had been conducted on the presumption that Elk Hills oil cost $4.50 a barrel to extract, Occidental was soon pulling it out of the ground at a lower extraction cost. It did not take long for ugly talk to swirl around the oil industry that the auction had not been conducted on a level playing field.

A full review of the documents relating to the sale could have settled such unworthy suspicions, but these same documents werein the custody of the Department of Energy, and Secretary Richardson obdurately refused to release them. Occidental chairman Irani has been hailed for his perspicacity in acquiring the Elk Hills reserve, but the $470,000 he has contributed in soft money to Clinton, Gore and the Democratic Party since 1972 is plainly no less shrewd an investment. Refreshing the Gore family coffers is of course an old and hallowed tradition at Occidental, Hammer's old company. Al Jr.'s Occidental connections do not appear to have been so personally lucrative as they were for Albert Sr., although, as executor of his father's estate, Gore controls somewhere between $500,000 and $1 million's worth of the company's stock. He therefore has a fiduciary responsibility to keep an eye on such Occidental operations as the extensive drilling program in the country of the U'wa people in Colombia. The U'wa have been deeply opposed to the despoliation of their ancestral territory by Occidental, and have threatened to starve themselves to death if the program continues. The torrent of military hardware funneled to Colombia by the Clinton-Gore Administration will have afforded the residual benefit to Occidental and its shareholders of ending such obstructionism once and for all.

On May 27, 2000 Al Gore laid out his foreign policy and military strategy during a speech at West Point Military Academy. Gore announced that he would pursue a more robust form of Clintonism: highlighted by quicker interventions, less diplomacy and more firepower against "the rogue states...that represent the emerging threat to our country". He called this approach "Forward Engagement", a phrase redolent of Kissinger's "constructive engagement" which meant backing up brutes like Suharto, Somoza and Pinochet.

Like an auctioneer at Sotheby's, Gore rattled off the components of his strategy: a beefed up conventional army ready to "repel cross border invasions by conventional forces"; a new troupe of computer warriors so "we can defend cyberspace"; new technologies to help combat "asymmetrical threats" such as chemical and biological weapons; and, he concluded, the US must "maintain its nuclear strength." The objective of all this firepower is to what the Pentagon now calls "full-spectrum dominance."

Gore took the opportunity to denounce George W. Bush's recent call for deep cuts in the US's nuclear arsenal—cuts, Bush had suggested, that the US should consider making on its own. "Nuclear unilateralism will hinder, rather than help, arms control," Gore said. "Reductions alone don't guarantee stability. If you're not careful, you could have a reduction of missiles and a more dangerous world." This fealty to the nuclear weapons industry is hardly surprising, since in the course of his career Gore has voted for the neutron bomb, the B-2 bomber, the Trident II missile, the MX missile and the Midgetman. He has also backed the mini-Star Wars plan, a project that can't even hit the marks when the Pentagon fixes the tests. It will however channel an estimated $60 billion into the accounts of Boeing, Raytheon, TRW and Lockheed.

Of course, that's the main reason the defense contractors have always loved Gore. And he is prepared to do even more for them. Gore pledged to "create strong incentives [ie., tax breaks] for the defense industry to draw on our commercial technological prowess, and for the best commercial firms to bring their capabilities into the defense market."

14 TEMPLE OF DOOM

Gore and campaign finance; :from "Boy Scout" to "solicitor in chief". The Dutko-Gore two-step. An anatomy of Democratic bag men. Those White House coffee klatsches. Gore says an overdose of iced tea made him mioe potentially damning Whitehouse exchange.

The disclosure that Al Gore was a major player in the Donorgate campaign finance scandal came as a shock to many journalists who had spent years contrasting the supposed probity of the vice president with the morally beleagured president. Yet here was Gore, doing everything from shaking down Buddhist monks to using a credit card to make calls to potential donors from the White House. As Dan Balz *of The Washington Post* put it, "Gore has long been called the Boy Scout of the Clinton administration, a politician of such integrity and personal probity that even Clinton has complained about the vice president's glowing press."

Gore, of course, has never been a political Boy Scout, least of all when it comes to campaign finance. Between 1987 and 1992, he raised almost $2.5 million as a senator from Tennessee, according to the Center for Responsive Politics. Gore oversaw the telecommunications sector from his perch on the Senate Commerce Committee and raised nearly 10 percent of that $2.5 million from the communications barons. Today, Gore commands a fundraising network that is among the most polished in town, one that has been pumping away in the service of his 2000 presidential bid.

One of Gore's closest allies was the late Dan Dutko, head of The Dutko Group, a major beltway lobby shop that has made a specialty of representing telecommunications companies. Gore's relationship with Dutko, and with his other top fund-raisers, offers a revealing look at an issue that lies at the heart of the Donorgate scandal — the way in which lobbyists, consultants and other political fixers are able to win access to lawmakers and reap huge financial whirlwinds for their business clientele.

Dutko had been an intimate of Gore's since the mid-1980s and soon became one of his ablest fund-raisers. According to one Beltway veteran, the two men devised an especially effective technique by which Senator Gore would arrange a conference call with a group of about five telecommunications company officials and industry lobbyists. Dutko would participate in these calls as Gore's designated plant. After Gore made his pitch for cash, Dutko, professing to be moved by Gore's passionate interest in the telecommunications field, would agree to pony up a huge campaign contribution. Not wanting to appear to be cheap, the other conference callers would reluctantly match Dutko's offer and Gore would walk away with a nice haul.

The fundraising scam cemented a relationship that has flourished ever since, and coincides with Dutko's meteoric rise within the ranks of Democratic Party bag men. Though Dutko was fairly stingy about donating his own money — in the 1995-96 election cycle Dutko gave the Clinton/Gore campaign $1,000 and the DNC a paltry $700 — he was adept at extracting cash from others. In 1996, Dutko was named national finance vice chairman of the Clinton/Gore re-election campaign, as well as to the DNC's Financial Advisory Board, a group charged with prodding donors into doling out $350,000 or more. His colleagues on the board included Hollywood movie mogul Lew Wasserman and Steven Rattner, the New York Times reporter-turned-investment banker. Following Clinton/Gore's reelection, Dutko was put in charge of the Democrats' "Victory" fund, which raised millions for the 1998 off-year elections.

When not drumming up cash for Gore and the Democrats, Dutko tended to matters at his lobbying outfit, the Dutko Group, which remains—even after his death—one of the most powerful in town. Its clients include telecommunications firms such as COMSAT, the Competitive Telecommunications Association, DSC Communications Corporation, National Cellular Resellers Association and the Satellite Broadcasting and Communications Association. The Dutko Group also represents the Alliance for GATT, Citgo Petroleum and the American Plastics Council.

Dutko was a Democrat as is the company's current president, Mark Irion, a former staffer to ex-Senator Alan Dixon of Illinois. But, like many Washington lobby shops, The Dutko Group has been careful to cover all the bases. Its top officers include Kevin Tally, former chief of staff and campaign director to William Goodling, who now chairs the House Committee on Education and the Work Force, Ronald Kaufman, a deputy assistant to the President under George Bush, and Gary Andres, another former Bush staffer and between 1994 and 1996 a member of the "Thursday Group," the elite troupe of Republican lobbyists and activists who met weekly with the House Republican leadership to plot strategy on the Contract With America.

Thanks to his link with Gore, Dutko tended to be in the right place at the right time. He was one of 831 guests who stayed overnight at the Lincoln Bedroom during Clinton's first term and was invited to a June 1996 state dinner with Irish Prime Minister Mary Robinson. He was also in the crowd at a May 1996 DNC fund-raiser held at Gore's mansion, an affair that raised several million dollars and which Dutko described to the press as "a very tasteful and modest event."

Dutko attended at least two of the White House notorious coffee klatsches where money was prised from the pockets of those in attendance. Irion was on hand for a session hosted by Gore in November of 1995. That event was for members of the Democratic National Committee's Environmental Leadership Council, though the Dutko Group's interest in ecology does not appear to extend beyond its representation of a firm called Empire Sanitary Landfill, Inc.

Dutko's access served his clients well. Take DSC, a Texas-based phone switching and computer equipment manufacturer. In 1998, DSC was battling with several foreign competitors to win a $36 million deal with Telmex, Mexico's state-run telecommunications company. The company faced serious obstacles to winning the contract, especially as one of its chief's rivals, Alcatel of France, owned a five percent share of Telmex and was considered to have the inside track.

DSC asked Dutko for help and the lobbyist put the company in touch with officials at the Commerce Department. Soon, the late Commerce Secretary Ron Brown was on the job for DSC, writing and calling Telmex chieftain Jaime Chico Pardo to press the firm's case. In early June of 1995, DSC announced that it had won the contract, and a few weeks later it sent a $25,000 donation to the Democrats. At Dutko's suggestion, DSC sent an additional $100,000 to the Democratic National Committee last year, a gesture which earned the firm's CEO, James Donald, a thank you call from Dutko's friend, Al Gore.

Perhaps the best known of Gore's financial warlords has been Nathan Landow, a Bethesda, Maryland developer. Landow raised millions for Jimmy Carter in 1976 and stood in line to be rewarded with a post as ambassador to the Netherlands. Then, amid some disobliging news stories, Landow withdrew his name from consideration. A decade later he surfaced once more as the man behind IMPAC 88, a political action committee backed by developers who derived much of their wealth from federal construction contracts and discussed here in an earlier chapter on Gore's '88 run. Though he lost badly, Gore gained the unswerving support of Landow and his associates, who raised millions on his behalf in the last decade.

Landow was invited to two coffee klatsches at the White House. At the April 12, 1996 gathering in the Map Room of the White House, Landow was accompanied by two executives from the National Homebuilders Association, an organization that had often hurled harsh invective at Gore's environmental agenda. Also in attendance was Peter Knight and Beth Alpert, from Gore's vice-presidential staff. Later that afternoon Landow wrote a $25,000 check to the DNC.

It was Dick Morris who came up with the idea of inviting corporate bigwigs and donors with fat wallets to the White House for face-to-face gatherings with the Clintons and Gores. It would be a way to prime the river of soft money that he would need to run the issue ads that would ultimately propel the Clinton-Gore team to its big win over Bob Dole. These events became known as the White House coffee klatsches. They were responsible for raising $3.5 million for the DNC.

Between January 1, 1995 and August 23, 1996 1,500 people were invited to the White House and the Vice President's Mansion for some face time with the Clintons, the

Gores and their top aides. By far the most heavily represented group were the Washington lobbyists, arriving in a familiar torrent of names: Patton, Boggs, and Blow, the most influential firm on the Hill; Skadden, Arp, the Republican lobby-shop; the PR house of Hill & Knowlton; Mickey Kantor's old firm, Manatt, Phelps, and Phillips; and Davis, Polk and Wardwell, the law offices of Robert Fiske, the first special prosecutor in the Whitewater scandal.

Chasing close on the lobbyists' heels were the bankers, bond traders and mutual fund operators, including executives from Morgan Stanley, Lehman Brothers, Goldman Sachs, and Chase Manhattan. One intriguing session, surely ripe for the scrutiny of a special prosecutor, occurred on May 13, 1996 between the top sixteen bankers in the country, the President of the United States, the Comptroller of the Currency, and the Secretary of the Treasury.

Third in frequency was the telecommunications sector headlined by what must have been a tense session with Sumner Redstone, owner of the controlling interest in cable giant Viacom, and the company's CEO, Frank Biondi, who Redstone fired soon thereafter. Also making an appearance were executives from Time/Warner, Disney, Knight-Ridder, Miramax and the Wall Street Journal, whose editorial page pounds out a daily anti-Clinton drumbeat. Remember that in this period the largest "reform" of telecommunications since 1932 was in progress, with billions at stake. Telecommunications companies infused the Democratic Party with nearly $20 million.

Next came the health care and insurance lobbies, intent on killing any new initiative for a national health care system. The insurance company most frequently sending its executives to sip coffee with the president was Travelers Group, whose executives attended no less than seven White House klatschs, one of them ennobled by Travelers' CEO Sanford Weill, at $50 million a year the highest paid corporate executive in 1995. Everyone at the table knew Weill's position on product liability lawsuits: he wanted them limited.

Close behind was the energy and oil companies. Executives from Enron, Exxon, Amoco, Arco, and Phillips all graced the White House with appearances. The most frequent visitor from the fossil fuel sector was Stan McLelland, the executive vice-president of Valero Energy of San Antonio. Valero was a big supporter of NAFTA because the firm had embarked on a joint venture with the Mexican oil company PEMEX. Valero was also mustard-keen on the Mexican bailout and on US help to Mexico in suppressing any attacks by insurgent groups on PEMEX facilities. McLelland wrote personal cheques to the tune of $130,000 to the DNC in the run-up to the '96 election.

The rest of the 1,500 names consisted mostly of Democratic Party loyalists and functionaries from the public interest movement mustered by the White House to coopt their clientele and guide them towards acommodation with the requirements of the corporate sector present at the klatsches.

The most frequent single visitor to the klatsches was Alfonso Fanjul, anti-Castro resident of southern Florida and the most prominent member of the family that owns Flo-Sun Inc., which manages vast plantations of sugar cane around the southern shore of Lake Okeechobee in Florida. Hence Fanjul maintained a keen interest in aborting any environmental legislation that might inhibit his company's capacity to discharge phosphorus into the Everglades.

Fanjul showed up at the klatsches five times, including an October 13, 1995 session with Al Gore who, at that very moment, was crafting a another "win-win" compromise protecting the sugar lords while throwing a morsel to the establishment greens by going through the motions of protecting the nation's most famous wetland. The next time Fanjul visited the White House on December 18, 1995 he was in the company of Jeffrey Leonard, the manager of the Global Environment Fund, a group advocating the virtues of green capitalism. (In the fraught Oval Office encounter on Presidents Day, February 19, 1996, when Bill Clinton felt he had to tell Monica Lewinsky their love must end, he interrupted this intimate exchange to take a call from Fanjul at 12:42 p.m., having kept the sugar baron on hold for eighteen minutes, then parleying with him for another 22 minutes. The Starr report is precise on the times, though Lewinsky only remembered the phone caller as "Fanuli.")

For pleasing pairings at the klatsches it was hard to beat the May 7, 1995 session where Beth Dozoretz, a vice president of the First Hospital Corp. exchanged pleasantries with Tina Flournoy, an executive with tobacco giant Philip Morris.

Justice Department investigators homed in on whether the Democratic National Committee was knowingly recycling the "soft money" contributions extorted at these klatsches and other venues by Clinton and Gore into the Morris-scripted ads that were designed to bolster Clinton and Gore's re-election campaigns. The second major question was whether the DNC was knowingly soliciting contributions from foreign nationals. These two issues came together most illuminatingly at a December 15, 1995 coffee klatsch in the White House attended by Clinton, Gore and the Indonesian-born gardener, Arief Wiriadinata who had contributed $455,000 to the DNC. The DNC ultimately returned these donations after discovering that Wiriadinata had not filed federal income tax returns in 1995. A White House videotape of that event surfaced in mid-2000 in which Wiriadinata approaches Clinton and Gore and says, "James Riady sent me." Riady was the son of Mokhtar Riady, an Indonesian billionaire, and the US Justice Department suspected that he had laundered money from his father through conduits such as the redoubtable gardener. On the videotape Gore is heard to say excitedly, "We oughta show Mr Riadi the tapes, some of the ad tapes." This appeared to confirm that Gore was entirely aware of what such contributions were paying for.

By mid-July of 2000, Attorney General Janet Reno was once again on the hotseat over Al Gore. For the fourth time in three years, her own investigators from the Justice Department had urged her to appoint a special prosecutor to look into Gore's fundraising activities during the 1996 election campaign. Reno had rejected earlier calls from special investigator Charles LaBella and FBI director Louis Freeh. This time, the investigator, Robert Conrad, a prosecutor with the DoJ's Office of Professional Responsibility, added another charge: Gore may have lied about his role during interviews with federal investigators.

Gore has never been ashamed of his facility to raise campaign cash. Indeed, he has often boasted about his prowess. In a 1996 memo, Gore wrote: "I did three events this week which where projected to raise $650,000 and...actually raised $800,000. Tipper and I were supposed to do $1.1 million, and it looks like we will be closer to $1.3 million." But when Gore's central role in the 1996 Clinton/Gore cash machine came to light, he acted like a young boy caught with a hand in the cookie jar, stuttering his excuses, shifting his story and, when all else failed, claiming to suffer from a kind of convenient political amnesia.

The Buddhist temple fiasco, as unsavory as it was, doesn't appear to have involved any illegal activity by Gore himself. The temple and some of Gore's fundraisers may have conspired to use the monks and nuns as pass-throughs for illegal contributions. But there is no evidence that Gore knew about the scam. Still, Gore, in trying to defend himself, went farther, claiming that he wasn't aware that the temple event was a fundraiser. It was, he offered, merely a "community outreach event". When memos surfaced refuting Gore's story, he clumsily changed it yet again, calling the session a "donor maintenance event". None of the stories had the ring of truth to them, perhaps because Gore never learned Clinton's political greatest skill: the gift for nuance.

Gore also came under scrutiny for 52 telephone calls he made from his office in the White House seeking campaign money. One of the people Gore called described being bullied by the Veep; another said he felt like the victim of a "shakedown". The calls, which raised several hundred thousand dollars, were made on a Clinton-Gore campaign phone card. Much of the money raised ended up in so-called "hard" money accounts, specifically for the Clinton/Gore campaign and not the so-called party-building ads. These calls appeared to violate campaign finance laws and the Pendleton Act, which strictly prohibits political fundraising from taking place on federal property.

After the Washington Post's Bob Woodward broke a story on the calls, Gore rushed forward to try to clear his name in a hastily arranged White House press conference on May 2, 1997. It proved to be one of the most bizarre performances in modern politics, with a robotic Gore saying that he had been advised "that there is no controlling legal authority or case, that there was any violation of law whatsoever in the manner in which I asked people to contribute to our election campaign."

When Gore's quavering performance was derided on newscasts and joked about on the Tonight Show, he tried to blame it all on his lawyer, Charles Burson. Burson, an old friend of Gore's from Tennessee, may have advised him of the law, but he certainly didn't tell the Veep sputter the strange phrase eight times, as if he were melting down like Hal the computer in Kubrick's 2001.

The attention of the investigators from the Justice Department looking into this mess quickly focused on a key meeting that took place on November 21, 1995, involving Gore, Clinton and the DNC officials. In 1997 investigators asked Gore whether he discussed the telephone calls at this session. According to an FBI summary, Gore said that "discussions of fundraising calls for him and the president would not have been discussed." Gore also told the investigators at that time "the number of telephone calls to be made by the President and the Vice President was never discussed with him and he doubts that the issue was ever discussed with the President."

But Gore was undermined by his own aide, David Strauss, who took notes of the meeting. Strauss wrote: "VP: 'Is it possible to do a reallocation for me to take more of the events and the calls?'" The notes show Gore being allocated 10 calls. Another note records Gore's assent to the plan: "VP: 'Count me in on the calls.'" When interviewed about this by prosecutors and FBI agents Gore continued to deny all and on more specific matters resorted to that old standby "I don't recall"—23 times. When FBI agents confronted Gore with another of Strauss' damning notes, this one regarding the allocation of "hard" money, the vice president froze for a moment and then offered a novel excuse: He must have been in the bathroom at the time this was being discussed, having overdosed on iced tea.

15 PLAYING THE GREEN GAME

The Arch Druid charges that Clinton and Gore have done more harm to the environment than the Republicans. Gore's trail of broken promises. How his green relations team armtwisted forest defenders. A horrible salvage rider. Missiles for dead whales. The not-so-great McGinty. Spooking for Monsanto. Saving dams and killing salmon.

The official version of the political battles over the environment in the late 1990s goes something like this:

As the Republican Visigoths swept into control of the 104th Congress, in January of 1995, trembling greens predicted that not an old-growth tree, not an endangered species would be spared. The Republicans' threats were terrible to behold. They proposed to open the Arctic National Wildlife Refuge to oil drilling. They vowed to establish a commission to shut down several national parks; to relax standards on the production and disposal of toxic waste; to turn over enforcement of clean water and air standards to the states. They uttered fearsome threats against the Endangered Species Act. They boasted of plans to double the amount of logging in the National Forests.

Then, the official myth goes on, the president, Gore and the national greens fought off the Visigoths.

American politics thrives on simple legends of virtue combating vice. As regards the environment, the Republican ultras did not carry all before them. They didn't need to. Clinton and Gore had already done most of the dirty work themselves. The real story begins back in the early days of the administration, when Clinton and Gore had what might be called an environmental mandate and a Democratic Congress to help them move through major initiatives. But the initiatives never happened. Instead, those early years were marked by a series of retreats, reversals and betrayals that prompted David Brower, the grand old man of American environmentalism, to conclude that "Gore and Clinton have done more harm to the environment than Reagan and Bush combined."

The first environmental promise Al Gore made in the 1992 campaign, he soon shattered. It involved the WTI hazardous waste incinerator in East Liverpool, Ohio, built on a floodplain near the Ohio River. The plant, one of the largest of its kind in the world, was scheduled to burn 70,000 tons of hazardous waste a year in a spot only 350 feet from the nearest house. A few hundred yards away is East Elementary School, which sits on a ridge nearly eye-level with the top of the smokestack.

On July 19, 1992, Gore gave one of his first campaign speeches on the environment, across the river from the incinerator, in Weirton, West Virginia, hammering the Bush Administration for its plans to give the toxic waste burner a federal air permit. "The very idea is just unbelievable to me", Gore said. "I'll tell you this, a Clinton-Gore Administration is going to give you an environmental presidency to deal with these problems. We'll be on your side for a change." Clinton made similar pronouncements on his swing through the Buckeye State.

Shortly after the election, Gore assured neighbors of the incinerator that he hadn't forgotten about them. "Serious questions concerning the safety of the East Liverpool, Ohio, hazardous waste incinerator must be answered before the plant may begin operation", Gore wrote. "The new Clinton/Gore administration will not issue the plant a test burn permit until all questions concerning compliance with the plant have been answered."

But that never happened. Instead, the EPA quietly granted the WTI facility its test burn permit. The tests failed, twice. In one trial burn, the incinerator eradicated only 7 percent of the mercury found in the waste, when it was supposed to burn away 99.9 percent. A few weeks later the EPA granted WTI a commercial permit anyway. They didn't tell the public about the failed tests until afterward.

Gore claimed his hands were tied by the Bush Administration, which had promised WTI the permit only a few weeks before the Clinton team took office. But by one account, William Reilly, Bush's EPA director, met with Gore's top environmental aide Katie McGinty in January 1993 and asked her if he should begin the process of approving the permit. In this version of events apparently McGinty told Reilly to proceed. McGinty said later that she had no recollection of the meeting.

Gore persisted in maintaining that there was nothing he could do about it once the permit was granted. A 1994 report on the matter from the General Accounting Office flatly contradicted him, saying the plant could be shut down on numerous grounds, including repeated violations of its permit.

"This was Clinton and Gore's first environmental promise, and it was their first promise-breaker", says Terri Swearington, a registered nurse from Chester, West Virginia, just across the Ohio River from the incinerator. Swearington, who won the Goldman Prize in 1997 for her work organizing opposition to WTI, has hounded Gore ever since, and during the

2000 campaign she was banned by Gore staffers from appearing at events featuring the vice president.

The decision to go soft on WTI may have had something to do with its powerful financial backer. The construction of the incinerator was partially underwritten by Jackson Stephens, the Arkansas investment king who helped bankroll the Clinton-Gore campaign. According to EPA whistleblower Hugh Kaufman, during the period when the WTI financing package was being put together Stephens Inc. was represented by Webb Hubbell, who later came into Clinton's Justice Department and was indicted during the Whitewater investigation, and the Rose law firm, to which Hillary Clinton belonged. Over the ensuing seven years, the WTI plant has burned nearly a half-million tons of toxic waste, 5,000 truckloads of toxic material every year, spewing chemicals such as mercury, lead and dioxin out of its stacks and onto the surrounding neighborhoods. The inevitable illnesses have followed.

Up in the Douglas fir forests of the Pacific Northwest, a similar saga of betrayal unfolded. In the late 1980s and 1990s federal judge William Dwyer, a Reagan appointee, rocked the Bush Administration when he sided with environmentalists in a series of lawsuits involving the northern spotted owl. Dwyer ruled that the fierce pace of Forest Service logging in ancient forests was driving the spotted owl, and more than 180 other species that dwell in the deep forests west of the Cascade Mountains, to extinction. In 1991, Dwyer handed down an injunction halting all new timber sales in spotted owl habitat. He famously cited the Bush Administration forest plan for "a remarkable series of violations of environmental laws".

Then along came Bill Clinton and Al Gore. At a rally in Portland, Oregon, on the eve of the 1992 election, Gore vowed to "end the standoff" over the fate of the Northwest forests once and for all. In fact, the standoff was serving the owl pretty well. By 1993, new timber sales in the Northwest had declined from 20 million board feet a year in 1982 to 2 million board feet. What was to come would drive the owl even closer to extinction.

Within days of taking office, the Clinton-Gore team set its sights on getting Dwyer's injunction lifted and the big logs rolling back to the sawmills. The scheme was to become a template for the way Clinton and Gore would handle environmental disputes for the remainder of their term. convene a staged "town hall" style meeting, put out a pre-fab plan and induce your liberal friends to swallow their principles and sign off on it. This shadow play was the April 1993 Forest Summit, a orgy of consensus-mongering that saw some of the nation's leading environmentalists hunkering down with executives from Weyerhaeuser. The event, orchestrated by Gore and Katie McGinty, is best remembered for the administration's bid to censor the opening remarks of a local historian, who wanted to put the session in its proper context by describing the social effects from a hundred years of conscienceless logging by an industry that had treated its workers as ruthlessly as it had treated salmon streams.

Shortly after the Portland summit the political arm-twisting began. Gore's so-called "green relations team", led by McGinty, was sent to palaver with environmentalists in the region. "They told us that during the campaign they'd made commitments to the timber lobby and the Northwest delegation that logging would be restarted before the end of 1993", Larry Tuttle later recalled. Tuttle, who formerly headed the Oregon Natural Resources Council (a lead plaintiff in the original spotted owl suit), now runs the Portland-based Center for Environmental Equity. "They made it clear that if greens wanted to get some of the provisions we wanted in the new forest plan, we had to offer up something in return." The Clinton emissaries wanted the plaintiffs in the spotted owl case to go to Judge Dwyer and ask him to release for clear-cutting some of the sales he had halted. Many of the big national groups, including the Wilderness Society, National Wildlife Federation and the Sierra Club Legal Defense Fund, were ready to throw in the towel that very moment. Local groups still held out.

Then Clinton and Gore summoned Bruce Babbitt, secretary of the interior and former president of the League of Conservation Voters. Babbitt came carrying a big stick. The former Arizona governor knew exactly how to scare the hell out of his former colleagues—-by threatening them with "sufficiency language", a legal device that would allow federal agencies, such as the Forest Service and the BLM, to violate laws like the Endangered Species Act with impunity. Unless they were willing to go along, Babbitt told the spotted owl plaintiffs, the Clinton Administration to ask Congress to enact a legislative rider that would overturn the injunctions and insulate the new plan from any future environmental lawsuits. The deal was struck over the dissent of grassroots groups.

Judge Dwyer had no choice. He had to let the injunction go, and he had to approve the new Clinton forest plan. There simply wasn't any opposition to it. However, the judge did issue a warning: if any one element of the plan was not implemented, its legal standing would crumble and an even more sweeping injunction could be in the offing.

For the greens who'd folded, the pay-off was scarcely worth it. The plan didn't stop the logging of ancient forests. In fact, more than 35 percent of the remaining spotted owl habitat was put into the free-fire zone called "the matrix", where logging could go forward. But even the remaining 65 percent of old-growth forest was not safe. Although the plan sequestered these lands in a category called Old Growth Reserves, such zones were not, in fact, off limits to logging. The plan's fine print allowed these lands to be, in Babbitt's unforgettable phrase, "cut for their own good". Ecological logging—considered a joke during the Bush era—came into its own with a vengeance during Clinton-Gore time.

Next came the salvage logging rider a spending bill, signed by Clinton in 1995. Brent Blackwelder, president of Friends of the Earth, issued the dire judgement that "the salvage rider was arguably the worst single piece of public lands legislation ever signed into law." The bill consigned millions of acres of National Forest lands across the country to the chainsaw, and contained language exempting the sales from all environmental laws and from any judicial review. The consequences were especially dire in the Pacific Northwest. Gore later called this rider the administration's biggest mistake on the environment. But it was just one of many.

By 1998, the evidence was irrefutable. The Clinton-Gore plan was driving the owl to extinction much faster than the old cutting plans of the Bush era that Dwyer had forbidden. In an April 1999 report, the Forest Service's own biologists found that across its range the spotted owl was declining at more than 8 percent per year since the Clinton plan had been put into effect. In California, the rate was even higher, more than 10 percent per year. But the most rapid decline was being seen on the Olympic peninsula, Washington state, where the owls, isolated by geographical features such as the Puget Sound and surrounded by millions of acres of corporate land clearcut by Weyerhaeuser, Simpson, ITT-Rayonier and John Hancock, were plummeting at the alarming rate of 12.3 percent per year.

At that rate the Olympic peninsula owls will be extinct in 2005 and maybe sooner. In all, the spotted owl population under the Clinton-Gore administration declined more in five years than the plan's environmental impact statement predicted it would decline under a worst-case scenario over forty years.

The fall of 1993 saw Gore broker a bizarre deal to trade missiles for dead whales. On September 23 of that year he entertained Norway's prime minister, Gro Brundtland, at the White House. Brundtland, a fellow Harvard grad and a longtime friend of the vice president, sought Gore's backing for Norway's effort to overturn the International Whaling Commission's ban on the hunting of minke whales in the northeast Atlantic Ocean. For years this had been Norway's aim. But they'd had little success with the Bush Administration.

Early in 1993 the Norwegian fleet flouted international law by killing nearly 300 whales, supposedly for "scientific" and "experimental" purposes, although a later investigation disclosed that Norwegian minke whale meat had ended up in the fish markets of Japan. American environmental groups lashed out at Norway and demanded that the US take action to punish the rogue whalers. Under a US law known as the Pelly Amendment, the Commerce Department could have imposed trade sanctions on nations that violate the whaling ban. (This amendment has now been neutered as an "unfair trade barrier" by the WTO."

But Norway had so far escaped without even a mild rebuke. In part this was because Norway had softened up Congress and Clinton's Commerce Department through a $1.5 million influence-peddling campaign that was led by the lobby firm Akin Gump, home of former DNC chairman Robert

Strauss and that master of persuasion Vernon Jordan.

At the time of his meeting with Brundtland, Gore had several things on his mind. One was the situation in Bosnia. The Norwegians had one of the largest contingents of troops on the ground there, and Brundtland was under pressure to pull the peacekeepers out, a move that Gore, who was overseeing much of the Bosnian crisis for the administration, was desperate to avoid. Second, Gore was less than enthusiastic about an outright ban on whaling, feeling that it would impede his efforts to secure free trade pacts.

A White House transcript of the meeting, marked confidential by Gore's national security adviser, Leon Fuerth, records Brundtland denouncing environmental groups as "extremists" and liars. She tells the vice president that she doesn't want her nation's whaling fleet monitored "because that would allow Greenpeace to track them and disrupt our activities". Then Brundtland went on, "We do feel bullied, even by you simply evaluating the use of sanctions.... Especially after several nations in the IWC have tried to change the organization from a whale monitoring mission to a forum to ban whaling outright."

Gore tried to placate the Norwegian prime minister, agreeing that the environmental groups had unfairly beat up on Norway. "As in arms control, there are those who attempt to exploit uncertainty for their own ends", Gore said. "This strengthens my argument for the need of a scheme that will allow resumption [of whaling] while removing the basis of suspicion that the RMS [i.e., new international whaling rules] will be violated."

In the end, Gore agreed that the Clinton Administration would refrain from imposing sanctions on Norway and would work with Brundtland to weaken whale protection regulations at the IWC. To seal the agreement, Gore and Brundtland forged an arms deal involving the sale of $625 million worth of air-to-air missiles made by Raytheon to the Norwegian military.

Across the board, setbacks for the greens came at a dizzying pace during the Clinton Administration. A plan to raise grazing fees on Western ranchers was shelved after protests from two Western senators, one of whom, Max Baucus from Montana, later marveled at how quickly the administration caved. The EPA soon succumbed to pressure from the oil industry and automakers on its plans to press for tougher fuel efficiency standards, a move Katie McGinty defended by saying enviros were "tilting at windmills" on the issue. In the winter of 1994 the White House fired Jim Baca, the reform-minded director of the Bureau of Land Management, after his attempts to take on the ranching and mining industries riled Cecil Andrus, the governor of Idaho.

Tax breaks were doled out to oil companies drilling in the Gulf of Mexico. The Department of Agriculture okayed a plan to increase logging in Alaska's Tongass National Forest, the nation's largest temperate rainforest. The Interior Department, under orders from the White House, put the brakes on a proposal to outlaw the most grotesque form of strip mining, the aptly-named mountaintop-removal method. With Gore doing much of the lobbying, the administration pushed through Congress a bill that repealed the ban on the import of tuna caught with nets that also killed dolphins. The collapse was rapid enough to distress so centrist an environmental leader as the National Wildlife Federation's Jay Hair, who likened the experience of dealing with the Clinton-Gore Administration to "date rape".

The White House quashed a task force investigating timber fraud on the National Forests, which had uncovered several hundred million dollars' worth of illegal timber cutting by big corporations, including Weyerhaeuser. The task force was disbanded, some of its investigators reassigned to, as one put it, "pull up pot plants in clearcuts".

As ugly as things got, the big green groups never abandoned Gore, swallowing his line that he was "after all, only the vice president". It is a hallmark of the Gore style that he knows how to deftly exploit public interest groups even as he betrays their constituents. Like the Christian right during the Bush era, the Beltway greens felt there was nowhere else to turn. They had never trusted Clinton, who as governor had allowed the fouling of the White River and shamelessly pandered after corporate cash during the primaries.

They had pinned their hopes on Gore. They remembered him as the one who had held the first hearings on Love Canal and helped usher the Superfund law into being. Here was the man who popularized the term "global warming" and had warned of the dangers of the deterioration of the ozone layer. Here was the man who had led a contingent of Democratic senators to the 1992 Earth Summit in Rio, where he chastised George Bush's indifference to the health of the planet. Here was the man who had written Earth in the Balance, which called for the environment to be the "central organizing principle" of the new century and stressed strict environmental discipline for the Third World.

But as Brent Blackwelder of Friends of the Earth pointed out, during all his years in Congress, Gore's record on environmental issues was far from sterling. In fact, he voted for the environment only 66 percent of the time, a rating that put him on the lower end of Senate Democrats. Moreover,

Blackwelder says, Gore functioned rarely as a leader in Congress but more as a solo operator pursuing his own agenda.

That agenda, from the beginning, has been in line with his roots as a New Democrat. Gore has been a tireless promoter of incentive-based, or free-market, environmentalism, often remarking that "the invisible hand has a green thumb." Since the mid-1980s, Gore has argued that the bracing forces of market capitalism are potent curatives for the ecological entropy now bearing down upon the global environment. He has always been a passionate disciple of the gospel of efficiency, and a man suffused with an inchoate technophilia.

But Gore was also shrewd. He knew the environmental movement from the inside out, knew well that what the big green groups based in DC craved most was access. As vice president, he arranged to meet at least once a month with the Gang of Ten, the CEOs of the nation's biggest environmental outfits. It became a way for Gore to cool their tempers and deflect their gripes from him to the president, or more often, to Cabinet members such as Robert Rubin, Ron Brown, Mack McLarty or Lloyd Bentsen. Moreover, Gore made sure to seed the administration with more than thirty executives and staff members from the ranks of the environmental movement itself, headlined by Babbitt, the former president of the movement's main PAC. Others came from the Wilderness Society, National Audubon Society, Environmental Defense Fund, Sierra Club and the Natural Resources Defense Council.

This experience was a new one for environmental lobbyists who had lived through the exile of the Reagan-Bush era. "It was good to have people in the White House call you by your first name", Brock Evans, once regarded as the most effective green lobbyist in DC, reflected at a gathering of environmental activists in Oregon in 1993. Evans' gratified cry summed it all up. Official greens got a bit of access, and that was about it.

The main conduit to the ear of power was Katie McGinty, formerly on Gore's Senate staff. Few people are closer to Gore than McGinty, one of only two staffers permitted to call the Veep "Al". (The other is Leon Fuerth.) McGinty grew up in Philadelphia, the daughter of an Irish-American cop in Frank Rizzo's police force. She got a degree in chemistry at St. Joseph's University and soon went to work for ARCO, the oil/chemical giant. A few years later McGinty pursued a law degree from Columbia in the Science, Law and Technology program. Before joining Gore's Senate staff, she did a stint in DC as a lobbyist for the American Chemical Society, where she fine-tuned the techno-speak that Gore finds irresistible in a staffer. In answering a reporter's question about her favorite hobbies, McGinty once said, "Hiking and reading books on civic realization." It was a response only Gore could find exciting. McGinty became Gore's top environmental aide in 1990, helped him research Earth in the Balance and accompanied him to the Earth Summit in Rio de Janeiro in 1992.

In 1993, McGinty, then only 29, was tapped to head the White House Office of Environmental Policy, a newly created panel that Gore pushed for to give him more of a presence inside the White House. The move didn't sit well with members of Congress or with some Clinton staffers, who felt Gore was grasping too much power. Ultimately, the office was merged with the Council on Environmental Quality, which oversees compliance with environmental laws by federal agencies. McGinty was named as its chair.

The years from 1993 to 1996 were bleak ones for environmentalists, as Clinton and Gore retreated from one campaign pledge after another. "Katie seemed out of the loop most of the time she was there", a seasoned environmental lobbyist told the authors at the time. "Or that's how she made you feel. Katie's great talent was to seduce you on the phone. She made you feel as if she was your best friend, a secret Earth First!er, who was shocked and pained when the inevitable betrayals came. Katie never delivered bad news herself, but she was always there to console us. She was very, very adroit at soothing irate enviros, calming them down so that they wouldn't attack the administration."

At the height of the budget negotiations in 1998, McGinty shocked many in DC when she abruptly announced that she was resigning from her post and was moving to India to take a job at the Tata Research Institute in New Delhi. TERI, as it's known, is an obscure sustainable development group that receives funding from the UN and works on energy, biotech and forestry issues. McGinty's husband, Karl Hausker, an employee of the Center for Strategic and International Studies (an outpost of the national security establishment), had been assigned to India. Many thought McGinty would stay in DC, where her power in the administration would increase as the 2000 election approached. But apparently Tipper Gore convinced McGinty that she should follow her man.

Tipper had taken an unusual interest in McGinty's personal life. In 1995, she learned that McGinty had repeatedly postponed her marriage to Hausker, citing the "crushing workload" that kept her tied down at the White House. Evidently eager that McGinty cement her union and therefore leave Washington, Tipper intervened, handled the wedding arrangements and shipped the newlyweds off on a monthlong honeymoon to Australia's Great Barrier Reef and the rainforests of Papua, New Guinea.

In 2000, McGinty returned to the United States from

India. It didn't take her long to find a job—not with the Gore campaign but as the legislative affairs director of Troutman Sanders, a DC law firm with a reputation for defending the worst corporate polluters and using its lobbying might to carve up environmental legislation. In these unsavory surroundings, McGinty stayed true. "There would be no higher priority I would have", she had once said, "than to help or serve Al Gore." Opportunity did not dally. In the spring of 2000 McGinty co-founded a group called Environmentalists for Gore, designed to undercut the growing sentiment for greens to support Bill Bradley in the Democratic primary contests. Bradley had been endorsed by Friends of the Earth in 1999, and this slap in the face had set off alarm bells in the Gore camp.

Among McGinty's labors for Gore in 2000 was her input in his energy plan, which promises $68 billion in subsidies and tax breaks for utilities. It so happens that among the biggest clients of McGinty's new firm, Troutman Sanders, are American Electric Power, the Southern Company and the Edison Electric Institute, one of the main opponents of stringent new air pollution standards. When confronted with this confluence of interest, McGinty answered irrefutably, "I provide advice and have provided advice to anyone who asks me. Does the vice president ask for my views? Absolutely. Do people in the business community ask me for my views. Absolutely. And is that anything new? Absolutely not."

Another Gore protégé, Carol Browner, landed the key post of EPA administrator. She had served as Gore's legislative director from 1989 through 1991, before leaving to become the head of Florida's Department of Environmental Regulation. During her tenure in Florida, Browner took two particularly high-profile stands. The first was a capitulation to sugar-growers and developers which allowed continued (though

259

slightly filtered) dumping of pesticide-laced water into the Everglades. Second, Browner allowed the Walt Disney Company to destroy 800 acres of vital wetland habitat in central Florida, in exchange for a pledge from the eco-imagineers at Disney World to recreate several thousand acres of "wetlands", a feat which remains well beyond the capacities of modern science.

At EPA, Browner wasted little time in promoting ideas, such as wetland trading, that during the Bush administration had met with howls of derision from the green lobby. One of her very first actions was to put the imprimatur of the EPA on the Everglades deal she had brokered a year earlier in Florida. This was a precedent of sorts — the first time the federal government had officially sanctioned the pollution of a national park.

Following Gore, Browner initiated a campaign to reinvent the EPA by beginning to peel away "excessive environmental regulations". The theme here echoes back to the late 1970s and the writings of Stephen Breyer, then an aide to Senator Ted Kennedy, who Clinton elevated in 1994 to a spot on the US Supreme Court. Breyer argued that federal regulations should be evaluated through two tests: risk assessment and cost/benefit analysis. The costs of pollution control would be weighed against the heavily discounted benefits of human health and environmental quality — a certain recipe for more hazardous waste landfills, dioxin-belching incinerators and higher cancer rates.

Browner's first target was the so-called Delaney Clause in the Food and Drug Act, which placed a strict prohibition against any detectable level of carcinogens in processed food. Though long the bane of the American Farm Bureau and the Chemical Manufacturers' Association, the Delaney Clause remained inviolate, even through the Reagan and Bush years. Within months of taking office Browner announced that she felt this standard was too severe and moved to gut it. "We just don't have unlimited financial resources to enforce all these measures and that can create a backlash", Browner complained. "So we need to be realistic. We need the strongest possible standards, but we need flexibility in how to achieve those standards."

Al Gore has always been fascinated with the CIA and the technology of snooping. In 1994, he ordered the agency to conduct an analysis of the causes behind the collapse of nation states. Gore was hoping to prove his thesis that environmental factors, such as deforestation, overpopulation, desertification and poor sanitation, were the prime culprits. So the CIA spent the next six months entering more than 2 million pieces of information in its computers to come up with an answer. The result: the CIA's analysts reported that civilizations fall because of extreme poverty and high rates of infant mortality.

But Gore didn't give up on the spooks at Langley. In 1998 he convinced Clinton to issue an executive order expanding the agency's charter to include two new projects: the environment and free trade. The CIA quickly adapted to its new mission. In the summer of 1999 the *London Daily Telegraph* reported that the CIA had been spying on Michael Meacher, environment minister for the Blair government, presumably because Meacher—-nearly alone among the Blairites-—had been skeptical about Monsanto's plans to dump genetically engineered, or GE, crops on Europe.

The snooping came to light after the *Telegraph* made Freedom of Information Act requests to several US government agencies asking for any files on British ministers and elected

261

officials. Most agencies replied that they had no files, while a few kept short biographical briefs, which they duly turned over. The exception was the Environmental Protection Agency, headed by Al Gore's former staffer, Carol Browner. The EPA replied that it had a file on Meacher but refused to turn it over, saying it "originated within the Central Intelligence Agency". The CIA also refused to release the file.

Meacher had drawn fire not only from Monsanto but from the US State and Commerce departments for his recalcitrance on GE crops. He had taken the position that such crops should not be commercially grown in Europe until they have been proved not to pose health problems or environmental risks. Meacher had also moved to reformulate a government panel on genetically engineered crops by reducing the number of industry representatives. The US was maintaining that any restrictions on Monsanto's ability to market its GE crops was an unfair restraint on trade. Gore himself made frequent calls to members of the Blair government to drive home the point.

Meacher expressed astonishment that the CIA had a file on him, and said he had no idea what the reason might be. Chris Prescott, head of Friends of the Earth's London office, offered one. "The immediate fear is that the CIA is working hand in glove with Monsanto to do anything they can to force this technology down our throats, whatever Democratic politicians have to say. What business is it of the CIA's to worry about any politician's views about biotechnology products?" Apparently, Prescott missed Clinton's new directive to the Agency made at Gore's instigation. Some wondered how thick the file might be on Prince Charles, Britain's most outspoken foe of genetically engineered crops.

For Gore in particular, the Republican victory in 1994 was

of great assistance in fending off even the very modest beseechings of America's green organizations. All he had to do was point toward the supposedly awful threat posed by his old friend Gingrich and the Republicans. The bad faith was mutual. Environmental organizations were themselves ecstatic to have a real threat to raise money with. When James Watt became Reagan's interior secretary, outfits like the Sierra Club and Wilderness Society raised millions with mailshots quoting his foolish ideas. Indeed, the swelling memberships of green organizations at that time undercut militancy, as the newly flush green organizations invested in high-salaried lobbyists, new office suites and all the familiar paraphernalia of institutionalized DC public interest groups.

The election of Clinton and Gore in 1992 saw a shriveling of membership and revenues for the big green organizations. People sign on to such groups when they see a danger. With the advent of the new administration, they thought the threat had dwindled. November 1994 brought the Republicans into control of the Hill, and within weeks an avalanche of mailshots burdened postal carriers from Anchorage to Key West. They all had the same theme. Unless the recipient sent money at once, there wouldn't be a Douglas-fir left standing, a grizzly bear alive, an Arctic tundra unstained by oil, a coast free of the blood of dolphins and whales, an acre of the interior West safe from the miners' excavators, an Everglades untainted by pesticide. The political message was as simple. Only Clinton and Gore could save America's natural heritage.

Happy to have a constituency that regarded them as indispensable, Clinton and Gore did put up a few token fights, battling Republican efforts to slash the budgets of the EPA and Parks Service, fending off Senator Bob Dole's regulatory reform bill and successfully beating back property rights legislation,

263

long sought by the real estate lobby.

But then in 1996 came disaster for the big green organizations and fresh problems for the White House. In the elections that year the American people made it clear that they valued the environment and strongly disapproved of the proposed onslaughts on it by Gingrich and the Republicans. The Gingrich threat was thrown back. The big green outfits now faced the same problem as had the Pentagon when Communism collapsed. The White House no longer had Gingrich as an alibi. The 1998 elections compounded the problem. The people issued the same verdict as in 1996, this time so vociferously that Gingrich was forced to quit as speaker of the House.

By mid-1999 many greens were beginning to review the Gore record and ask what he'd done for the environment in all those White House years when America had as its most ardent green champion the most influential vice president in American history. David Brower put it pithily: "Environmentalists and progressives cannot endorse rhetoric, and that's the greenest thing we've seen from the vice president. I first thought he was just keeping bad company. So I created the bumper sticker 'Free Al Gore!' and even got him delivered a sweatshirt with the slogan on it. But things have gotten even worse since then. And Gore seems to have fumbled the ball even on an issue as noncontroversial as offshore oil drilling."

In the fall of 1999, Michael Dorsey, a progressive environmentalist and the only black member of the Sierra Club board, began to raise serious questions as to whether the board should endorse Gore in 2000. He drew up a bleak list of Gore's failures. Among them:

- Gore had failed to save forests both in the United States and worldwide and was instead pushing for a global free trade agreement on timber with no conservation measures.
- At the start of 1999 the administration killed the Biosafety Convention being negotiated in Cartagena, Colombia, because it wanted to protect the interests of biotechnology firms.
- Although Gore launched an initiative against sprawl in 1999, he was simultaneously promoting sprawl in Florida by supporting the scandal-ridden expansion of Homestead Air Force Base into another major airport situated between Everglades National Park and Biscayne National Park.
- Gore had broken his commitment to clean water in Appalachia. Further, the administration's failure to enforce the strip mining law had resulted in the removal of entire tops of mountains, the filling of valleys with rubble, and the obliteration of more than 1,000 miles of streams.
- In 1992, Gore promised to keep offshore oil and gas drilling away from the Florida coastline. He never followed through on this promise, despite opposition to such drilling by both Florida Democrats and Republicans.
- Gore had demanded that chemical manufacturers begin new tests on nearly 2,800 chemicals. If they wouldn't volunteer to do the tests, he'd force them to do so in what is called the High Production Volume (HPV) Challenge. In these tests animals are forced to ingest or inhale a chemical in increasing doses until half are dead. In all, Gore's plan would kill an estimated 800,000 birds, fish, rats, mice, and other animals. It would cost taxpayers at least $14 million.
- Gore had quit on his commitment to protect marine mammals. The administration had undermined protections for giant sea turtles and dolphins as it bowed to pressure from

Mexico, Thailand, India and Pakistan to weaken US laws.

• In 1996, Gore directly ordered the EPA to slow down its implementation of tougher pesticide standards that were required by the Food Quality Protection Act.

• Gore broke his commitment to protect wetlands.

That wasn't the full extent of the indictment, nor was Dorsey alone. Friends of the Earth issued its own list of Gore's failures, and endorsed Bill Bradley, saying, "When Gore got into a unique position of power to lead, he failed in serious and perplexing ways and even opened the way for Draconian erosions of existing environmental protections at home and abroad." Among the failings cited by the group: a poor performance on his signature issue, protection of the ozone layer. Gore had weakened the phase-out date for methyl-bromide. More broadly, he'd failed to push for any initiative designed to curb the power of multilateral institutions such as the World Bank, IMF and WTO, prime instigators of environmental destruction and human misery.

On the subject of global warming, a threat to which Gore had devoted much of his book, greens found grave fault with the vice president. At the crucial Kyoto conference in December of 1997 he brokered a deal that pledged the United States to reduce its so-called greenhouse gas emissions to 7 percent below what they were in 1990 by the year 2012. This was a signal backsliding from targets Gore himself had proclaimed in earlier years, and was far below a European proposal of 15 percent. Moreover, the levels themselves would be "voluntary" on developing nations, and the industrial nations could meet them by using pollution credits, thus solving the crisis on paper while exacerbating it in fact.

Not only was the agreement weak, greens charged, but

two years later the US had done nothing to implement the Kyoto accords, disappointing though they were. The only real winner in this debacle turned out to be the nuclear power industry, which has used the global warming scare to revive its sagging fortunes. At Gore's behest, the Department of Energy has tripled federal spending for research and development on commercial nuclear reactors, from $40 million to $120 million a year, and has pushed nuclear trade pacts to sell reactors to China, Argentina and Brazil.

Will the American environmental movement ever learn its lesson? Certainly the endorsements of mid-2000 were not encouraging. In late July, Ralph Nader sent a letter to the board of the Sierra Club, at that time meeting in Utah's Wasatch Mountains to decide which candidate to endorse. Only a few days earlier the administration had said flatly that it would not consider breaching four dams on the Snake River in the Northwest, mainly in Idaho, in order to save numerous runs of salmon from extinction. "This was in effect Wednesday's headline front page", Nader said: "'Clinton-Gore Administration will not breach dams to save salmon.' Will this be Sunday's headline, inside page, 'As expected, Sierra Club endorses Gore.'"

True to form, the Sierra Club duly endorsed Al Gore.

16 THE PROZAC LADY

*From It Takes a Village to It Takes a Shrink, a
Drug Company, and a Psychotropic.*

We left Tipper entering amid the throes of depression
following the accident to Albert III and Gore's prolonged
absence writing Earth in the Balance. On the campaign trail
she and Bill Clintion, late owls, stayed up chatting, with the
governor lending a sympathetic ear to Tipper's accounts of her
depressed mother. After the election Tipper became the White
House anchor on mental health, and before long she was an
impresario crucial to the promotion of America's new Great
Depression, launched in the form of a study released at the end
of 1993 purporting to show that the cost of depression to
America was just under $44 billion a year. A cascade of bogus
statistics followed this bald calculation, including a grotesque
estimate that America's 18,400 suicides in 1990 cost Uncle Sam
$7.5 billion in lost productivity and that 60 per cent of the
self-slaughterers did so because of depression. And the other
40 percent?

Along with Dr Fred Goodwin, head of the National
Institute of Mental Health, Tipper Gore promptly hailed the
report as indicative of the vital necessity of a huge boost in the
nation's health spending in this area. Press stories recording
her observations and those of Goodwin almost entirely failed to
note that both the report and the press conference were
underwritten by Eli Lilly, the pharmaceutical company making
Prozac, an anti-depressant launched in 1987 and by the early

Nineties doing $760 million in sales and being heavily touted as the cure for America's Great Depression. Goodwin's NIMH excitedly rode the boom, claiming that no less than 52 million American adults, a fifth of the population, had a diagnosable mental illness. Eli Lilly seems to have semi-permanent parking rights at the White House. George Bush Sr was a director after he left the CIA and when he became vice president the company had ready access, in the form of Mitch Daniels, the company's vice president for corporate affairs, who shuttled between company hq in Indianapolis and the Reagan and Bush White House.

Presumably spurred into action by eight years of contemplating Ronald Reagan, President Bush announced "The Decade of the Brain" in 1990, signalling enhanced federal interest in mental health. Drug companies and public interest groups circled the trough. The consequent campaign was a marvel of synergy in action. The psychiatric profession was under pressure from insurance companies and state budget authorities to cut back on time-consuming and therefore expensive psychiatric consultations and counselling sessions and to use pharmacological treatments. The advantage of Prozac and other serotonin reuptake inhibitors is that unlike barbiturates they could be prescribed without fear that the patients would, either by accident or design, take overdoses and do themselves in.

So Lilly and kindred companies underwrote studies to show Americans in vast numbers were depressed or otherwise nuts. Tipper and less exalted flacks for the drug companies performed their role by denouncing the "stigma" of depression and by claiming that it was a complaint as directly treatable by chemicals as a physical ailment. Public interest organizations like the National Alliance for the Mentally Ill and the National

Mental Health Association played their part too. No less than eighteen drug firms gave NAMI $11.72 million between 1996 and mid-1999, with the leading corporate donor being Eli Lilly. It gave $2.87 million, and released a Lilly executive, Jerry Radke, to work at NAMI, in what the group's director, Laurie Flynn, described as "strategic planning". Marveling at her acumen, Clinton named Flynn to the national bioethics advisory commission. She has had her critics. NAMI "reduces human distress to a brain disease, and recovery to taking a pill" was the acid assessment of Sally Zinman of California Network of Mental Health Clients.

Each year National Depression Screening Day became Tipper's equivalent of the Trooping of the Color for the British monarch, with National Childhood Depression Awareness Day being rolled out in 1997, to ensure that no tot was overlooked in the drive to get Americans to put the Prozac bottle up on the shelf next to the aspirin and Alka-Seltzer.

October 30, 1999, found the Prozac cabal in New Orleans with Tipper being honored as one of the winners of the Eli Lilly Schizophrenia Reintregration awards, presented in conjunction with the American Psychiatric Association's annual meeting of the Institute of Psychiatric Services. The APA's contribution has been to widen definitions of mental illness in its Diagnostic and Statistical Manual of Mental Disorders to include speculative conditions such as Attention Deficit and Hyperactivity Disorder, which in turn requires the child or tot to be dosed with psychotropic drugs. In New Orleans Tipper made a graceful speech: "It is because of companies like Lilly that people can receive the innovative, pharmaceutical based health care solutions they need to live better lives."

The Columbine shootings in the spring of 1999 were followed by a White House conference on youth violence. Since it was by that time a matter of some public comment that many homicidal teens, including one of the Columbine shooters, had been on psychtropic drugs, the matter had to be handled with delicacy by the White House drug boosters. Hillary Rodham Clinton carried the burden with aplomb, telling the crowd that "I think that part of what we've got [to do], though, is to reflect how we can both identify and get help to children who need it, whether or not they want it or are willing to accept it." In other words, the First Lady was advocating the forced drugging of kids with Ritalin, Prozac, Luvox or kindred psychotropic drugs.

By early 2000 methodical reports were confirming what many Americans knew anyway. In many schools kids are being loaded up with psychotropic drugs, and the age level for recipients is dropping down to infancy. The "mental health" complex has shrugged off such concerns, and the Second Lady along with the Second Man continued to supply the rhetorical accoutrements for the pharmaceutical salesfolk. By now Tipper had gone public with her own bouts of depression a decade earlier. For his part Gore called for the training of teachers to spot mental illness, after which diagnosis the kids would presumably be compulsorily dosed with psychotropics. The chief legal counsel for the Department of Education in Rhode Island promptly sent out an advisory noting that "concerns have arisen about teachers and other school personnel 'recommending' that parents consider placing their child on medication." The counsel advised that under federal law school personnel must refrain from making statements that could be construed as offering medical advice or making medical decisions. Not to worry. The worried teacher can always call up a social worker and express concern about little Billy. Then the social worker can pay a call on little Billy's folks, or maybe little Billy's single parent/mom. And if the folks or the single-parent resist the social worker's suggestion that they put little Billy into "counselling", aka doses of psychotropics, then little Billy could very well find himself in a new home.

Tipper's achievement is to have converted the difficulties of her childhood and of being with Al into a national malady.

The late Christopher Lasch typified the coercive, therapeutic liberalism of the Clintons and the Gores very well in the final passage of his great book *Haven in a Heartless World:* "Today the state controls not merely the individual's body but as much of his spirit as it can preempt; not merely his outer but his inner life as well; not merely the public realm but the darkest corners of private life, formerly inacccessible to political domination. The citizen's entire existence has now been subjected to social direction, increasingly unmediated by the family or other institutions to which the work of socialization was once confined. Society itself has taken over socialization or subjected family socialization to increasingly effective control. Having thereby weakened the capacity for self-direction and self-control, it has undermined one of the principle sources of social cohesion, only to create new ones more constricting than the old, and ultimately more devastating in their impact on personal and political freedom."

WHY WE FOUNDED COUNTERPUNCH

By Alexander Cockburn and Jeffrey St Clair

Seven years ago we felt unhappy about the state of radical journalism. It didn't have much edge. It didn't have many facts. It was politically timid. It was dull. So we founded CounterPunch. We wanted it to be the best muckraking newsletter in the country. We wanted it to take aim at the consensus of received wisdom about what can and cannot be reported. We wanted to give our readers a political roadmap they could trust.

Seven years later we stand firm on these same beliefs and hopes. We think we've restored the honor of muckraking journalism in the tradition of our favorite radical pamphleteers, Edward Abbey, Peter Maurin and Ammon Hennacy, Appeal to Reason, Jacques René Hébert, Tom Paine and John Lilburne.

Every two weeks CounterPunch gives you jaw-dropping exposés on: Congress and lobbyists; the environment; labor; the National Security State.

"CounterPunch kicks through the floorboards of lies and gets to the foundation of what is really going on in this country," says Michael Ratner, attorney at the Center for Constitutional Rights. "At our house, we fight over who gets to read CounterPunch first. Each issue is like spring after a cold, dark winter."

Sign me up for CounterPunch:

❏ $40 one year   ❏ $75 two years   ❏ $30 low income   ❏ $100 institutions
Please send subscription to:

_____

_____

_____

CounterPunch PO Box 228 Petrolia, CA 95558
Call 1-800-840-3683 to subscribe by credit card.

ACKNOWLEDGEMENTS

This book could not have been completed without the aid of our friend JoAnn Wypijewski, for her scrutiny of the manuscript under combat conditions. Thanks also to our friend and and erstwhile CounterPunch colleague Ken Silverstein for allowing us to adapt an article that he and Jeffrey St. Clair wrote for In These Times on Gore's fundraising network. Likewise, Patrick and Andrew Cockburn shared a wealth of information on the Gulf War and its aftermath, as well as the Gore family's relationship to the former Soviet Union and present-day Russia. Our thanks to Christy Ward, to Laurence Pantin, also to Joe and Karen Paff, and Dave and Becky Grant, part of the CounterPunch team.

Mark Greenfield and Sharon Banis, at Total Graphics, achieved the impossible as did Colin Robinson and the Verso crew.

Two recent biographies of Gore were invaluable to us: Robert Zelnick's *Gore: a life* and Bill Turque's *Inventing Al Gore*. Also helpful were magazine and newspaper profiles by David Maraniss and Ellen Nakashima in the Washington Post, Alex Jones in the New York Times, Gail Sheehy in Vanity Fair, Julia Reed in Vanity Fair, Louis Menand and Peter Boyer in the New Yorker, Katherine Boo and Myra McPherson in the Washington Post and Richard Berke in the New York Times. Gore Vidal's portrait of the Gore family's historical roots was fun to read and loaded with catty details. Equally important was Charles Lewis' dissection of Gore's political career and his fundraising machine in *The Buying of the Presidency 2000*.

We also found several memoirs of Clintontime useful, particularly the duelling perspectives of Dick Morris and George Stephanopoulos. Bob Woodward's account of the first Clinton budget, *The Agenda*, remains a crucial text for understanding how the undermining of the New Deal began. (His reporting for the Washington Post on the 1996 fundraising scandals and the career of Peter Knight was also valuable.) Elizabeth Drew's account of the 1996 campaign, *Whatever It Takes*, contains important insights into how Gore spearheaded welfare reform and how he sought to undermine the Democrats' chances to take back the House.

Public Citizen opened a storehouse of information on the economic and environmental consequences of trade pacts, such as NAFTA and GATT. The Center for Defense Information, Project on Government Oversight and the Federation of American Scientists shared information on the Clinton military budget, the history of the nuclear arms control movement, and the political economy of the defense industry. Thanks also to Frank Von Hippel for his memories of Midgetman. Rock critic Dave Marsh and anti-censorship activists Phyllis Pollack opened their huge files on Tipper's crusade against popular music. Larry Tuttle gave us an inside account of what it was like for an environmentalist to deal with the new Clinton/Gore administration. Another key resource was the catalogue of Al Gore's congressional voting record maintained by Americans for Democratic Action. For a flavor of the diverse characters and corporations that have bankrolled Gore's political career we recommend a visit to the Center for Responsive Politics' website, www.opensecrets.org and the more detailed one at FEC Info www.tray.com/fecinfo/.

Jeffrey St Clair owes a life-long debt to Kimberly Willson-St. Clair for her unsparing advice, encouragement, tolerance and final injunction to "get the damn book finished before the election". Alexander Cockburn has his affectionate debts too to Daisy Cockburn and to Barbara Yaley for their endless indulgences towards, and support for, a deadline writer. He will repay, he swears he will.

INDEX

Abzug, Bella 189
Adams, John 162
Ahlerich, Mitch 113-4
Ahtissaari, Martti 226
Aitcheson, Jack 14-15, 50
Aitcheson, Margaret Carlson
    14-15, 140
al-Attar, Leila 212
Albright, Madeleine 213, 224-6
Alexander, Gov. Lamar 85
Allison, Graham 22
Andrus, Gov. Cecil 254
Anslinger, Harry 98-9
Arafat, Yasir 126
Armistead, Donna 14-16, 32, 146
Aspin, Rep. Les 66, 80, 84-5,
    151, 219
AuCoin, Rep. Les 84
Azoff, Irving 108

Babbitt, Gov. Bruce 20, 125-6,
    134, 151, 178, 250-1
Baca, Jim 254
Baker, James 97
Baker, Sen. Howard 63-4, 85
Baker, Susan 97, 100-1, 109-10
Balz, Dan 233
Barak, Yahud 70
Baucus, Sen. Max 254
Bayh, Sen. Evan 200
Beckel, Bob 133-4
Beilin, Yossi 67,
Bennett, William 106
Bennis, Warren 154

Bentsen, Sen. Lloyd 27, 151, 153,
    155-7
Bevill, Rep. Tom 62-3
Biafra, Jello 115-6
Biondi, Frank 239
Blackwelder, Brent 251, 255-6
Blair, Tony 261-2
Blitzer, Wolf 212
Blumenthal, Sidney 21
Boggs, Rep. Hale 12-3, 45,
Boggs, Tommy 179
Boland, Edward 124
Bonior, Rep. David 50, 162
Boren, Sen. David 157
Bradley, Sen. Bill 3, 57, 86, 134-
    5, 163-4, 170-1, 266
Brazile, Donna 154
Breaux, Sen. John 19, 36, 53,
    157
Breyer, Stephen 260
Brock, Sen. Bill 26-7, 51,
Brodie, Bernard 81
Brower, David 63, 246, 264
Brown, Ron 236
Browner, Carol 150, 259-61
Browning, Gov. Gordon 10
Brundtland, Gro 252-5
Buchanan, Patrick 163
Bumpers, Sen. Dale 59-60
Bush, Gov. George W. 16, 116,
    168, 203
Bush, President George 68-9, 86-
    8, 92-4, 133, 143, 145, 160,
    163, 210-1, 235, 246, 248, 269

Byrd, Sen. Robert 156

Caddell, Patrick 23-4, 122
Cardoso, Michael 95
Carrick, William 122-3
Carter, President Jimmy 63, 78, 153
Carville, James 144
Chafee, Sen. John 64
Chalabi, Ahmad 216
Chase, Allen 35-6
Chaucer, Geoffrey 17
Chernomyrdin, Viktor 226-30
Christopher, Warren 94, 143, 145, 153, 220
Churchill, Winston 16, 69,
Cisneros, Henry 115-6
Clark, Blair 20
Clark, Gen. Wesley 224-5
Clinton, Chelsea 4
Clinton, Hillary Rodham 48, 112, 145, 147-8, 172, 174, 193, 248, 271
Clinton, President Bill 7, 17, 22, 48, 64, 77, 92, 96, 143-5, 147-8, 155-7, 169-70, 172, 177-8, 184-5, 189-93, 200-2, 207-8, 211-2, 216, 224-5, 248-9, 268
Coelho, Tony 230-1
Cohen, Gilbert 40
Conrad, Robert 242-3
Cook, Lowdrick 229-30
Coop, C. Everett 106-7
Cooper, Gen. Kenneth 28

Coors, Joseph 98
Crotty, William 121
Cuomo, Gov. Mario 94, 120
Cutrer, Tommy 49

Daley, William 161
Danforth, Sen. John 103-5
Daniels, Mitch 269
Davis, Gov. Gray 168
Davis, John 17
Delabar, Bob 29
Deutch, John 218-9
Diallo, Amadou 203, 207
Dicks, Rep. Norm 84
DiMaggio, Joe 44
Dine, Tom 71
Dingell, Rep. John 53, 54,
Dobson, Rev. James 110-1
Dodd, Sen. Christopher 196
Dole, Sen. Robert 90-1, 194
Dornan, Rep. Robert 58
Dorsey, Michael 264-6
Downey, Rep. Thomas 50, 52,
Doyle, Frank 175
Dukakis, Gov. Michael 123, 128-34
Dutko, Dan 234-6
Dwyer, Judge William 248-50

Edelman, Peter 158, 193-4, 198-9
Edgar, Rep. Bob 62
Eisenhower, President Dwight D. 11, 188

Ernst, Harry 6
Eskew, Carter 107-8
Estrich, Susan 134
Evans Jr., Silliman 38
Evans, Brock 256-7
Exon, Sen. James 104-5

Fall, Albert 230
Fanjul, Alfonso 240-1
Farnsworth, Anne Labouisse
    18-9
Feinstein, Fred 177
Ferraro, Rep. Geraldine 129-30
Fish, Rep. Hamilton 68-9
Flowers, Gennifer 144-5
Foley, Rep. Thomas 188
Ford, Rep. Harold 135
Frampton, George 151
Freeh, Louis 242
Freud, Sigmund 18
Friedman, Harvey 67
Friedman, Thomas 211
Fuerth, Leon 71, 79-81, 85, 87-8,
    93-4, 148, 212, 218-9, 253,
    257
Furtseva, Yakaterina 43-4

Galbraith, Amb. James 221
Gaskin, Stephen 39
Gephardt, Rep. Richard 50,
    122-5, 162, 195-6
Gergen, David 158-60
Gilligan, Don 18
Gingrich, Rep. Newt 65, 93, 188,

191, 195-6, 263-4
Glasser, Ira 203
Gonzalez, Elian 205
Goodwin, Dr. Fred 268-9
Gore Sr., Sen. Albert 2, 8-15,
    23-4, 44-6, 49, 119, 146
Gore, Albert, Jr. (b. March 31,
    1948): overview of basic
    political and personal defects
    1-7; St Albans, first love and
    Tipper, 12-16; Harvard,
    Martin Peretz and Richard
    Neustadt 17-22; Gore and
    Vietnam, 22-29; inhaling of
    marijuana, 29-30; Vanderbilt
    Divinity School and three
    books that shaped Gore's
    environmental outlook 31-38;
    stint at The Tennessean 38-9;
    Gore's shady muckraking 39-
    41; beneficiary of Armand
    Hammer 42-7; kills off
    Tipper's career 47-8; first
    congressional race 48-51;
    unloved by House colleagues
    52-3; early rapport with tv
    cameras 53-54; fear of Oak
    Ridge's clout 55; lousy voting
    history in Congress on gays,
    abortion, and race 55-9;
    support for Clinch River
    breeder reactor and Tellico
    dam 59-63; friendship with
    Newt Gingrich 65; love for

CIA's covert ops 66; serf to Israeli lobby 67-70; disgraceful behavior to Richard Marius 71-5; apprenticeship as armchair nuclear wargamer 76-82; hires Leon Fuerth 79-80; Midgetman fiasco 83-5; Pentagon's friend 86-7; Iraq and pro-war posturing 87-94; Gore's views on proper sex posture to engender male heir 95; oily remarks to Frank Zappa 106; comportment at hearings on dirty music 108-9; backpedaling to Hollywood 108; his 88 bid for Democratic nomination 119-135; his money men 120-122; his record on *contra* funding 123-4; humiliation at the polls 126; he stays in race to cut down Jackson 128-131; use of Willie Horton 131-5; falls among shrinks 136; use of Albert 111's accident 136-8; empty pledge to Tipper 139; writes Earth in the Balance 139-143; aboard the Clinton campaign 144-7; establishes himself in White House 148; his aides Peter Knight and Thomas Grumbly 148-152; sets up therapy and soul-

baring at Camp David 152-4; his "Coolidgeonomics" 155; BTU tax imbroglio 156-7; welcomes Gergen 158-9; his role in pushing through NAFTA 160-5; his debate with Ross Perot 163-5; empty promises on green benefits of treaty 167-9; relations with AFL-CIO 169-171; assigned task of "reinventing" government 172-3; public enthused 174; tears up government regs 175-6; sells off government assets 178-9; GAO questions supposed savings wrought by "Reinvention"; wretched failure of effort to reinvent Pentagon 181-4; anger of Blacks in Government 184-7; Democratic setbacks in 1994 bring Gore and Dick Morris together 188-191; assault on welfare 193-4; Gore pushes Clinton to sign bill of shame 195; Democrats suspect Gore stabbbed them in the back to spite Gephardt 195-7; effects of welfare bill 197-201; Gore eager accomplice in Clinton's assault on Bill of Rights 201-207; failure of Clintonomics 208-9; Gore lead player in

setting Iraq policy 210-212;
deadly aspects of sanctions
described 213-5; asked about
deadly nature of sanctions on
Iraqi civilians, Gore laughs
217-8; Gore and the Balkans
220-234; Gore amd
Chernomyrdin compared 226-
8; Elk Hills deal 230-1; the
Pentagon's man 231-2; Gore's
campaign finance history 233-
8; White House coffee
klatsches 239-244; Gore's
betrayals on environment
245-267; attack on Pacific
Northwest forests 248-252;
revealing colloquy with Gro
Buntland 252-254; disillusion
of green groups 253-6; Katie
McGinty 257-9; Carol
Browner 259-260; his love of
CIA 261-2; green groups'
disillusion deepens 264-6; but
illusions still abound 267.
Gore III, Albert 4, 24, 95-6,
136-7
Gore, Grady 9-10
Gore, Kristin 95
Gore, Pauline LaFon 8-9, 23-4,
38, 146
Gore, Sarah 4, 95
Gore, Tipper 2-4, 6, 14-5, 18, 23-
4, 26-7, 29-30, 46-8, 54, 72,
95-118, 119, 136-40, 144, 147,
258-9, 268-78
Gortikov, Stanley 99-100, 102-3
Graham, Katharine 38
Gramm, Sen. Phil 92-3
Grassley, Sen. Charles 182-3
Green, Rev. Al 197
Greenberg, Stanley 130, 174
Greenspan, Alam 155
Grumbly, Thomas 151-2

Haddox, Maurice 40
Hair, Jay 161-2, 254
Hammer, Armand 27, 42-7, 50,
146, 228
Harding, President Warren 229-
30
Harkin, Sen. Tom 52, 86, 124
Harrison, Gilbert 20
Hart, Sen. Gary 123
Hastert, Rep. Dennis 204
Hausker, Karl 258-9
Heflin, Sen. Howell 140
Helms, Sen. Jesse 58-9, 189, 216
Hertzberg, Hendrik 21
Hitchens, Christopher 216
Hoffa Jr., James 171
Holbrooke, Amb. Richard 222-3
Hollings, Peatsy 100-1
Hollings, Sen. Ernest 85-6, 103-4
Hoover, J. Edgar 44
Hopkins, Jane 152-4
Horton, Willie 120, 131-4
Howar, Barbara 13
Howar, Pam 97-8, 100

Hubbell, Webb 248
Hull, Cordell 10
Humphrey, Sen. Hubert H. 6-7, 8, 20
Hundt, Reed 147-8, 151
Hunger, Frank 50, 150
Hunger, Nancy Gore 142-3
Hussein, Saddam 88-90, 93, 210-4
Hyde, Rep. Henry 57-8, 205-6

Ickes, Harold 144
Irani, Ray 230-1
Irion, Mark 235-6

Jackson, Rev. Jesse 69, 96, 120-43, 163, 166
Jackson, Sen. Henry 82-3
Janklow, Mort 140
Johnson, President Lyndon B. 22, 39,
Johnston, Sen. Bennett 156
Jordan, Vernon 150
Jost, Ken 50

Kahn, Herman 81
Kamarck, Elaine 173-4, 187
Kantor, Mickey 94, 108, 151, 161, 165-6
Kasten, Sen. Robert 124
Kaufman, Hugh 248
Kefauver, Diane 14, 16
Kefauver, Sen. Estes 14, 38

Kelly, Michael 74-5
Kennedy, David 39
Kennedy, President John F. 22, 53
Kennedy, Sen. Edward 124, 133, 260
Kennedy, Sen. Robert F. 39
Kerrey, Sen. Bob 153
Khrushchev, Nikita 43
King, Larry 145, 163-5
Kinsley, Michael 21
Kirk, Paul 132-3
Kissinger, Henry 83, 232
Knight, Peter 29-30, 147-52
Koch, Mayor Ed 70, 128-30
Kokoshin, Andrei 227
Kopkind, Andrew 19
Koppel, Ted 126
Kortunov, Andrei 228
Krenik, Mark 182

LaBella, Charles 242
Lake, Anthony 218
Landow, Nathan 23-4, 95, 120-2, 237-8
Laurence, Dr. Lance 136
Leahy, Sen. Patrick 64
Lenin, V.I. 43
Leo, Alan 28
Letterman, Dave 174
Lewinsky, Monica 241
Lewis, Anthony 220
Lott, Sen. Trent 189, 216

INDEX

Lovelock, James 141
Lowenstein, Allard 19
Lynn, Barry 110-2

Madonna, 97
Maplethorpe, Robert 59
Marius, Richard 71-5
Marsh, Dave 96
Marx, Karl 18
Matthews, Chris 204
McCarthy, Sen. Eugene 19, 82, 137
McCurdy, Rep. David 157-8
McCurry, Mike 170
McFarlin, Ben 49
McGinty, Katherine 247-50, 150, 254, 257-9
McGrory, Mary 70
McKellar, Sen. Kenneth 9-10
McLarty, Thomas "Mack" 157, 172
McLelland, Stan 240-1
McWherter, Gov. Ned 49
Meacher, Michael 261-2
Meese, Edwin 111
Menand, Louis 21
Merleau-Ponty, Maurice, 37, 39
Metzenbaum, Sen. Howard 189
Meyers, Dee Dee 159
Miller, Alice 136, 142-3
Miller, Henry 97
Miller, Rep. George 50
Miller, Robert 183

Milosevic, Slobodan 219-20, 222, 225-6
Mitchell, Sen. George 88-91
Mondale, Sen. Walter 51, 120, 129-30
Morley, Jefferson 20-1
Morris, Dick 54, 104, 189-90, 201, 220, 224, 238, 241
Moynihan, Sen. Daniel Patrick 194-5, 197-8
Muller, Danny 217-9
Myers, Rep. John 65-6

Nader, Ralph 166, 171, 267
Neel, Roy 50, 74, 148
Neustadt, Richard 17, 21-3, 27
Nevius, Sally 97-8, 109
Niebuhr, Reinhold 36
Nixon, President Richard M. 26-7, 187
Nunn, Sen. Sam 66, 84, 88-9, 94, 158

O'Bannon, Gov. Frank 200
O'Leary, Hazel 152
O'Neill, Rep. Thomas 52, 77
Osborn, Fairfield 32-3, 34
Osborn, Henry F. 32
Osbourne, David 152, 173

Panetta, Rep. Leon 155, 180-1, 191, 194-5
Peretz, Martin 1, 17-21, 27-8, 70-1, 85, 130-1, 219-20

Perle, Richard 216
Perot, Ross 145, 161-5
Perry, William 219
Peters, Tom 152
Phillips, Kevin 51
Pollack, Phyllis 101, 117-8
Pollin, Robert 7, 208-9
Pope, Carl 35,
Powell, Gen. Colin 158
Price, Hugh 198
Prince, 96
Pryor, Sen. David 139
Pusey, Nathan 20

Quayle, Sen. Dan 3, 96, 147, 175-6

Rabin, Yitzhak 68
Radke, Jerry 269-70
Rattner, Steve 235
Reagan, President Ronald 51, 66, 78, 85, 87, 106, 121, 187, 269
Redstone, Sumner 239
Reedy, George 38
Reich, Robert 155, 193-4
Reilly, William 247-8
Reisner, Marc 61-2
Reno, Janet 201, 242
Riady, James 242
Richardson, Rep. Bill 221, 231
Ritter, Frank 47
Robertson, Rev. Pat 74
Robinson, Mary 236

Robinson, Walter King 42
Rockefeller, Laurence 34
Rogers, Stanley 49
Romash, Marla 71-2
Roosevelt, President Franklin D. 10-1, 156
Roosevelt, President Theodore 14
Rosenblat, Roger 18
Rostenkowski, Rep. Dan 51, 188
Rubin, Robert 195-0

Sagan, Carl 65
Sanger, Margaret 33, 35
Sasser, Sen. James 59
Schiff, Karenna Gore 4, 47, 95-6, 154, 220-1
Schlesinger, Andrew 39
Schlesinger, James 78
Schorr, David 169
Schultze, Charles 61-2
Schumer, Sen. Charles 206
Scowcroft, Gen. Brent 83
Segal, Eric 3
Sexton, Dwayne 55
Sexton, Mary Sue 55
Shalala, Donna 193-4
Shamir, Yitzhak 69, 130-1
Sherrill, Robert 6
Shriver, Tom 40
Siegenthaler, John 23, 38-40, 48-9
Siljander, Rep. Mark 56-7
Simon, Sen. Paul 46-7, 86, 123, Simon, Greg 179

Simpson, Sen. Alan 90-1
Smith, Sam 205
Somoza, Gen. Anastasio 123-4
Sprey, Pierre 80-1
Springsteen, Bruce 101
Squier, Bob 145, 190
Stephens, Jackson 248
Stephanopoulos, George 144,
    152-4, 159, 172, 184-5, 191,
    220
Stevenson, Adlai 38
Strauss, David 244
Strickland, Rep. Tom 179-80
Swaggert, Rev. Jimmy 197
Swearington, Terri 247-8
Sweeney, John 170-1

Talbott, Strobe 79
TeSelle, Eugene 32, 36-7
Thomases, Susan 144
Thurmond, Sen. Strom 2, 26, 122
Timbers, William 179-80
Toffler, Alvin 65
Townsend, Chris 177
Tudjman, Gen. Franjo 220
Turque, Bill 24,
Tuttle, Larry 249-50

Vidal, Gore 9-10, 53
Vogt, William 33-4
Voles, Lorraine 72-4, 138-9
Von Hippel, Frank 83-4

Warnecke, John 29-30, 39
Warnecke, Nancy 29-30
Wasserman, Lew 235
Watt, James 64, 263
Wertheimer, Fred 121-2
Westmoreland, Gen. William
    25-6
Wheelis, Allen 136
Whitehurst, Fredrick 212
Will, George 98
Wilson, William 41
Winternitz, Helen 71-2
Wiriadinata, Arief 242
Wirth, Sen. Tim 50, 64, 145, 151
Wirth, Wren 145
Wolf, Naomi 154
Woodward, Bob 155, 221, 243
Woolsey, Adm. James 82-3, 85,
    93-4
Wright, Rep. Jim 52

Yarborough, Sen. Ralph 28
Young, Rep. Don 65

Zappa, Frank 102-3, 105-7
Zelnick, Robert 36, 73-4
Zinman, Sally 270